COMPLETE HOCKEY RECORDS

Dan Diamond saw his first NHL hockey game in 1961. He redesigned the *NHL Official Guide & Record Book* in 1984, creating the game's most respected reference source. He edited both the *Total Hockey* encyclopedia and the NHL's *75th Anniversary Commemorative Book* and has asked Gordie Howe for his autograph in six different decades.

As a boy, **Eric Zweig** filled his school news books with game reports instead of current events. He is the author of two hockey novels, *Hockey Night in the Dominion of Canada* (1992) and *Fever Season* (2009), and several non-fiction books for adults and children. Eric has worked with Dan Diamond and Associates, consulting publishers to the NHL, since 1998.

Bill Bernardi saw his hockey playing days come to an end long before they ever truly began. No, an injury wasn't to blame – his less-than-graceful skating ability was the actual culprit. Thankfully, the press box and the editor's chair provided a safe haven for the bruised ego of Bernardi, who has written about various levels of hockey for a number of leading newspapers and the highly respected PA SportsTicker before serving as the NHL Editor for SportsDirect Inc.

First published by Carlton Books Limited in 2011
Reprinted with updates 2012, 2014
This edition published 2016

Carlton Books Limited
20 Mortimer Street
London W1T 3JW

ISBN: 978-1-78097-744-7

Project art editor: Luke Griffin
Designers: Sally Bond and Katie Baxendale
Picture research: Paul Langan
Production: Rachel Burgess
Editorial: Vanessa Daubney and Chris Hawkes
Project editor: Matt Lowing

Printed in Dubai

COMPLETE HOCKEY RECORDS

2016 EDITION

DAN DIAMOND, ERIC ZWEIG AND BILL BERNARDI

CARLTON BOOKS

CONTENTS

INTRODUCTION

Welcome to *Complete Hockey Records*, a book spanning the breadth and depth of the world's fastest game as played in North America and Europe by men and women, both amateur and professional, for three centuries.

Conversations about hockey are almost as spirited as the game itself. Emotions run high. Tempers grow short. And one never knows if there's a referee nearby should the gloves fall to the ice.

With that in mind, *Complete Hockey Records* would like to provide a peaceful solution while furthering the discussion of the sport that fuels our fire. And how do we do that? Well, with stories, pictures, charts and anecdotes that can whet the appetite of any hockey fan – and with facts and statistics that have the power to settle all arguments and keep the penalty boxes empty.

Turn the page and the journey starts with the sport's modest beginnings, as it works its way from frozen ponds to several associations which predate the National Hockey League. The Original Six had a

charm all its own before the Expansion Era ultimately paved the way to the league we know today. With pages detailing all 30 NHL clubs, the reader can relive his favorite team's glory days while taking a closer look at the personalities that made them so.

Complete Hockey Records also has plenty of stories on the game's greats, and the legendary names of Wayne Gretzky, Bobby Orr and Gordie Howe won't be too hard to find. With that said, active stars like Sidney Crosby, Alex Ovechkin or Carey Price won't be left out of the discussion, either.

If the Olympic flame captures your heart, this book brings it to light as we detail each Winter Games tournament – as well as a Summer Games rendition in Antwerp in 1920. The years eventually pass and memories of Soviet Dominance, the Miracle on Ice and

Canada's winning top honors in both Vancouver (2010) and Sochi (2014) will bring us back to the present.

Reliving memories has its place, but *Complete Hockey Records* likes to be part of the conversation – and what better way than to test the mettle of the reader? So, let's test that theory with a few questions, shall we? Which legendary player trails only Gretzky in goals? You'll find that answer on Page 51. There's a strong chance you got that one, so let's really test your love of the game by asking you to name the three players that have won both the Hart Trophy and the Conn Smythe Trophy in the same year. Page 103 will let you know if your shot was either on the mark or wide of the goal.

Speaking of trophies, hockey's hardware is also on display in this book – with the greatest of them all (the Stanley Cup) having several pages to itself. Page 94 will allow the reader to relive the dynasties of the men that fought tooth and nail to capture the oldest trophy awarded in North American team sports.

Whether you loved them or hated them, the Montreal Canadiens enjoyed a stranglehold on the Stanley Cup for various parts of the late 1950s through the 1970s before the New York Islanders reveled in a four-year run at the top. Then along came Gretzky, and Edmonton basked in its day in the sun for the majority of the remainder of the 1980s.

But this book discusses more than just the NHL. There are stories regarding other professional leagues, colleges and both the U-20 and U-18 tournaments, while light is shed on two players with promising futures despite having yet to make their NHL debuts: Connor McDavid and Jack Eichel.

Finally, a special tip of the hat is extended to both Dan Diamond and Eric Zweig for their significant contributions, the photo archives of the Hockey Hall of Fame and Getty Images as well as the design and editorial team at Carlton Books.

So, now that my introduction has reached its conclusion, please turn the page so your conversation can begin in earnest. But remember, keep the gloves down.

Bill Bernardi, 2015

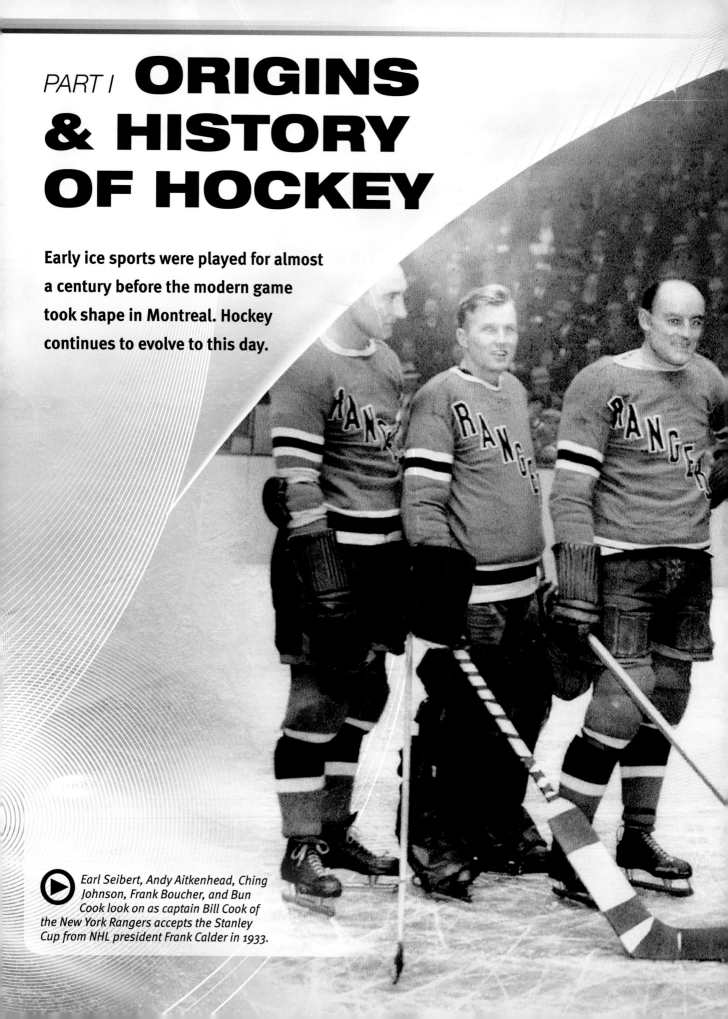

PART I ORIGINS & HISTORY OF HOCKEY

Early ice sports were played for almost a century before the modern game took shape in Montreal. Hockey continues to evolve to this day.

Earl Seibert, Andy Aitkenhead, Ching Johnson, Frank Boucher, and Bun Cook look on as captain Bill Cook of the New York Rangers accepts the Stanley Cup from NHL president Frank Calder in 1933.

INTRODUCTION: PUTTING THE GAME ON ICE

The city of Montreal was where the game of hockey first came indoors from frozen lakes and rivers. The first demonstration of "modern" hockey took place at Montreal's Victoria Skating Rink on March 3, 1875, yet hockey was not truly "invented" anywhere. In fact, it evolved over a lengthy period of time. Ball and stick games were played on the frozen waterways of Nova Scotia in the early 1800s and may have been played in the United States a decade or two before that. In Europe, Dutch paintings display skaters playing games that look a lot like hockey as early as the mid-1500s.

◀ *Ball and stick games, such as this one depicted in a painting from Holland that was a form of golf on ice, predate modern hockey by some 300 years.*

THE WINDSOR CLAIM

Much of the evidence to prove that Windsor, Nova Scotia is the birthplace of hockey comes from the reminiscences of a character named Sam Slick in a book called *The Attaché*, written by Thomas Chandler Haliburton in 1844. Haliburton was born in Windsor in 1796 and graduated from King's College in 1815. In his book, Sam Slick recalls boys "whoopin' like mad with pleasure" while playing "hurley on the long pond on the ice."

HOCKEY DEFINED

A very old root word, *hok* or *hak*, refers to a bent or curved piece of wood or metal similar to the English word "hook." In French, the word *hoquet* comes from the same root and means "curved stick" or more specifically, "shepherd's crook." By the 1840s, the word hockey (or *hawkey*) was common in English, although it usually referred to a curved stick and only rarely to a game played with one.

RICKET

A poem in a Halifax magazine from 1829 includes the lines:

Now at ricket with hurlies some dozens of boys, Chase the ball o'er ice, with a deafening noise.

An 1859 story in the *Boston Evening Gazette* entitled "Winter Sports in Nova Scotia" describes ricket as a game played on ice, where the players wear skates and use a hurley to shoot a ball through their opponent's ricket – which was a goal between two stones on the ice.

HURLING

An Irish team sport with Gaelic origins that may date back more than 2,000 years, hurling is played with a stick called a hurley and a ball (sliotar). The object is to hit the ball through your opponent's goalposts. Students at King's College in Windsor, Nova Scotia are believed to have adapted the field game of hurling for the ice on Long Pond in about 1800. In Ireland, hurling was standardized in 1887.

SHINTY

The game of shinty likely shares similar Gaelic origins with hurling, though it developed differently while being played in Scotland. Today, it resembles field hockey more closely than hurling, though the key differences between the two include hitting the ball out of the air and using both sides of the stick. Shinty was also popular in Nova Scotia and the term "shinny" for informal hockey games may well have derived from shinty.

EARLY REFERENCES

One of the first written references to the word "hockey" in relation to a sport dates back to a letter from Arctic explorer Sir John Franklin, written on November 6, 1825. "Till the snow fell," he wrote, "the game of hockey played on the ice was the morning's sport." British soldiers later wrote about "hockey on the ice" at Chippewa Creek, near Niagara Falls, in 1839 and in Kingston, Ontario in 1843.

THE FIRST GAME

The March 3, 1875 game took place at the Victoria Skating Rink and featured two teams of nine men aside; the team captained by James Creighton won 2-1. A report in the Montreal *Gazette* claimed: "Hockey, though much in vogue on the ice in New England is not known much here." The Montreal *Daily Witness* wrote: "In order to spare the heads and nerves of the spectators a flat piece of board was used instead [of a ball]."

JAMES G.A. CREIGHTON

Born in Halifax, Nova Scotia, on June 12, 1850, James George Aylwin Creighton grew up playing early versions of hockey. Educated in civil engineering, employment opportunities took him to Montreal by 1872, where he played football and joined the Victoria Skating Club. Creighton soon brought in sticks from Halifax and introduced his new friends to the winter game that he had grown up playing. He drafted a set of rules and took part in the first public display of hockey on March 3, 1875.

FIRSTS FOR MCGILL

On February 1, 1877, the *McGill University Gazette* reported that the Montreal school had formed a hockey team. This team is believed to be the first formed solely for the purpose of playing hockey. On February 21, 1881, the McGill Hockey Club posed at the Crystal Palace Skating Rink for what is thought to be the first official photograph of a hockey team. Then, in 1883, McGill won the first hockey championship at the Montreal Winter Carnival.

MONTREAL WINTER CARNIVAL

The Montreal Winter Carnival's hockey tournament was a big success in 1883, so boosting the popularity of the sport. Tournaments were held again in 1884, 1885, 1887, and 1889. On February 4, 1889, Canada's new governor-general, Lord Stanley of Preston, witnessed his first hockey game as part of that year's Winter Carnival. The Montreal Victorias beat the Montreal Amateur Athletic Association 2-1.

BANDY

Similar to field hockey on ice, bandy's roots can be traced back to Russia in the 1700s and possibly as early as the tenth century; links to hockey date to its debut in England, circa 1813. Bandy also became popular in Finland and Sweden in the 1890s. Many of the first hockey players in those countries, as well as Russia, were already skilled at bandy. Today, the game is still popular there.

 Two girls teams play bandy in Sweden, circa 1900.

ORIGINS OF THE NATIONAL HOCKEY LEAGUE

The Amateur Hockey Association of Canada, formed on December 8, 1886, was the sport's first national hockey league. Through a series of mergers and reformations over the next 30-plus years, this association would eventually evolve into the National Hockey League. So many leagues came and went in the early years of the game that it would have been impossible to predict that the NHL was soon to become the sport's dominant organization. From as few as three teams located within a few hundred miles of each other in its early years, the NHL has grown to become the international league of 30 teams that we know today.

◀ *The Montreal Hockey Club pose with several trophies, including the Stanley Cup and the much larger trophy representing the championship of the Amateur Hockey Association of Canada.*

GOING PRO

The first professional hockey leagues were formed in Western Pennsylvania and northern Michigan in the early 1900s. In Canada, the game remained strictly amateur until the Montreal Wanderers and Ottawa Senators pushed forward a rule allowing professionals to play alongside amateur players in the Eastern Canada Amateur Hockey Association in November of 1906. The Manitoba Hockey League quickly followed suit. In 1908, the Ontario Professional Hockey League was organized and would last four seasons through 1911.

AMATEUR HOCKEY ASSOCIATION OF CANADA

The first season of the Amateur Hockey Association of Canada (AHAC) began on January 7, 1887. The league lasted for 12 seasons and played its final game on March 5, 1898. Despite its national name, the AHAC only ever comprised of teams from Montreal, Quebec City, and Ottawa. As champions of the AHAC in 1893, the Montreal Hockey Club (better known as the Montreal Amateur Athletic Association team) became the first winners of the Stanley Cup.

LEAGUES LINKING THE AHAC TO THE NHL

Amateur Hockey Association of Canada (AHAC)	1887–98
Canadian Amateur Hockey League (CAHL)	1899–1905
Federal Amateur Hockey League (FAHL)	1904–07*
Eastern Canada Amateur Hockey Association (ECAHA)	1906–08
Eastern Canada Hockey Association (ECHA)	1909
Canadian Hockey Association (CHA)	1910
National Hockey Association (NHA)	1910–17
National Hockey League (NHL)	1917 to present

*The FAHL was not a true link between these leagues, but the first home of the Montreal Wanderers, who soon joined the ECAHA and were later part of the formation of the NHL.

CHAMPIONS OF THE NHA

1909–10	Montreal Wanderers*
1910–11	Ottawa Senators*
1911–12	Quebec Bulldogs*
1912–13	Quebec Bulldogs*
1913–14	Toronto Blueshirts*
1914–15	Ottawa Senators
1915–16	Montreal Canadiens*
1916–17	Montreal Canadiens

*Also won the Stanley Cup.

THE BIRTH OF THE NATIONAL HOCKEY ASSOCIATION

In November 1909, the Eastern Canada Hockey Association re-formed as the Canadian Hockey Association. Ambrose O'Brien of Renfrew, Ontario, had been trying to get his hometown team into the ECHA. Instead, he banded with the Montreal Wanderers to form a new league called the National Hockey Association. Early in the 1909–10 season, the Ottawa Senators and Montreal Shamrocks left the CHA for the new league and the NHA became the sport's top organization.

◀ This photo of the 1916 Montreal Canadiens depicts the team with the Stanley Cup and the O'Brien Trophy, which was emblematic of the National Hockey Association championship.

THE END OF THE NHA

World War One had an impact on professional hockey in that many National Hockey Association players had joined the armed forces while the fans wondered whether it was right for others to still be playing. In 1916–17, the NHA had a team of soldiers called the 228th Battalion, but before the season came to an end the men were sent to serve overseas. Faced with the threat of further player losses the following season, the NHA suspended operations in November 1917.

THE BIRTH OF THE NHL

Other owners never liked Eddie Livingstone, who had owned teams in Toronto since 1914. Getting rid of him was the main reason why his fellow owners formed the National Hockey League to replace the NHA. Toronto may not have had a team in the NHL's first season at all, had the Quebec Bulldogs not dropped out due to a lack of players. Ownership of the Toronto club was then handed over to the Toronto Arena Company.

Meetings were held throughout November 1917 to dissolve the NHA and then form the NHL. Often, the date given for the formation of the NHL is November 22, 1917. However, the meetings held that day ended with no decision made. A second meeting was set for November 24, but was postponed until November 26. It was on that day, at the Windsor Hotel in Montreal, that the formation of the NHL was formally announced.

THE ORIGINAL FOUR

The Montreal Canadiens, Montreal Wanderers, Ottawa Senators, and Toronto Hockey Club (soon to become known as the Arenas, later the St Patricks and then the Maple Leafs) were the NHL's original teams. After a fire destroyed the Westmount Arena on January 2, 1918, the Wanderers dropped out, but the return of the Quebec Bulldogs in 1919–20 restored the league to four teams. Quebec's comeback would prove short-lived, however, as the Hamilton Tigers replaced the Bulldogs the following season.

SPLIT SEASONS

From 1917–18 through 1920–21, the NHL used a split-season format. The schedule was divided into two halves and playoffs featured the first-place team from the first half playing the first-place team from the second half to decide a champion. (Ottawa won both halves in 1919–20 so there was no NHL playoff that year.) The NHL champion then had to play the winners of the Pacific Coast Hockey Association for the Stanley Cup.

EXPANSION BEGINS

The Roaring Twenties brought great prosperity to the NHL. In the fall of 1924, the league added the Montreal Maroons and also expanded to the United States with the formation of the Boston Bruins. A year later, the NHL dropped the Hamilton Tigers after a strike by its players and added the New York Americans and the Pittsburgh Pirates. In 1926–27, the New York Rangers joined the NHL, along with new teams in Chicago and Detroit.

PACIFIC COAST INNOVATIONS

Though it was the rival National Hockey Association that would later become the NHL, it was the Pacific Coast Hockey Association (PCHA) who modernized the game. Brothers Lester and Frank Patrick formed the league in 1911, building Canada's first artificial ice rinks in British Columbia with money from the sale of their father's lumber business. They went on to introduce many new rules that redefined the way the game was played. Some of their refinements may well have been borrowed from smaller leagues, but the Patricks were the ones who introduced them to a wider audience. Although the PCHA was gone by 1924, it changed the game of hockey forever.

THE PATRICK BROTHERS

The Patricks were raised in Montreal, where the oldest brother (Lester) grew up to star with the Montreal Wanderers when they won the Stanley Cup in 1906 and 1907. The family then relocated to Nelson, British Columbia, but Lester and Frank returned East to star with the Renfrew Millionaires during the NHA's first season of 1909–10. In addition to running the PCHA, both brothers served as team owners, coaches, general managers, and players: Lester in Victoria and Frank in Vancouver.

An image from the first set of hockey cards ever produced shows Lester Patrick in the uniform of the Renfrew Millionaires in 1910.

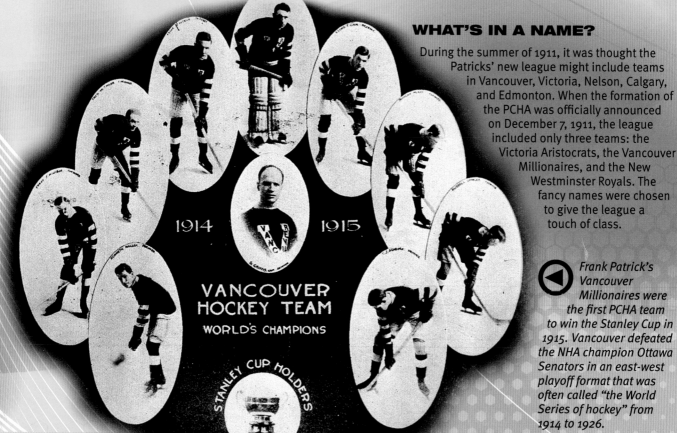

1914 1915

VANCOUVER HOCKEY TEAM
WORLD'S CHAMPIONS

STANLEY CUP HOLDERS

WHAT'S IN A NAME?

During the summer of 1911, it was thought the Patricks' new league might include teams in Vancouver, Victoria, Nelson, Calgary, and Edmonton. When the formation of the PCHA was officially announced on December 7, 1911, the league included only three teams: the Victoria Aristocrats, the Vancouver Millionaires, and the New Westminster Royals. The fancy names were chosen to give the league a touch of class.

Frank Patrick's Vancouver Millionaires were the first PCHA team to win the Stanley Cup in 1915. Vancouver defeated the NHA champion Ottawa Senators in an east-west playoff format that was often called "the World Series of hockey" from 1914 to 1926.

THE FIRST GAME

The showcase of the PCHA was the huge 10,000-seat arena in Vancouver, but the smaller 4,000-seat rink in the British Columbia capital of Victoria had the honor of hosting the first game on January 2, 1912. New Westminster beat the home team 8-3. "With all due reverence for cricket," reported the *Victoria Times*, "we think hockey is a trifle faster. For genuine thrills, hockey has every other game faded to a shadow."

CYCLONE TAYLOR

Frederick Wellington "Cyclone" Taylor is considered by many to be pro hockey's first superstar. Taylor had played with the Patrick brothers in Renfrew and they signed him for the Vancouver Millionaires for the 1912–13 PCHA season. Having previously been a defenseman, Taylor played center and rover in Vancouver and won five PCHA scoring titles in a six-year stretch from 1913–14 to 1918–19. He also led the Millionaires to a Stanley Cup title in 1915.

THE FIRST CHANGES

Though the National Hockey Association dropped the position of rover and introduced six-man hockey in 1911–12, the PCHA stuck with the old seven-man game. Still, the Patricks soon came up with other ways to make the game better. Among their first innovations was allowing goalies to drop to the ice to make a save. In the NHA and other leagues, goalies had to remain standing at all times. The NHL adopted this PCHA rule in its very first season.

THE FORWARD PASS

In an effort to reduce delays caused by offsides, the PCHA became the first hockey league to allow forward passing in 1913–14. Blue lines were painted on the ice to divide the rink into zones and forward passing was permitted inside the neutral zone. (It would be five more years before forward passing was introduced to the NHL.) The PCHA was also the first major league to officially tabulate assists and to assign uniform numbers to its players.

EAST VS. WEST

In the fall of 1913, the NHA and the PCHA signed a "peace treaty" to stop each other from raiding talent from the rosters of rival teams. Among other matters that the leagues agreed upon was that their two league championships should meet annually in a hockey version of baseball's World Series. From 1914 until 1926, teams from the NHA and the NHL would face teams from the West in an annual series for the Stanley Cup.

SOUTH OF THE BORDER

The PCHA was the first Canadian hockey league to include teams from the United States. The New Westminster franchise moved to Portland, Oregon, for the 1914–15 season and one year later, an expansion club was granted to Seattle, Washington. In 1917, the Seattle Metropolitans became the first American team to win the Stanley Cup, beating the Montreal Canadiens three games to one in a best-of-five series.

CHAMPIONS OF THE PCHA

1911–12	New Westminster Royals
1912–13	Victoria Aristocrats
1913–14	Victoria Aristocrats
1914–15	Vancouver Millionaires*
1915–16	Portland Rosebuds
1916–17	Seattle Metropolitans*
1917–18	Vancouver Millionaires
1918–19	Seattle Metropolitans
1919–20	Seattle Metropolitans
1920–21	Vancouver Millionaires
1921–22	Vancouver Millionaires
1922–23	Vancouver Maroons
1923–24	Vancouver Maroons

*Also won the Stanley Cup.

PLAYOFF PAYOFF

In the early days of hockey, playoffs were arranged only to break a deadlock when two or more teams tied for first place. The NHA introduced the split-season playoff format for the 1916–17 season, but it was the PCHA who introduced the first truly modern playoff format the following year. The PCHA playoff system called for the first-place team to meet the second-place finishers, and the first such playoff in 1918 saw second-place Vancouver upset first-place Seattle.

END OF AN ERA

A new league to rival the NHL and the PCHA was introduced in 1921–22 with the formation of the Western Canada Hockey League. A year later, the PCHA began to play an interlocking schedule with the WCHL, though each league maintained separate standings. After the 1923–24 season the PCHA's Seattle club folded. As a result, Frank Patrick's Vancouver team and Lester Patrick's Victoria club joined the WCHL and the PCHA was no more.

NHL ORIGINAL SIX

Having grown to 10 teams before the end of the 1920s, the NHL was hit hard by The Great Depression of the 1930s. By the early years of World War Two, the league was reduced to just six clubs. The era of the NHL's "Original Six," which ran from 1942–43 until 1966–67, has been called the golden age of professional hockey; the league functioned as a sort of exclusive club where only about 100 players had steady jobs. With the advent of the 70-game schedule in 1949–50, teams faced each other 14 times during the regular season, so rivalries were intense.

THE GOOD, THE BAD, AND THE UGLY

Toronto, Detroit, and Montreal dominated the NHL during the "Original Six" era. In the 25 seasons between 1942–43 and 1966–67, the Maple Leafs (nine times), Red Wings (five), and Canadiens (10) combined to win the Stanley Cup on 24 occasions. The New York Rangers failed to even make the playoffs 18 times during the era; Chicago missed the playoffs 13 times and Boston 11 times, including eight straight seasons between 1959–60 and 1966–67.

CARRY ON

It was at the NHL meetings in late September 1942 that the New York Americans suspended operations, leaving the league with just six teams. There were fears that the entire league would shut down, but NHL president Frank Calder announced: "[Government] authorities have recognized the place which the operations of the league hold in the public interest and have, after lengthy deliberation, agreed that in the interest of public morale the league should carry on."

RED LINE MEANS MORE RED LIGHTS

With some 80 players called away to military service, the NHL took action to improve the quality of play by introducing the center red line in 1943–44. Prior to this innovation, teams could pass the puck forward in any zone, but not across the blue line. Allowing passes all the way up to center ice greatly improved the offensive action. Just one year later, Maurice Richard scored 50 goals in 50 games during the 1944–45 season.

Gordie Howe broke into the NHL with Detroit in 1946–47 and starred with the Red Wings for 25 years through 1970–71.

Detroit's Red Kelly and Gordie Howe defend against Montreal's Maurice Richard in front of the Red Wings goalie Terry Sawchuk.

SAWCHUK'S SHUTOUTS

In his first two seasons in the NHL, Terry Sawchuk saw every minute of action in goal for the Detroit Red Wings. He had 44 wins and 11 shutouts in 1950–51, then enjoyed 44 wins with 12 shutouts in 1951–52. In the playoffs that year, Sawchuk posted eight straight wins as Detroit swept their semifinal and final series en route to the Stanley Cup. Sawchuk posted four shutouts in those eight games and had a 0.62 goals-against average.

STREAKERS

The Detroit Red Wings finished in first place in the NHL standings for seven straight seasons from 1948–49 to 1954–55. Red Wings superstar Gordie Howe was the NHL's top scorer four years in a row, from 1950–51 to 1953–54. The Montreal Canadiens reached the Stanley Cup finals for 10 straight springs from 1951 to 1960, winning the championship six times. Between 1956 and 1960, the Canadiens won a record five straight Stanley Cup titles.

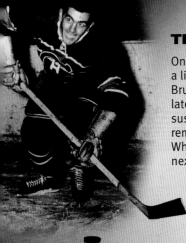

THE RICHARD RIOT

On March 13, 1955, Maurice Richard punched a linesman during an altercation with Boston Bruins defenseman, Hal Laycoe. Three days later, NHL President Clarence Campbell suspended Richard for the season's three remaining games and all of the playoffs. When Campbell attended the Canadiens next home game on March 17, he was pelted with garbage. The game was canceled after a tear-gas canister was set off in the Forum during the first intermission. Outside, a full-fledged riot broke out.

Montreal's Maurice Richard played the game with a fiery intensity that sometimes got the better of him.

TAKING CHICAGO TO THE TOP

The Chicago Blackhawks had missed the playoffs 10 times in 11 years when an 18-year-old rookie named Bobby Hull joined the team in 1957–58. By the 1960–61 season, the Blackhawks were Stanley Cup champions. Over the next few seasons, Hull and teammate Stan Mikita would begin to rewrite the NHL record book. Good as the Blackhawks were, it was not until the 1966–67 season that they finally finished first overall in the NHL standings.

"ORIGINAL SIX" TOP 10 SINGLE-SEASON GOAL TOTALS

54	Bobby Hull, Chicago, 1965–66
52	Bobby Hull, Chicago, 1966–67
50	Maurice Richard, Montreal, 1944–45*
	Bernie Geoffrion, Montreal, 1960–61
	Bobby Hull, Chicago, 1961–62
49	Gordie Howe, Detroit, 1952–53
48	Frank Mahovlich, Toronto, 1960–61
47	Gordie Howe, Detroit, 1951–52
	Jean Beliveau, Montreal, 1955–56
45	Maurice Richard, Montreal, 1946–47**
	Jean Beliveau, Montreal, 1958–59

*50-game season, **60-game season (all others are 70.)

TWO CLOSE TO CALL

During the 1962–63 season there was a four-team race for first place, with only five points separating first from fourth in the tightest finish in NHL history. The Maple Leafs finished on top with 82 points on a record of 35-23-12. Chicago was just one point back with 81, followed by Montreal (79) and Detroit (77). One year later, in the playoffs of 1964, both semifinal series and the Stanley Cup Finals all went to seven games.

A young Bobby Hull (who would later switch to number 9) quickly established himself as the most dangerous goal scorer in the NHL.

"ORIGINAL SIX" TOP 10 SINGLE-SEASON ASSIST TOTALS

62	Stan Mikita, Chicago, 1966–67
59	Stan Mikita, Chicago, 1964–65
58	Jean Beliveau, Montreal, 1960–61
	Andy Bathgate, Tor., NYR, 1963–64
56	Bert Olmstead, Montreal, 1955–56
	Andy Bathgate, NY Rangers, 1961–62
55	Ted Lindsay, Detroit, 1949–50
	Dickie Moore, Montreal, 1958–59
54	Elmer Lach, Montreal, 1944–45*
52	Three players tied

*50-game season (all others are 70.)

"ORIGINAL SIX" TOP 10 SINGLE-SEASON POINT TOTALS

97	Bobby Hull, Chicago, 1965–66 (54G–43A)
	Stan Mikita, Chicago, 1966–67 (35G–62A)
96	Dickie Moore, Montreal, 1958–59 (41G–55A)
95	Gordie Howe, Detroit, 1952–53 (49G–46A)
	Bernie Geoffrion, Montreal, 1960–61 (50G–45A)
91	Jean Beliveau, Montreal, 1958–59 (45G–46A)
90	Jean Beliveau, Montreal, 1960–61 (32G–58A)
89	Stan Mikita, Chicago, 1963–64 (39G–50A)
87	Bobby Hull, Chicago, 1963-64 (43G–44A)
	Stan Mikita, Chicago, 1964–65 (28G–59A)

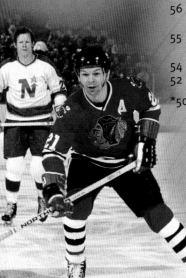

Stan Mikita starred for Chicago well beyond the end of the "Original Six" era in 1967, playing with the Blackhawks from 1958 until 1980.

"ORIGINAL SIX" TEAMS TO REACH 100 POINTS

101	Detroit Red Wings, 1950–51 (70 GP 44-13-13)
100	Detroit Red Wings, 1951–52 (70 GP 44-14-12)
	Montreal Canadiens, 1955–56 (70 GP 45-15-10)

THE EXPANSION ERA

On March 11, 1965, the NHL announced plans to double in size from 6 to 12 teams. Official acceptance for new franchises was given to ownership groups in Los Angeles, San Francisco (Oakland), St. Louis, Pittsburgh, Philadelphia, and Minneapolis-St. Paul on February 8, 1966. On June 6, 1967, an Expansion Draft allowed the Kings, Seals, Blues, Penguins, Flyers, and North Stars to choose 20 players from a pool of unprotected "Original Six" talent. Under pressure from a new rival league called the World Hockey Association that began operation in 1972, the NHL continued to add teams and by the 1974–75 season had grown to 18 franchises.

THE NEW ALIGNMENT

For the 1967–68 season, the 12-team NHL was split into East and West divisions with the expansion clubs together in the West. The first four teams in each division qualified for the playoffs, which now consisted of three best-of-seven rounds; the quarterfinals and semifinals determined the champion of each division, with the two division winners meeting for the Stanley Cup. This guaranteed an expansion club would meet an established team in the final round.

THE 100-POINT PLATEAU

On March 2, 1969, Phil Esposito's first of two goals in a 4-0 win over Pittsburgh made him the first player in NHL history to record 100 points in a single season. Esposito finished the year with 49 goals and 77 assists for 126 points. Bobby Hull (58-49-107) and Gordie Howe (44-59-103) also topped 100 points that year. Aged 41 at the time, Howe remains the oldest player ever to hit the century mark.

Red Berenson starred with St. Louis from 1967 to 1971 and again from 1974 to 1978. He served as team captain in 1977–78.

SINGING THE BLUES

Though the Philadelphia Flyers finished first in the West in 1967–68, the St. Louis Blues would emerge as playoff champions in each of the first three seasons. Ex-Montrealers Dickie Moore, Doug Harvey, Jacques Plante, and Red Berenson led the Blues but could not beat the Canadiens, who swept St. Louis in the Stanley Cup Finals of 1968 and 1969. The Blues fared no better against Boston in 1970, dropping four straight to Bobby Orr and the Bruins.

FROM WORST TO FIRST

As the 1970s dawned, the NHL's weakest franchise of the 1960s was poised for greatness. Bobby Orr had joined the Bruins in 1966–67 and a year later Boston acquired Phil Esposito from the Blackhawks. In the spring of 1970, the Bruins won their first Stanley Cup title since 1941; they won again in 1972. The New York Rangers were also much improved, though it would take until 1994 to win their first Cup since 1940.

Boston's Bobby Orr (left) and Phil Esposito would rewrite the NHL record book in the early 1970s while building the Bruins into a powerhouse.

DRYDEN'S DEBUT

After playing just six games (and winning them all!) late in the 1970–71 season, Ken Dryden earned the Canadiens starting job in goal for the playoffs and was brilliant in Montreal's seven-game upset of Boston in the quarterfinals. The Canadiens once more went seven games against Chicago in the Finals to win the Stanley Cup. Frank Mahovlich set playoff records with 14 goals and 27 points, but it was Ken Dryden who won the Conn Smythe Trophy as playoff MVP.

Ken Dryden played just eight seasons in the NHL between 1970–71 and 1978–79, but he helped the Montreal Canadiens win the Stanley Cup six times.

A GEOGRAPHICAL ODDITY

When the NHL added the Buffalo Sabres and Vancouver Canucks for the 1970–71 season, both new clubs were placed in the same division, meaning that the league's most western-based club (Vancouver) was playing in the East Division. The Canucks remained in the East until 1974–75, when the NHL was realigned into four divisions that dropped their geographic designations and took the names of famed NHL builders James Norris, Charles Adams, Lester Patrick, and Conn Smythe.

BUILT FOR SUCCESS

The New York Islanders set records for futility with a 12-60-6 record as an expansion team in 1972–73, but with draft choices such as Denis Potvin, Bryan Trottier, and Mike Bossy, the Islanders reached the playoffs in just three years and quickly became an elite team. After several playoff disappointments, the Islanders won the Stanley Cup in 1980 on an overtime goal by Bob Nystrom and went on to secure the Cup four years in a row.

THE WORLD HOCKEY ASSOCIATION

When the WHA began play in the fall of 1972, it marked the first time that the NHL's dominance of professional hockey had been challenged since the collapse of the Western Hockey League in 1926. Bobby Hull's defection to the Winnipeg Jets in June of 1972 proved the new league was serious. After seven seasons and several failed franchises, the Edmonton Oilers, Winnipeg Jets, Quebec Nordiques, and New England (Hartford) Whalers entered the NHL from the WHA in 1979–80.

THE BROAD STREET BULLIES

The Philadelphia Flyers of the mid-1970s were a talented team: Bobby Clarke was a three-time MVP, while Rick MacLeish, Bill Barber, and Reggie Leach were 50-goal scorers and Bernie Parent was a brilliant goalie. Still, it was rough play and intimidation – goon hockey – that set the Flyers apart. The Flyers became the first 1967 expansion team to win the Stanley Cup when they beat the Bruins in 1974. In 1975, they beat the Sabres to win again.

Bobby Clarke was the heart and soul of the Philadelphia Flyers and led the team in scoring every season from 1970–71 through 1975–76.

EXPANSION TIMELINE AND ENTRANCE FEES

67–68	California Seals	$2 million		79–80	Hartford Whalers	$6 million
	Los Angeles Kings	$2 million			Quebec Nordiques	$6 million
	Minnesota North Stars	$2 million			Winnipeg Jets	$6 million
	Philadelphia Flyers	$2 million		91–92	San Jose Sharks	$50 million
	Pittsburgh Penguins	$2 million		92–93	Ottawa Senators	$50 million
	St. Louis Blues	$2 million			Tampa Bay Lightning	$50 million
70–71	Buffalo Sabres	$6 million		93–94	Mighty Ducks of Anaheim	$50 million
	Vancouver Canucks	$6 million			Florida Panthers	$50 million
72–73	Atlanta Flames	$6 million		98–99	Nashville Predators	$80 million
	New York Islanders	$6 million		99–00	Atlanta Thrashers	$80 million
74–75	Kansas City Scouts	$6 million		00–01	Columbus Blue Jackets	$80 million
	Washington Capitals	$6 million			Minnesota Wild	$80 million
79–80	Edmonton Oilers	$6 million				

SUMMIT SERIES & BEYOND

From 1920 to 1952, it was a given that Canadian teams would dominate international hockey, but the Soviet Union entered the scene in 1954 and by the early 1960s it was obvious that the Canadian amateur teams could no longer keep up. Hockey fans in Canada remained convinced their top professionals could put the Russians in their place, but it took until the final minute of the final game for Team Canada to emerge victorious in the 1972 Summit Series. The series gave a huge boost to international hockey and opened the door for European talent to begin making its way into the NHL.

◀ Canadian players like Pete Mahovlich did not expect the level of talent they saw in Soviet stars such as Vladimir Petrov.

THE SERIES GETS STARTED

Inside the Montreal Forum the atmosphere was as hot as the weather. The Canadian fans expected a coronation and thought they would get it when Team Canada jumped out to an early 2-0 lead, but the Soviets soon settled into their game of short passes and tireless skating. Much better conditioned than the NHL athletes, who were unaccustomed to summer training, the Soviets tied the score before the first intermission and went on to a 7-3 victory. A nation was stunned.

THE SUMMIT SERIES, GAME BY GAME

Sept. 2/72	USSR 7	Canada 3	at Montreal
Sept. 4/72	USSR 1	Canada 4	at Toronto
Sept. 6/72	USSR 4	Canada 4	at Winnipeg
Sept. 8/72	USSR 5	Canada 3	at Vancouver
Sept. 22/72	Canada 4	USSR 5	at Moscow
Sept. 24/72	Canada 3	USSR 2	at Moscow
Sept. 26/72	Canada 4	USSR 3	at Moscow
Sept. 28/72	Canada 6	USSR 5	at Moscow

BOOED ON HOME ICE

Team Canada gave a much better effort in winning game two at Toronto, but let a 4-2 lead slip away in a 4-4 tie in Winnipeg, two nights later. The home fans were frustrated and unhappy with their team's rough play against the smooth-skating Soviets. Indeed, fans in Vancouver booed Team Canada throughout the game there. Afterward Phil Esposito went on television and expressed his personal disappointment. Espo's speech helped get his team back on track and rallied the country's support.

HENDERSON'S HEROICS

After losing the first game in Moscow, Team Canada needed three straight wins. With Cold War tensions tightening, Paul Henderson came to the rescue. He scored the winning goal in game six and then scored a beautiful goal with just 2:06 remaining to win game seven. Canada was trailing 5-3 entering the third period in game eight, but after goals from Phil Esposito and Yvan Cournoyer, Henderson scored the series winner with just 34 seconds remaining.

▶ Phil Esposito (number 7) hugs Paul Henderson (in the red helmet) who has leapt into the arms of Yvan Cournoyer after scoring the winning goal for Team Canada in the last minute of the final game in 1972.

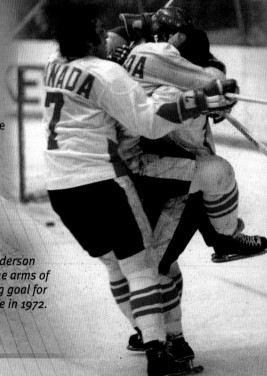

BATTLING THE RED ARMY

During the 1975–76 NHL season, two teams from the Soviet Union came to North America for a special exhibition dubbed "Super Series '76." On December 31, 1975, Moscow's Central Red Army visited Montreal. Though the Canadiens dominated play, the end result was a 3-3 tie in a contest many consider to be the greatest game ever played. On January 11, 1976, the Stanley Cup champion Philadelphia Flyers defeated the Red Army 4-1 in an emotionally charged match that saw the Soviets retreat to their dressing room midway through the first period to protest the rough play by the Flyers.

SUPER SERIES SUMMARY

In all, there were nine Super Series played between 1976 and 1991. Over the years, 21 NHL teams played a total of 98 games against six different Soviet clubs, plus the Soviet national team who competed in the 1983 series. Overall, the Soviet teams posted a record of 55-33-10 against NHL competition. Soviet teams were often boosted with top stars from other clubs, which was frequently offered as a reason for their dominance.

PERMISSION GRANTED

Sergei Priakin was the first Russian to play in the NHL with the permission of the Soviet Union. The Soviet Wings and national team player was allowed to join the Calgary Flames in 1988–89. Though he played just three seasons before returning to Europe, Priakin paved the way for Soviet stars such as Vladimir Krutov, Sergei Makarov, Igor Larionov, and Viacheslav Fetisov plus others from behind the Iron Curtain to enter the NHL without defecting.

 Sergei Makarov won the Calder Trophy as rookie of the year after joining the Calgary Flames in 1989–90.

STANLEY CUP FIRSTS

Sergei Priakin received a ring when Calgary won the Stanley Cup in 1989, but he had not played enough games to have his name engraved on the trophy. The first Russians to get their names engraved on the Cup were Alexei Kovalev, Alexander Karpovtsev, Sergei Nemchinov, and Sergei Zubov when they won it with the New York Rangers in 1994. Igor Larionov, Slava Kozlov, and Viacheslav Fetisov were the first to take the Stanley Cup home to Russia after Detroit's 1997 victory.

SUPER SERIES '76, GAME BY GAME

Date	Soviet Team		NHL Team	
Dec. 28/75	CSKA (Red Army)	7	New York Rangers	3
Dec. 29/75	Krylya Sovetov (Soviet Wings)	7	Pittsburgh Penguins	4
Dec. 31/75	CSKA (Red Army)	3	Montreal Canadiens	3
Jan. 4/76	Krylya Sovetov (Soviet Wings)	6	Buffalo Sabres	12
Jan. 7/76	Krylya Sovetov (Soviet Wings)	4	Chicago Blackhawks	2
Jan. 8/76	CSKA (Red Army)	5	Boston Bruins	2
Jan. 10/76	Krylya Sovetov (Soviet Wings)	2	New York Islanders	1
Jan. 11/76	CSKA (Red Army)	1	Philadelphia Flyers	4

SUCCESS IS SWEDE

The first NHL player born and raised in Europe was Sweden's Ulf Sterner, who spent four games with the New York Rangers in 1964–65. Thommie Bergman joined the Detroit Red Wings in 1972–73, but it was Borje Salming, who made his NHL debut with the Toronto Maple Leafs the following year, who truly paved the way for future Europeans. Salming withstood constant challenges in his early years and went on to star in the NHL for 17 seasons.

 Borje Salming starred in Toronto for 16 of the 17 seasons he played in the NHL.

A DIFFERENT WORLD

Unlike the NHL, the rival World Hockey Association was far quicker to accept European players. Vaclav Nedomansky, the 30-year-old captain of the Czechoslovakian national team, defected to join the Toronto Toros in 1974, but most of the Europeans in the WHA were Scandinavians who were free to come to North America without incident. Anders Hedberg and Ulf Nilsson joined the Winnipeg Jets in 1974–75 and became huge stars on a line with Bobby Hull.

 Anders Hedberg (left) and Ulf Nilsson were huge stars in the WHA before signing big contracts with the NHL's New York Rangers in 1978.

PART II HOCKEY AT THE WINTER OLYMPICS

Whether an amateur tournament or a competition open to the pros, hockey has provided many of the most memorable moments in Winter Olympic Games history.

▶ Canada's Sidney Crosby, left, backhands the puck past the extended left pad of Sweden's Henrik Lundqvist in the gold-medal game of the 2014 Sochi Olympics. The Canadians breezed to a 3-0 triumph and became the first team in over 20 years to claim the gold in consecutive Olympic tournaments.

OLYMPIC HOCKEY HISTORY

Hockey has been part of every Olympic Winter Games since 1924. In fact, the sport even predates the Winter Olympics. The first Olympic hockey tournament was held in 1920 at a spring sports festival in conjunction with the Antwerp (Summer) Games. Counting that original 1920 tournament, Canada has won Olympic gold in hockey on nine occasions – one more than Russia, which won seven times as the Soviet Union from 1956 to 1988, and then as the Unified Team in 1992. Once exclusively an amateur tournament, limited numbers of professionals were allowed to compete from 1988 onward. Since 1998, there has been full NHL participation at the Olympics.

CHAMONIX, 1924

Known at the time as the International Week of Winter Sport, one year later the competition in Chamonix, France, was officially dubbed the first Winter Olympics. Canada's Toronto Granites romped to victory in the hockey tournament, outscoring their opponents 110-3 in five games, including a 33-0 rout of Switzerland. The United States was almost as dominant, sweeping aside its European opponents before dropping a 6-1 decision to Canada in the gold medal game. Great Britain took bronze.

Great Britain (white) takes on Sweden in the opening game for both teams at the 1936 Winter Olympics. The British team won 1-0.

GARMISCH-PARTENKIRCHEN, 1936

Teams from 15 countries competed at the 1936 Winter Olympics, including Italy, Japan, and Latvia, who were all making their Olympic debut. With a team comprised almost entirely of Canadians of British descent, Great Britain surprised Canada's Port Arthur Bearcats with a 2-1 victory in the semifinal round and went on to win the gold medal. Canada settled for silver, while the United States took bronze despite a stunning 2-1 loss to Italy in the opening round.

ST. MORITZ, 1948

After World War Two wiped out the Games of 1940 and 1944, the Olympics returned in 1948, following a 12-year absence. The United States sent two teams backed by different sanctioning organizations and wound up being disqualified. Canada, represented by the RCAF Flyers (a team made up of air force servicemen), and Czechoslovakia both finished with 7-0-1 records (6-0-1 officially), including a scoreless tie against each other. However, Canada won gold because of a better overall goal differential.

ANTWERP, 1920

The Winnipeg Falcons, who received their only real competition from a team of American all-stars, represented Canada at the first Olympic hockey tournament. They defeated Czechoslovakia 15-0, the United States 2-0, and Sweden 12-1 to win the gold medal. The US took silver, while the Czechs secured the bronze. Falcons captain Frank Fredrickson went on to star in the Pacific Coast Hockey Association and the NHL, and was later inducted into the Hockey Hall of Fame.

LAKE PLACID, 1932

The economics of the Great Depression kept many European teams at home, so only four countries took part in the Olympic hockey tournament at Lake Placid, New York. Each team played the others twice in a double-round robin format. Canada took the gold medal, thanks to a 2-1 win over the Americans followed by a tie game that remained 2-2 through three overtime periods. Germany gained the bronze, with only Poland finishing out of the medals.

The RCAF Flyers won a gold medal for Canada at the 1948 St. Moritz Games.

OSLO, 1952

It took a goal with 20 seconds remaining to give Canada's team a 3-2 win in their game against Sweden, but that victory proved to be the difference as the Edmonton Mercury claimed gold after a 3-3 tie with the United States and finished the tournament undefeated at 7-0-1. The Americans had to settle for silver, while Sweden took bronze by beating Czechoslovakia 5-3 in a sudden-death game after the two teams finished tied in the round-robin standings.

CORTINA D'AMPEZZO, 1956

Two years after winning in their debut at the World Championship, the Soviet Union entered the Winter Olympic hockey tournament for the first time and emerged with a gold medal. Led by Vsevolod Bobrov, who tied for the tournament lead with nine goals, the USSR went undefeated in seven games. The United States took silver, while the Kitchener-Waterloo Dutchmen of Canada lost to both the USA and USSR, settling for the bronze.

SQUAW VALLEY, 1960

The Americans had been gradually building toward these Olympics and were quite open about their goal of winning at home in 1960. Led by goalie Jack McCartan and two sets of talented brothers (the Christians and the Clearys), they did indeed win gold. Canada, again represented by the Kitchener-Waterloo Dutchmen, claimed the silver medal, while the Soviets settled for bronze. Australia competed for the first time and finished last among the nine nations.

⏺ *The USA's 2-1 victory over Canada at Squaw Valley in 1960 marked the first time the Americans defeated Canada in Olympic competition.*

LAKE PLACID, 1980

⏻ *Vladimir Krutov of the Soviet Union fends off a German player during a game at the 1988 Winter Olympics.*

Led by coach Herb Brooks, who had been the last player cut from the 1960 Olympic champions, a group of unknown American college students pulled off a stunning victory over the Soviets and went on to win an Olympic gold medal that was quickly dubbed "The Miracle on Ice." Goalie Jim Craig was the biggest US hero and one of 13 players on the 20-man roster who went on to play in the NHL.

CALGARY, 1988

The decision prior to the 1988 Calgary Games to open the hockey competition to "professionals" cleared the way for NHL players to compete at the Olympics for the first time. Despite the presence of Andy Moog, Jim Peplinski, and several other NHLers, Canada could finish no better than fourth. The gold medal-winning Russians, of course, had no NHL players in their lineup, but did feature 19-year-old Alexander Mogilny, who would later go on to NHL stardom.

GOLD MEDALS WON IN THE OLYMPICS SINCE 1920

9	Canada
8	USSR/CIS/Russia
2	USA
	Sweden
1	Great Britain
	Czech Republic

THE BIG RED MACHINE: SOVIET DOMINANCE

What the Soviets called "Canadian Hockey" was first introduced in 1932, but it was slow to catch on. The first hockey league in the Soviet Union began in 1946, but the big breakthrough came in 1948 when the Moscow Selects had a win and a tie in three games versus LTC Prague of Czechoslovakia. In 1954, the Soviet national team entered the World Championship for the first time and won it. The first Olympic gold medal came two years later. From 1963 to 1972, the Soviets won nine consecutive World and/or Olympic Championships. They remained a dominating force until just after the collapse of the Soviet Union, late in 1991.

FIRST GOLD IN '56

After winning the World Championship in 1954, the Soviets appeared to take the 1955 tournament too lightly and were beaten by Canada's well-prepared Penticton Vees. Determined not to repeat their mistake in their first Olympic appearance, the Soviets swept through the tournament without a defeat, posting a perfect 7-0 record and blanking the Americans 4-0 and Canada 2-0 in their last two games. *The New York Times* considered Russia's rapid rise in hockey to be "bordering on the impossible."

STARTING THE STREAK

After going down to the final day before claiming the World Championship in 1963, and then needing a win by Czechoslovakia over Sweden to clinch top spot, the Soviet victory at the 1964 Innsbruck Olympics was much simpler. Though their games with Canada, Sweden, and Czechoslovakia were close, the Soviets posted another perfect 7-0 record to take the gold medal. A late change in the tie-breaking procedure saw Canada slip to fourth place behind the Swedes and Czechs.

ANATOLI TARASOV

A player in the early days of his country's hockey program, Anatoli Tarasov is generally regarded as architect of Soviet domination of international amateur hockey. He and Arkady Chernyshev coached the Soviet Union to their streak of nine straight championships before Tarasov retired after the 1972 Sapporo Olympics. He was inducted into the Hockey Hall of Fame as a builder in 1974. Tarasov was a strong believer in conditioning and wrote many books on hockey.

VSEVOLOD BOBROV

The first captain of the Soviet national team, Vsevolod Bobrov, was named best forward at the World Championship in 1954 and tied for the scoring lead with nine goals in seven games at the 1956 Olympics. In league play in the Soviet Union, he scored a stunning 254 goals in just 130 games. Bobrov later coached the Soviet national team, serving behind the bench at the 1972 Summit Series and winning World Championships in 1973 and 1974.

PILING UP THE NUMBERS

The 1968 Winter Games in Grenoble marked the last time that the Olympic, World and European hockey titles were all decided in one tournament. After opening with five straight wins, the Soviets lost 5-4 to Czechoslovakia but bounced back to beat Canada 5-0 and claim gold. It was Russia's sixth straight title, tying Canada's record from 1920 to 1932. They also won 39 straight games before their streak was snapped, tying a Canadian record from 1936 to 1948.

ANATOLI FIRSOV

A forward with brilliant skills and an extremely hard slap shot, Anatoli Firsov played in the Soviet league with Spartak Moscow (1958–61) and CSKA Moscow (1961–74), scoring 344 goals in 474 league games and winning nine championships. Internationally, he played at every tournament from 1964 to 1972, winning three Olympic gold medals and five additional titles at separate World Championships. Firsov is one of the greatest players in the history of Soviet hockey.

▶ *Soviet star Anatoli Firsov tries to get the puck past Canadian goalie Wayne Stephenson during the 1968 Grenoble Olympics.*

FOUR IN A ROW

Despite having a win erased by a positive drug test for codeine during an outbreak of flu, Czechoslovakia could still defeat the USSR with a win in the final game of the 1976 Olympic tournament. Instead, the Soviets rallied from down 2-0 and 3-2 to pull out a 4-3 win with two quick goals late in the third period. The gold medal for the Soviet Union matched Canada's stretch of four straight Olympic titles between 1920 and 1932.

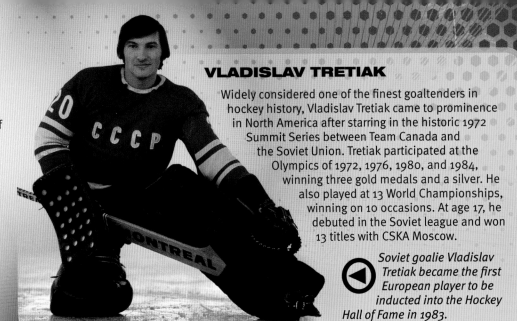

VLADISLAV TRETIAK

Widely considered one of the finest goaltenders in hockey history, Vladislav Tretiak came to prominence in North America after starring in the historic 1972 Summit Series between Team Canada and the Soviet Union. Tretiak participated at the Olympics of 1972, 1976, 1980, and 1984, winning three gold medals and a silver. He also played at 13 World Championships, winning on 10 occasions. At age 17, he debuted in the Soviet league and won 13 titles with CSKA Moscow.

Soviet goalie Vladislav Tretiak became the first European player to be inducted into the Hockey Hall of Fame in 1983.

BACK ON TOP

After losing to the Americans at Lake Placid in 1980, the Russians romped through the 1984 Olympic tournament in Sarajevo. The USSR was a perfect 5-0 in group play during the opening round, outscoring their opponents 42-5, including a 10-1 win over Sweden that carried over into the medal round. Following this, the Soviets beat Canada 4-0 and Czechoslovakia 2-0 to claim gold. This marked the first of two gold medals for Soviet stars Viacheslav Fetisov, Vladimir Krutov, Igor Larionov, and Sergei Makarov.

Americans Steve Christoff and Mike Eruzione surround Sergei Makarov of the Soviet Union at Lake Placid in 1980.

SOVIET/RUSSIAN OLYMPIC RESULTS, 1956–2014

1956	USSR	Gold
1960	USSR	Bronze
1964	USSR	Gold
1968	USSR	Gold
1972	USSR	Gold
1976	USSR	Gold
1980	USSR	Silver
1984	USSR	Gold
1988	USSR	Gold
1992	Unified Team	Gold
1994	Russia	Fourth
1998	Russia	Silver
2002	Russia	Bronze
2006	Russia	Fourth
2010	Russia	5th to 8th
2014	Russia	5th to 8th

END OF AN ERA

With the dissolution of the Soviet Union in December 1991, athletes of the former Soviet Republics competed together at the 1992 Albertville Games under the name "Unified Team." The hockey team comprised only ethnic Russians, but wore no logo on their uniforms. When they scored a 3-1 win over Canada in the gold-medal game, the Olympic anthem was played in lieu of a national anthem. Twenty of the 23 players on the Unified Team went on to play in the NHL.

Members of the former Soviet "Unified Team" celebrate their gold medal victory in 1992.

THE OPEN ERA: 1998 TO 2015

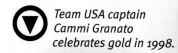

Team USA captain Cammi Granato celebrates gold in 1998.

Future NHLers had represented Canada and the United States at the Winter Olympics since the first hockey tournament in 1920. However, it took an agreement reached in 1995 before the NHL fully committed itself to Olympic participation in 1998. That year, a total of 122 NHL players took part, launching an "open era" that has produced some of the greatest hockey in history. In the 2014 Sochi Games, there were 149 NHLers competing – with at least one on each of the rosters of the 12 countries. The 1998 Games also marked the debut of women's hockey at the Olympics.

NAGANO (MEN'S), 1998

The NHL shut down its regular season for two weeks to allow players to compete at the Winter Olympics. With the United States having surprised Canada at the World Cup of Hockey two years earlier, it was expected the two teams would battle it out for gold, but the US struggled and Canada was eliminated by the Czech Republic in a semifinals shootout. Dominik Hasek then posted a shutout in the gold medal game as the Czechs beat Russia 1-0.

Goalie Dominik Hasek led the Czech Republic to its first hockey gold at the Nagano Olympics.

NAGANO (WOMEN'S), 1998

Women's hockey made its debut at the Olympic Games in Nagano in 1998. Having won all of the medals available at the previous World Championships, Canada, the United States, and Finland were clearly the class of the Women's Olympic tournament. Canada had captured every previous world title, but it was the Americans who won the first Olympic gold. As American captain Cammie Granato led her teammates in celebration, the Canadian women could not conceal their disappointment.

SALT LAKE CITY (MEN'S), 2002

Though Canadian men were out to win the country's first Olympic gold in hockey since 1952, the team struggled in the early going. A 2-1 win over Finland in the quarterfinals got Canada on track while a stunning upset by Belarus took top-ranked Sweden out of the way in the semifinals. Canada played its best hockey in the gold medal game, where Martin Brodeur and Mario Lemieux led the team to a 5-2 win over the United States.

SALT LAKE CITY (WOMEN'S), 2002

Canadian women were out to avenge their loss of 1998, but the USA had a 31-0-0 record during its pre-Olympic schedule, including eight straight wins against the Canadians. Canada fell behind Finland 3-2 in the semifinals before Hayley Wickenheiser sparked a five-goal outburst. Wickenheiser then scored the go-ahead goal in the gold medal game as Canada took a 3-1 lead on the USA and held on for a 3-2 victory.

Hayley Wickenheiser led Canadian women on a mission of revenge in 2002.

SENSATIONAL SELANNE, 2014

Teemu Selanne capped a phenomenal Olympic career with two goals to lead Finland to a 5-0 triumph over the United States in the bronze-medal contest of the 2014 Sochi Games. Selanne finished his record-tying sixth and final Winter Olympics with four tallies and two assists en route to being named the Most Valuable Player of the tournament. The Finn holds the Olympic scoring record with 43 points (24 goals, 19 assists) and became the oldest player to win a medal in hockey at 43 years, 234 days.

TORINO (MEN'S), 2006

Led by tournament scoring leaders Teemu Selanne and Saku Koivu, Finland remained undefeated until their archrivals from Sweden beat them in the gold medal game. Nicklas Lidstrom scored the go-ahead goal 10 seconds into the third period and goaltender Henrik Lundqvist withstood a late Finnish flurry to give Sweden a 3-2 victory. Slovakia were undefeated until they lost against the Czech Republic in the quarterfinals. The Czechs went on to beat Russia in the bronze medal game.

▲ *The Swedish team stands together in celebration after winning gold in 2006.*

TORINO (WOMEN'S), 2006

While Canadian women cruised to their second straight gold medal, the Games of 2006 featured the biggest upset in the history of women's hockey. Swedish goalie Kim Martin led her team to a stunning 3-2 shootout upset of the Americans in the semifinals, stopping 37 out of 39 shots and then making saves on four shootout attempts. Canada beat the Swedes 4-1 in the final game, while the Americans bounced back to beat Finland 4-0 and take the bronze medal.

CUMULATIVE MEDAL STANDINGS, WOMEN'S OLYMPIC HOCKEY, 1998-2014

	G	S	B	Total	Last Medal
1. Canada	4	1	0	5	Gold 2014
2. USA	1	3	1	5	Silver 2014
3. Sweden	0	1	1	2	Silver 2006
4. Finland	0	0	2	2	Bronze 2010

CUMULATIVE MEDAL STANDINGS, MEN'S OLYMPIC HOCKEY, 1920-2014

	G	S	B	Total	Last Medal
1. Canada	9	4	2	15	Gold 2014
2. USSR/Russia*	8	2	2	12	Bronze 2002
3. USA	2	8	1	11	Silver 2010
4. Sweden	2	3	4	9	Silver 2014
5. Czechoslovakia/ Czech Republic	1	4	5	10	Bronze 2006
6. Great Britain	1	0	1	2	Gold 1936
7. Finland	0	2	4	6	Bronze 2014
8. W. Germany	0	0	2	2	Bronze 1976
9. Switzerland	0	0	2	2	Bronze 1948

* Soviet Union/Russia played as the Unified Team in 1992.

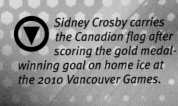

▼ *Sidney Crosby carries the Canadian flag after scoring the gold medal-winning goal on home ice at the 2010 Vancouver Games.*

SOCHI (MEN'S), 2014

After taking gold at the 2010 Vancouver Games, the Canada men's team repeated the feat in Sochi, Russia. Although favorites, the Canadians were hardly dominant en route to winning Group B honors – and then had to fend off upstart Latvia in the quarterfinal round. Montreal Canadiens goaltender Carey Price stopped all 31 shots he faced to make Dallas Stars captain Jamie Benn's second-period goal stand up in Team Canada's 1-0 triumph over the United States. The Canadians advanced to the final match, where Price was perfect again with 24 saves in his team's 3-0 victory over Sweden.

SOCHI (WOMEN'S), 2014

The Canadian women's team secured its fourth consecutive gold medal at the Olympics. Marie-Philip Poulin scored the tying goal late in the third period before netting the winner on a power play 8:10 into overtime as Team Canada rallied from a two-goal deficit for a 3-2 victory over the United States. Poulin wired a shot from the lower edge of the left circle past Jessie Vetter to earn Canada victory. The setback was all-too-familiar for the Americans, who have lost in the Olympic final to Canada in all three tries since winning the gold at the 1998 Nagano Games.

GOLDEN GOALS & MIRACLES ON ICE

Though Canada and the Soviet Union dominate much of the history of Olympic hockey, the competition at the Winter Games has created some of the greatest moments that the game has ever seen. Across the board, however, there is little to compare with the drama of the American triumph over the Soviets at Lake Placid in 1980. Swedish fans reveled in their victory over archrival Finland in 2006, while the Canadians rejoiced on home ice in 2010. The one-game elimination playoff system inaugurated in 1992 has increased the drama in recent years, but some dramatic moments occurred in the early years too.

CANADA VS. USA, 1932

The very first game of the 1932 Olympic hockey tournament turned out to be the most important one: the United States led Canada's Winnipeg Hockey Club 1-0 until Harold Simpson tied the game at 13:36 of the third period. Vic Lundquist got the winner for Canada at 7:14 of overtime. The game was played outdoors. A crowd of 7,000 packed the 3,000-seat indoor arena for the rematch, which ended in a 2-2 tie and clinched the gold for Canada.

CANADA VS. USA, 1920

Though seven countries took part in the spring hockey tournament held in conjunction with the 1920 Summer Olympics, everyone knew the European nations had no chance of winning. The game between the United States and Canada's Winnipeg Falcons on the third day of the tournament proved to be the true gold medal contest. A late goal by Frank Fredrickson broke open a scoreless game and led Canada to a 2-0 victory. A 12-1 win over Sweden the next day sealed the gold medal.

GREAT BRITAIN VS. CANADA, 1936

Though the biggest upset of the Olympic tournament was Italy's 2-1 overtime win over the Americans in the preliminary round, the key victory was Great Britain's 2-1 victory over Canada in the second. Goalie Jimmy Foster, born in Glasgow but raised in Winnipeg (all bar one member of the British team had grown up in Canada), was the star and Edgar Brenchley scored the winning goal with little time remaining. Great Britain went on to win gold, with Canada settling for the silver and the US taking the bronze.

 The Port Arthur Bearcats represented Canada at the 1936 Games in Garmisch-Partenkirchen, Germany.

USA VS. CZECHOSLOVAKIA, 1960

The USA had a perfect record of 6-0 on home ice in Squaw Valley, California (including a 2-1 win over Canada and a 3-2 victory over the Soviets), but still needed to beat Czechoslovakia in the final game to clinch gold. Trailing 4-3 after two periods, the Americans were advised by a Russian defenseman to take oxygen to restore their pep. It may have helped, as Roger Christian led a six-goal barrage en route to a 9-4 gold-medal victory.

USA VS. SWEDEN, 1980

The Americans were ranked seventh among the 12 teams at the Lake Placid Games and believed a fast start was important for even a chance of reaching the medal round. Goalie Jim Craig was brilliant in the opener against Sweden, but the Americans trailed 2-1 late in the third period. With Craig on the bench for an extra attacker, Bill Baker slapped home the tying goal with 27 seconds remaining. "It was a big point for us," said coach Herb Brooks.

 Bill Baker was a defensive defenseman with one big goal in the 1980 Olympics.

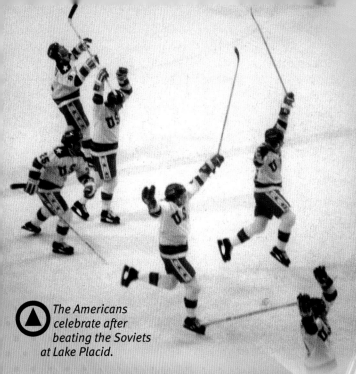

USA VS. SOVIET UNION, 1980

After the tie against Sweden, the USA won four straight games to reach the medal round and a date with the Soviet Union. Once again Jim Craig kept the Americans in the game, while a shaky Vladislav Tretiak was pulled at the end of the first period. Tied 3-3 midway through the third, captain Mike Eruzione scored the go-ahead goal at the 10-minute mark and the USA held on to win: "Do you believe in miracles? ... *Yes!*"

The Americans celebrate after beating the Soviets at Lake Placid.

USA VS. FINLAND, 1980

Even with their win over the Soviets, the USA still faced the prospect of finishing out of the medals heading into the final day of action at Lake Placid. As they had for most of the tournament, the Americans gave up the first goal in their game against Finland. They were trailing 2-1 after two. Dave Christian, whose father and uncle both played with the 1960 US team, set up two goals in the third period as the Americans rallied for a 4-2 gold medal victory.

SWEDEN VS. CANADA, 1994

With the decision to stagger the Summer and Winter Games, the 1994 Lillehammer Olympics took place just two years after the 1992 Albertville Games. The exciting hockey tournament reached a thrilling conclusion with a shootout in the final game between Sweden and Canada. The winning goal on a trick shot by Peter Forsberg gave the Swedes their first-ever Olympic championship. Tomas Jonsson, Hakan Loob, and Mats Naslund became the first players to win World, Olympic, and Stanley Cup titles.

Peter Forsberg scores his first of two goals in the gold medal shootout in 1994.

CZECH REPUBLIC VS. RUSSIA, 1998

Dominik Hasek allowed only six goals in six games and posted two shutouts in leading the Czech Republic to its first Olympic gold in hockey at the Nagano Games. In a shootout, Hasek blanked all five Canadian shooters to give the Czechs a 2-1 victory in the semifinals and then kept goal-scoring leader Pavel Bure and his Russian teammates off the scoreboard in a 1-0 victory in the final game. Petr Svoboda scored the gold medal-winning goal.

BELARUS VS. SWEDEN, 2002

Sweden opened the Salt Lake City Olympics with three straight wins, but Belarus beat the Swedes in a stunning upset in the quarterfinals when Vladimir Kopat put a long shot past Tommy Salo with just 2:24 remaining to give the huge underdogs a 4–3 victory. Belarus could not capitalize on their unexpected chance of a medal, losing 7-1 to Canada in the semifinals and 7-2 to Russia in the bronze medal game. The Swedes bounced back to win gold in 2006.

CANADA VS. USA, 2010

As a rookie, Sidney Crosby had been left off Canada's team at the 2006 Olympics. However, he was there on home ice in Vancouver in 2010 and though he played well, he was not the dominant offense force that the fans had expected. Still, it was Crosby who scored the goal that gave Team Canada the first Olympic gold medal to be decided in overtime, sneaking a quick shot past American goalie Ryan Miller for a Canadian victory.

Canada's Sidney Crosby celebrates after beating Ryan Miller for the gold medal goal at the Vancouver Olympics.

PART III NHL TEAM RECORD BOOK

Which team scored the most goals?
Which won the most games?
Or the most in a row? Which was
the worst of all-time? The team
records let you know.

Captain Henrik Zetterberg, left, and the Detroit Red Wings had plenty for which to rejoice after the club extended its playoff streak to 24 consecutive seasons during the 2014–15 campaign.

TEAM RECORDS: WINS, LOSSES, & STREAKS

Over the years of its history, the length of the NHL season has ranged from as few as 18 games in 1918–19 to 84 games in the early 1990s. For 18 seasons from 1949–50 to 1966–67, the NHL season was 70 games long. Teams played 80 games a year for a similar 18-year stretch from 1974–75 to 1991–92 and have been playing an 82-game schedule since the 1995–96 season. Obviously, the longer the season the more opportunities there are for wins ... and for losses. In recent years, overtime and shootouts have also given teams more opportunities for wins and points.

THE 2012-13 CHICAGO BLACKHAWKS

The Chicago Blackhawks began the 2012–13 lockout-shortened season in impressive fashion, recording a point in their first 24 games (21-0-3) while also winning a franchise-record 11 in a row. The NHL's third-longest undefeated streak came to an unexpected halt at the hands of Colorado, which breezed to a 6-2 home victory on March 8, 2013. Chicago's run easily bested that of the Anaheim Ducks, who began the 2006-07 season with a then-record 16-game point streak. The Blackhawks overcame their brief stumble against the Avalanche en route to defeating Boston in the Stanley Cup.

▲ *Larry Robinson was the top offensive threat on a strong Canadiens defense in the 1970s.*

▼ *Eddie Shore (number 2) helps sprawled Bruins goalie Tiny Thompson cover a loose puck during a game in the early 1930s.*

MOST POINTS, ONE SEASON

132	Montreal Canadiens, 1976–77	60-8-12	80 GP
131	Detroit Red Wings, 1995–96	62-13-7	82 GP
129	Montreal Canadiens, 1977–78	59-10-11	80 GP
127	Montreal Canadiens, 1975–76	58-11-11	80 GP
124	Detroit Red Wings, 2005–06	58-16-8	82 GP
121	Boston Bruins, 1970–71	57-14-7	78 GP
	Washington Capitals, 2009–10	54-15-13	82 GP

THE 1929-30 BRUINS

The 1929–30 season was the first one in which the NHL allowed forward passing in all zones on the ice. No team was better prepared to take advantage of the new rules than the Boston Bruins who put up a record of 38-5-1 during the 44-game season for an .875 winning percentage that is still the best in history. Boston set another record that still stands (matched by the 1975–76 Philadelphia Flyers) with 20 straight wins on home ice.

THE LONGEST UNDEFEATED STREAK

After losing their second game of the 1979–80 season, the Philadelphia Flyers did not lose again for 84 days. Between October 14, 1979 and January 6, 1980, the Flyers went undefeated in 35 straight games, recording 25 wins and 10 ties. The Flyers broke the previous NHL record of 28 straight set by the 1977–78 Montreal Canadiens and broke the all-pro sports record of 33 games without a loss by the 1971–72 Los Angeles Lakers of the NBA.

The Islanders' Mike Bossy watches Philadelphia Flyers' defenseman Jimmy Watson closely.

LONGEST WINNING STREAK, ONE SEASON

17 Games	Pittsburgh Penguins, March 9 to April 10, 1993
15 Games	New York Islanders, January 21 to February 20, 1982
14 Games	Boston Bruins, December 3, 1929 to March 18, 1930
	Washington Capitals, January 13 to February 7, 2010

LONGEST LOSING STREAK, ONE SEASON

17 Games	Washington Capitals, February 18 to March 26, 1975
	San Jose Sharks, January 4 to February 12, 1993
15 Games	Philadelphia Quakers, November 29, 1930 to January 8, 1931
	Washington Capitals, January 13 to February 7, 2010

MOST LOSSES

71	San Jose Sharks, 1992–93	11-71-2 (24 pts)	84 GP
70	Ottawa Senators, 1992–93	10-70-4 (24 pts)	84 GP
67	Washington Capitals, 1974–75	8-67-5 (21 pts)	80 GP
61	Quebec Nordiques, 1989–90	12-61-7 (31 pts)	80 GP
	Ottawa Senators, 1993–94	14-61-9 (37 pts)	84 GP
60	New York Islanders, 1972–73	12-60-6 (30 pts)	78 GP

THE 1974-75 WASHINGTON CAPITALS

With a record of just 8-67-5 for 21 points in their first NHL season, the Washington Capitals of 1974–75 rank as the worst team in league history. Though other teams would lose more games, no one has ever posted a worse points percentage than the Capitals' mark of .131 that season. No team has ever won fewer games or collected fewer points since 1930–31 when the NHL season lasted just 44 games.

Michel Belhumer was a woeful 0-29-4 in 42 games in Washington during the Capitals' first two seasons.

HOME SWEET HOME

The Detroit Red Wings gave little indication of what was to come. After securing just one point in its previous three games at Joe Louis Arena, coach Mike Babcock's club set an NHL record by winning its next 23 straight at home. The Red Wings outscored their opponents by an 89-34 margin, collected four shutouts and registered five or more goals on eight separate occasions. The Vancouver Canucks put a stop to it all with a 4-3 victory on February 23, 2012. This home setback was Detroit's first since a 4-1 loss to Calgary on November 3, 2011.

Jimmy Howard's sensational play at home helped the Detroit Red Wings get a leg up on their adversaries.

WILD: AT HOME ON THE ROAD

Minnesota tied the 2005–06 Detroit Red Wings for the longest road winning streak in league history when it posted its 12th straight victory with a 4-2 triumph over Nashville on April 9, 2015. Jason Zucker scored twice and Jason Pominville netted the go-ahead goal with 2:03 remaining in the third period to continue the Wild's torrid stretch. Minnesota's run of good fortune ended in St. Louis two nights later in the regular-season finale, dropping a 4-2 decision for its first setback away from home since suffering a 3-2 loss in Vancouver on February 16.

TEAM RECORDS: GOALS FOR & AGAINST

In the early days of the NHL, hockey was a wide-open game with lots of scoring. But by the end of the 1920s, scoring had decreased drastically. More modern passing rules were introduced in 1929–30 and scoring production jumped. Defense returned to the forefront during the 1950s and though scoring would begin to creep up again in the 1960s it took expansion to really give the numbers a boost. The 21-team era of the 1980s was the true high-water mark for offensive production with teams combining to score approximately eight goals per game. Most of the NHL's major individual and team records were set during this era.

MOST GOALS, ONE SEASON

446	Edmonton Oilers, 1983–84	80 GP
426	Edmonton Oilers, 1985–86	80 GP
424	Edmonton Oilers, 1982–83	80 GP
417	Edmonton Oilers, 1981–82	80 GP
401	Edmonton Oilers, 1984–85	80 GP
399	Boston Bruins, 1970–71	78 GP

GOALS PER GAME

Wayne Gretzky's Edmonton Oilers of the 1980s were the most prolific offensive machine in the history of hockey. In addition to holding the top five spots for goals scored in one season, they also hold three of the top five positions in goals-per-game average. The 1983–84 Oilers averaged a record 5.58 goals per game. The second highest-scoring average of 5.38 belongs to the 1919–20 Montreal Canadiens. They scored 129 goals in just 24 games.

SEVEN THE HARD WAY

After being shut out in the first 40 minutes of their game versus Vancouver, the New York Islanders showed little in what was to come in the final 20. The Islanders erupted for a franchise record-tying seven goals in the third period en route to a 7-4 triumph over the Canucks on March 10, 2014. Josh Bailey, Ryan Strome and defenseman Calvin de Haan scored power-play goals 2:23 apart early in the session to erase New York's 3-0 deficit. Frans Nielsen, Matt Martin and Anders Lee also tallied before Cal Clutterbuck scored into an empty net for the Islanders, who matched the franchise's previous record for tallies in one period - which was set against the rival New York Rangers on Dec. 23, 1978. Vancouver yielded seven goals in a period for the third time in history (1983, 1985).

MOST GOALS, ONE TEAM, ONE GAME

On March 3, 1920, the Montreal Canadiens beat the Quebec Bulldogs 16-3. Four different Canadiens players scored three or more goals in the game. Didier Pitre had a hat trick in the first period and Newsy Lalonde scored three in the second before netting a fourth goal in the third period. Defenseman Harry Cameron also had four goals in the game while Odie Cleghorn collected one goal in each period to round out the foursome.

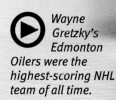 *A star since the early 1900s, Newsy Lalonde was the highest-scoring player of his day.*

MOST GOALS, BOTH TEAMS, ONE GAME

It was another big night for Newsy Lalonde when he scored six times in Montreal's 14-7 win over the Toronto St. Pats on January 10, 1920. The NHL record of 21 goals in a single game set that evening still stands. It was tied on December 11, 1985 in a 12-9 Edmonton Oilers victory over the Chicago Blackhawks. Wayne Gretzky tied an NHL record with seven assists including six on hat tricks by Jari Kurri and Glenn Anderson.

Wayne Gretzky's Edmonton Oilers were the highest-scoring NHL team of all time.

ONE-SIDED WIN

On January 23, 1944, the Detroit Red Wings beat the New York Rangers 15-0 for the highest scoring win by shutout in NHL history. Connie Dion faced only nine shots to earn his first shutout while Rangers goalie Ken McAuley made 43 saves but still surrendered all 15 goals. Of the 13 Red Wings in action that night, only Dion and defenseman Cully Simon failed to collect a point. Sid Howe had three goals and two assists.

MOST GOALS, ONE PERIOD

With Gilbert Perreault scoring a hat trick and Andre Savard notching two of his three goals on the night, the Buffalo Sabres exploded for nine goals in the second period en route to a 14-4 win over the Toronto Maple Leafs on March 19, 1981. With Toronto scoring three times itself, the two teams combined for a record 12 goals in the period ... though that mark would later be tied in Edmonton's 12-9 win over Chicago.

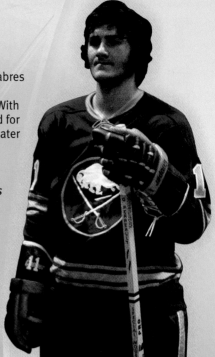

Gilbert Perreault's three goals against Toronto in Buffalo's 14-4 victory was one of 18 hat tricks in his career.

Brian Hayward tended goal for the San Jose Sharks in 1991–92 and 1992–93. During that time he posted a 3-18-1 record with a 5.39 goals-against average.

MOST GOALS AGAINST, ONE SEASON

446	Washington Capitals, 1974–75	80 GP
415	Detroit Red Wings, 1985–86	80 GP
414	San Jose Sharks, 1992–93	84 GP
407	Quebec Nordiques, 1989–90	80 GP
403	Hartford Whalers, 1982–83	80 GP
400	Winnipeg Jets, 1980–81	80 GP

WORST GOALS-AGAINST AVERAGE

The Quebec Bulldogs played just one season in the NHL in 1919–20 but set records for futility that will never be matched. With a record of 4-20-0, Quebec's eight points are an all-time low and their 177 goals-against in those 24 games give the Bulldogs a team average of 7.38. The New York Rangers of 1943–44 surrendered 310 goals in a 50-game season for a mark of 6.10, while Washington's total from 1974–75 is 5.58.

FEWEST GOALS, ONE SEASON

All-Time

33	Chicago Blackhawks, 1928–29	44 GP
45	Montreal Maroons, 1924–25	30 GP
46	Pittsburgh Pirates, 1928–29	44 GP

Minimum 70-Game Schedule

133	Chicago Blackhawks, 1953–54	70 GP
147	Toronto Maple Leafs, 1954–55	70 GP
	Boston Bruins, 1955–56	70 GP
150	New York Rangers, 1954–55	70 GP
	Buffalo Sabres, 2013-14	82GP

THE WORST OF THE WORST

The 1928–29 season was the low mark for goals scored in NHL history. This was the year in which Montreal's George Hainsworth recorded 22 shutouts in 44 games. The Chicago Blackhawks scored just 33 goals all season and were shutout 20 times. During one stretch of games from February 7 to 28, 1929, Chicago was shutout in eight straight games! Still, the Blackhawks only lost six of those games as two ended in scoreless ties.

SHOTS ON GOAL

The Boston Bruins fired 83 shots at the Chicago Blackhawks during a game on March 4, 1941. Chicago's Sam Lo Presti made 80 saves but still lost the game 3-2. On March 21, 1991, Boston fired 73 shots at Quebec Nordiques goalie Ron Tugnutt but only managed a 3-3 tie. On December 26, 1925, the New York Americans and Pittsburgh Pirates combined for 141 shots on goal. The Americans led 73-68 and won the game 3-1.

TEAM RECORDS: SCORING FAST & OFTEN

Fifty goals and 100 points have long been the milestones for excellence in a single season. Players began hitting these numbers on a regular basis in the 1970s and since then only a few seasons have passed without one or the other number being reached. Even so, some teams have hit these numbers more spectacularly than others. The 1970–71 Boston Bruins and the Edmonton Oilers of the 1980s put up numbers that were hard to match, though Mario Lemieux and the Pittsburgh Penguins did their best in the 1990s. A few other teams have had their milestone moments, too.

Wayne Gretzky (left) and Jari Kurri led a high-powered offense in Edmonton in the 1980s.

THREE FOR THREE

The Boston Bruins "Kraut Line" of Milt Schmidt, Woody Dumart, and Bobby Bauer became the first teammates in NHL history to finish 1-2-3 in NHL scoring during the 1939–40 season. Their feat was matched in 1944–45 when Montreal's "Punch Line" of Elmer Lach, Maurice Richard, and Toe Blake topped the scoring charts together. Detroit's "Production Line" of Ted Lindsay, Sid Abel, and Gordie Howe finished 1-2-3 in scoring in 1949–50.

MOST 100-POINT SCORERS

In addition to the four Bruins of 1970–71 (see below), there have been four other times when four teammates each topped 100 points:

Edmonton Oilers, 1982–83. 80GP. Wayne Gretzky, 71G-125A-196PTS; Mark Messier, 48G-58A-106PTS; Glenn Anderson, 48G-56A-104PTS; Jari Kurri, 45G-59A-104PTS.

Edmonton Oilers, 1983–84. 80GP. Wayne Gretzky, 87G-118A-205PTS; Paul Coffey, 40G-86A-126PTS; Jari Kurri, 52G-61A-113PTS; Mark Messier, 37G-64A-101PTS.

Edmonton Oilers, 1985–86. 80GP. Wayne Gretzky, 52G-163A-215PTS; Paul Coffey, 48G-90A-138PTS; Jari Kurri, 68G-63A-131PTS; Glenn Anderson, 54G-48A-102PTS.

Pittsburgh Penguins, 1992–93. 84GP. Mario Lemieux, 69G-91A-160PTS; Kevin Stevens, 55G-56A-111PTS; Rick Tocchet, 48G-61A-109PTS; Ron Francis, 24G-76A-100PTS.

Right winger Bobby Bauer (17), left winger Woody Dumart (14) and center Milt Schmidt (15) of the Bruins' Kraut Line.

FAST TRICK

Three members of the 1970–71 Boston Bruins combined to score the three fastest goals by one team in NHL history on February 5, 1971. John Bucyk scored at 4:50 of the third period as the Bruins wiped out an early 2-0 deficit and went ahead of the Vancouver Canucks 3-2. The Bruins got two more, with Ed Westfall scoring at 5:02 and Ted Green at 5:10, to give Boston three goals in just 20 seconds.

ONE-TWO-THREE-FOUR

In 1970–71, Phil Esposito set what seemed like two unbreakable scoring records when he scored 76 goals and collected 152 points. Bobby Orr set a record with 102 assists and finished second to Eposito with 139 points. Boston's John Bucyk (51-65-116) and Ken Hodge (43-62-105) rounded out the top four scorers that year. Four Bruins teammates equaled the feat in 1973–74 when Esposito (145), Orr (122), Hodge (105), and Wayne Cashman (95) all topped the charts.

MOST 50-GOAL SCORERS

The Edmonton Oilers are the only team in NHL history with three 50-goal scorers in one season ... and they did it twice! In 1983–84, Wayne Gretzky had 87 goals, Glenn Anderson had 54, and Jari Kurri had 52. In 1985–86, Kurri scored 68 goals, Anderson had 54 and Gretzky had 52. Gretzky was part of four other pairs of 50-goal scorers, including one with Bernie Nicholls of the Los Angeles Kings in 1988–89.

TRIPLE MILESTONES

On March 29, 1983, the Edmonton Oilers beat the Vancouver Canucks 7-3. Wayne Gretzky had a goal and three assists, including his 121st of the year to break his own single-season assist record. (Three years later, he'd push the record to an astounding 163.) Linemates Jari Kurri and Glenn Anderson also had big nights, as they became the first pair of teammates to reach the 100-point plateau in the same game.

ALL-TIME HIGHEST GOAL SCORING PAIRS

144	Edmonton Oilers, 1984-85	80GP	Wayne Gretzky, 73; Jari Kurri, 71
142	Edmonton Oilers, 1981-82	80GP	Wayne Gretzky, 92; Mark Messier, 50
141	Edmonton Oilers, 1983-84	80GP	Wayne Gretzky, 87; Glenn Anderson, 54
131	Pittsburgh Penguins, 1995-96	82GP	Mario Lemieux, 69; Jaromir Jagr, 62
129	Buffalo Sabres, 1992-93	84GP	Alexander Mogilny, 76; Pat LaFontaine, 53
127	Boston Bruins, 1970-71	78GP	Phil Esposito, 76; John Bucyk, 51
124	Los Angeles Kings, 1988-89	80GP	Bernie Nicholls, 70; Wayne Gretzky, 54
	Pittsburgh Penguins, 1992-93	84GP	Mario Lemieux, 69; Kevin Stevens, 55
122	Edmonton Oilers, 1985-86	80GP	Jari Kurri, 68; Glenn Anderson, 54
118	Boston Bruins, 1973-74	78GP	Phil Esposito, 68; Ken Hodge, 50

THE LUNCH PAIL GANG

The Boston Bruins of the late 1970s did not have the star power of earlier Boston teams, but coach Don Cherry's crew could outwork anyone and always ranked among the NHL's top-scoring teams. In 1977–78, the Bruins set a record with 11 20-goal scorers: Peter McNab, 41; Terry O'Reilly, 29; Bobby Schmautz, 27; Stan Jonathan, 27; Jean Ratelle, 25; Rick Middleton, 25; Wayne Cashman, 24; Gregg Sheppard, 23; Brad Park, 22; Don Marcotte, 20; and Bob Miller, 20.

DOUBLE MILESTONES

When Mario Lemieux and Kevin Stevens both notched their 50th goals of the season in a 6-4 win over the Edmonton Oilers on March 21, 1993, it marked the first time in NHL history that two teammates had reached the milestone in the same game. Three years later, on February 23, 1996, Lemieux and Jaromir Jagr both scored their 50th goals in a 5-4 win over the Hartford Whalers.

TWO GOALS IN THREE SECONDS

Jim Dowd scored on a rebound of his own slap shot with just 15.5 seconds remaining to put the Minnesota Wild up 3-2 on the Chicago Blackhawks on January 21, 2004. With the Chicago net empty, Richard Park scored his second goal of the game off the face-off to clinch a 4-2 victory. Park's goal came three seconds after Dowd's to set a record for the fastest two goals scored by one team.

▶ *South Korean-born Richard Park played three seasons with the Wild from 2001 to 2004.*

TWO GOALS IN TWO SECONDS

The Boston Bruins and St. Louis Blues broke an NHL record on December 19, 1987 by combining for two goals in two seconds late in the Blues' 7-5 victory at the Boston Garden. Boston's Ken Linseman scored at 19:50 of the final period to make it 6-5, but with Bruins goaltender Doug Keans on the bench in favor of an extra attacker, Doug Gilmour shot the puck into the open net at 19:52 to secure the St. Louis victory.

▶ *Jaromir Jagr (left) and Mario Lemieux were a dynamic duo for the Pittsburgh Penguins.*

TEAM RECORDS: PENALTIES, POWERPLAYS, & SHORTHAND GOALS

In the early days of the NHL, sportswriter Elmer Ferguson of the *Montreal Herald* was responsible for tracking the league's statistics. Later, an official scorer in each NHL city would send in a score sheet after each game listing goals, assists, and penalties. By 1955, all six NHL teams had statisticians who also tracked shots on goal by individual players, saves by goalies, and who was on the ice when a goal was scored. These sheets made it possible to determine if a goal was scored shorthanded or on the powerplay, but the NHL did not officially keep track of those totals until the 1963–64 season.

Ron Duguay was a member of the Rangers team that scored 111 powerplay goals in 1987–88.

SLUGFEST IN PHILLY

The Philadelphia Flyers and Ottawa Senators combined for an NHL-record 419 minutes in penalties on March 5, 2004. With the Flyers leading 5-2, Ottawa's Rob Ray tangled with Donald Brashear – which set off a melee between the remaining players on the ice. Another brawl followed the ensuing faceoff and the teams combined for a league-record 409 minutes of penalties in the third period alone. All told, the clubs totaled 19 major penalties, 17 minors, eight 10-minute misconducts and 20 game-misconducts.

MAN ADVANTAGE MILESTONES

The Pittsburgh Penguins of 1981–82 had a record of 31-36-13 and finished 13th in the overall standings with 75 points. Their 310 goals that season ranked only 15th, yet the Penguins set an NHL record that season with 99 powerplay goals. It would take until the 1987–88 season before any team topped 100 powerplay goals, with the Rangers (111), Penguins (110), Winnipeg Jets (110), Calgary (109), and Los Angeles (103) all breaking Pittsburgh's old record.

MOST PENALTY MINUTES, ONE SEASON

2,713	Buffalo Sabres, 1991–92	80GP
2,670	Pittsburgh Penguins, 1988–89	80GP
2,663	Chicago Blackhawks, 1991–92	80GP
2,643	Calgary Flames, 1991–92	80GP
2,621	Philadelphia Flyers, 1980–81	80GP

MOST POWERPLAY GOALS, ONE SEASON

119	Pittsburgh Penguins, 1988–89	80GP
113	Detroit Red Wings, 1992–93	84GP
111	New York Rangers, 1987–88	80GP
110	Pittsburgh Penguins, 1987–88	80GP
	Winnipeg Jets, 1987–88	80GP

DUCKS DOMINATING DISPLAY

The Anaheim Ducks struggled with their power play throughout the 2013-14 season, but one wouldn't know it when they faced Vancouver on January 15, 2014. Anaheim registered a franchise-best six power-play goals versus the league's best penalty-killing team en route to a 9-1 rout of the Canucks. The Ducks' half-dozen goals with the man advantage were just one fewer than the sum total of their previous 15 games. The nine tallies overall set a club mark for Anaheim, which settled for eight on two separate occasions.

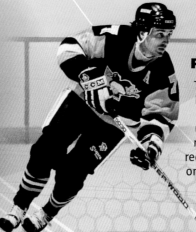

PENGUINS POWER PLAYERS

The acquisition of Paul Coffey by the Pittsburgh Penguins in 1987–88 was a huge boon to Mario Lemieux. No longer a lone superstar on an undermanned team, Lemieux took his game to the next level. He was on the ice for 110 of Pittsburgh's record 119 powerplay goals in 1988–89 with Coffey on the ice for 102. Lemieux led the league with 31 powerplay goals ... and set an NHL record with 13 shorthand goals.

Paul Coffey added pep to the Pittsburgh powerplay.

MORE DANGEROUS SHORTHANDED

In their five greatest offensive seasons, the Edmonton Oilers twice led the league in powerplay efficiency and finished second on two other occasions. Yet in those seasons from 1981–82 to 1985–86 the Oilers never scored more than 86 powerplay goals. Where Edmonton were truly more dangerous than anyone else was when they were a man short. The Oilers led the NHL in shorthand goals every year from 1982–83 through 1986–87 and then again in 1988–89 and 1989–90.

MOST SHORTHAND GOALS, ONE SEASON

36	Edmonton Oilers, 1983–84	80GP
28	Edmonton Oilers, 1986–87	80GP
27	Edmonton Oilers, 1985–86	80GP
	Edmonton Oilers, 1988–89	80GP

SHORTHAND IT TO THEM

Edmonton's record 36 shorthand goals in 1983–84 was three times the league average of 12 that season and as many as the next two best teams combined! (The Minnesota North Stars and New York Islanders each scored 18 that year.) Twelve different Oilers players scored shorthand goals, led by Wayne Gretzky's career-high 12. (He also had a career-high 20 powerplay goals that year.) Jari Kurri added five, while Mark Messier and Glenn Anderson had four apiece.

HAT TRICK OF SHORTHANDED GOALS

The Carolina Hurricanes thought they had the upper hand after Boston Bruins defenseman Matt Hunwick was whistled for a hooking penalty. They guessed wrong. The Bruins scored three times in a 64-second span to set an NHL record with a trio of shorthanded goals en route to a 4-2 victory on April 10, 2010. Daniel Paille opened the scoring 32 seconds into the second period before Blake Wheeler tallied 49 seconds later with a snap shot. Steve Begin capped the frenzy with his 100th career point prior to Hunwick exiting the penalty box.

MOST POWERPLAY GOALS AGAINST, ONE SEASON

122	Chicago Blackhawks, 1988–89	80GP
120	Pittsburgh Penguins, 1987–88	80GP
116	Washington Capitals, 2005–06	82GP
115	New Jersey Devils, 1988–89	80GP
	Ottawa Senators, 1992–93	84GP
114	Los Angeles Kings, 1992–93	84GP

MOST SHORTHAND GOALS AGAINST, ONE SEASON

22	Pittsburgh Penguins, 1984–85	80GP
	Minnesota North Stars, 1991–92	80GP
	Colorado Avalanche, 1995–96	82GP
21	Calgary Flames, 1984–85	80GP
	Pittsburgh Penguins, 1989–90	80GP

ONE POWERPLAY, THREE GOALS

On November 5, 1955, Jean Beliveau scored three goals in a span of 44 seconds for the Montreal Canadiens against Boston Bruins netminder Terry Sawchuk. Beliveau scored at 0:42, 1:08 and 1:26 of the second period while the Bruins had two players in the penalty box. After the season, the NHL changed the rules so that a player serving a minor penalty could come back on the ice when the other team scored a powerplay goal.

▶ *Jean Beliveau broke into the NHL in 1950 and starred with the Montreal Canadiens until 1971.*

SHORTHANDED DEVILS?

The New Jersey Devils scored nearly as many goals as they allowed while shorthanded during the 2011–12 season. The Garden State residents netted a league-best 15 such tallies and yielded just 27 while being shorthanded on 258 occasions. If one does the math – and we did – the Devils recorded an 89.53 percent efficiency rating, which eclipsed the post-expansion NHL mark of the 1999–2000 Dallas Stars (89.25 percent).

POWER (PLAY) OUTAGE

The Colorado Avalanche went six full games (March 10–20, 2012) without receiving one single power-play opportunity. By comparison, the Rocky Mountain representatives competed in just one contest over the previous 10 seasons without a man-advantage chance. Not surprisingly, Colorado finished with a league-low 223 power plays on the season – a full 20 fewer than the next team (New York Islanders).

TEAM RECORDS: PLAYOFF WINS, LOSSES, & STREAKS

No matter how good a team does in the regular season, the true mark of success comes in the playoffs. The NHL has changed its playoff format many times over the years but has been set up to allow 16 teams to make the playoffs since the 1979–80 season. It has taken 16 wins for a team to win the Stanley Cup since 1987. In the early years of the NHL, a playoff championship only gave the winning team a chance to play off against other league champions for the Stanley Cup, but since 1927 the Cup has been the NHL's playoff championship trophy.

MOST CONSECUTIVE PLAYOFF APPEARANCES

29	Boston Bruins (1968–96, inclusive)
28	Chicago Blackhawks (1970–97, inclusive)
25	St. Louis Blues (1980–2004, inclusive)
24	Montreal Canadiens (1971–94, inclusive)
24	Detroit Red Wings (1991–2015, inclusive)
21	Montreal Canadiens (1949–69, inclusive)

SCORCHING RED WINGS

The Detroit Red Wings may have changed conferences, but they didn't alter their winning ways. The Red Wings shuffled from the West to the East and overcame myriad injuries to slip into the playoffs for the 23rd consecutive season in 2013–14. The streak began during the 1990–91 season and continued through back-to-back Stanley Cup championships in 1997 and 1998 as well as title runs in 2002 and 2008.

WORKING OVERTIME

After dropping their first game of the 1993 playoffs to the Quebec Nordiques in overtime (and the second game in regulation time), the Montreal Canadiens went on a spectacular run to a Stanley Cup championship that included winning a record 10 games in overtime. The Canadiens won two overtime games against Quebec, three against the Buffalo Sabres, two against the New York Islanders, and three more against the Los Angeles Kings in the Stanley Cup Finals.

16 THE HARD WAY

After two straight losses to Buffalo knocked them out of the playoffs in 1975, the Chicago Blackhawks suffered four consecutive losses against Montreal in 1976, two straight against the Islanders in 1977, four in a row against Boston in 1978, and four against the Islanders in 1979. After 16 postseason losses in a row, Chicago finally snapped the streak on April 8, 1980 with a win over St. Louis in the opening game of 1980 playoffs.

 The Montreal Canadiens celebrate their Stanley Cup victory in 1993.

SWEETEST 16

Since all four rounds were expanded to a best-of-seven format in 1987, the Edmonton Oilers of 1988 managed to win the Stanley Cup in the fewest number of games. The Oilers lost just two times en route to winning the Stanley Cup that year, though their actual playoff record was 16-2-1 due to a power failure at the Boston Garden that forced game three of the Finals to end in a 3-3 tie.

THREE MORE TO 14

After winning the Stanley Cup in 1992 with 11 straight playoff victories, the Penguins won their first game of the 1993 postseason to tie the Edmonton Oilers' record of 12 straight playoff victories over two seasons. The Penguins ran their streak to 14 straight with two more wins before dropping a 4-1 decision to the New Jersey Devils. The Penguins bounced back to win their next game and take the series in five games.

OVERTIME & AGAIN

The Stanley Cup Finals of 1951 represent a unique occurrence in NHL history. The Toronto Maple Leafs dominated play against Montreal that year and won the series in five games, yet the spectacular performance of Canadiens goalie Gerry McNeil kept every game close. In fact, the series marks the only time that every game in an NHL playoff series went into overtime. The Canadiens are the only team ever to lose four overtime games in one series.

FIVE STRAIGHT OVERTIME GAMES

The Phoenix Coyotes and Chicago Blackhawks played five consecutive overtime games to begin their Western Conference quarterfinal series in 2012. After Mikkel Boedker scored his second straight overtime winner to give the Coyotes a 3-1 lead in the series, Blackhawks captain Jonathan Toews answered at 2:44 of the extra session in Game 5. It marked only the second time in league history that a series has opened with five straight overtime games. The other was the 1951 Stanley Cup Finals between Montreal and Toronto. Phoenix actually won in 60 minutes in Game 6 to claim its first postseason series victory since 1987, when the franchise was based in Winnipeg.

ROAD KINGS

The Los Angeles Kings tied a Stanley Cup playoffs record by winning 10 games on the road during their run to the title in 2012. They capped their dominance by winning the first two games of the Cup final on the road against New Jersey, which ironically shares the record. The Devils accomplished the feat en route to winning their first Stanley Cup title in 1995 – and again in 2000. Calgary also posted 10 road wins in 2004.

BEST OF SEVEN

The first best-of-seven series in the Stanley Cup Finals was played in 1939. The Boston Bruins needed only five games to beat the Maple Leafs. Two years later, Boston became the first team to win a seventh game when they beat Toronto four games to three in the semifinals. Boston then became the first team to sweep a seven-game series when they downed Detroit in four straight to win the 1941 Stanley Cup Finals.

MICHEL BRIERE

After missing the playoffs in their first two seasons after joining the NHL in 1967–68, the Pittsburgh Penguins made up for lost time in the spring of 1970. The Penguins became the first team in NHL history to win their first four playoff games when rookie Michel Briere scored at 8:28 of overtime for a 3-2 victory over the Oakland Seals and a four-game sweep. Tragically, Briere would die a year later after an automobile accident.

Michel Briere seemed destined for stardom following a solid rookie season until tragedy struck. He was in a coma for months before he died after a car crash.

ONE-GOAL SERIES

The Washington Capitals and Boston Bruins made NHL history in their 2012 Eastern Conference quarterfinal series as all seven games were decided by a single goal. Four games were decided in overtime and two others were decided with less than two minutes to play in the third period. Joel Ward cleaned up a rebound at 2:57 of overtime in Game 7 as the seventh-seeded Capitals eliminated the defending Stanley Cup champion Bruins.

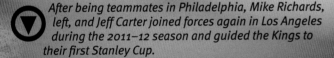

After being teammates in Philadelphia, Mike Richards, left, and Jeff Carter joined forces again in Los Angeles during the 2011–12 season and guided the Kings to their first Stanley Cup.

RICHARDS DOES IT AGAIN

Mike Richards holds the distinction of being on the ice for two of the four greatest comebacks in NHL history. After helping Philadelphia overcome a 3-0 deficit to stun Boston in the second round of the 2010 playoffs, Richards fueled Los Angeles to the same finish against San Jose in the first round of the 2014 postseason before guiding the Kings to their second Stanley Cup title in three years. Los Angeles forward Jeff Carter was also a member of the Flyers' contingent in 2010, but an injury prevented him from facing the Bruins. The 1942 Toronto Maple Leafs and 1975 New York Islanders also won a best-of-seven series after losing the first three games.

TEAM RECORDS: PLAYOFF SCORING

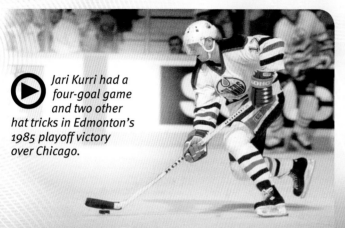

▶ *Jari Kurri had a four-goal game and two other hat tricks in Edmonton's 1985 playoff victory over Chicago.*

The road to the Stanley Cup is perhaps the toughest test in all of team sports. The NHL playoffs are a marathon, with teams playing nearly every other night for more than two months if they hope to go all the way. With the stakes raised so high, every moment takes on more meaning. The potential to be a hero is always there, which is what makes playoff moments so memorable. Whether it's a big goal to win in overtime or a key save to keep your team alive, more great moments happen in the postseason than at any other time of the year.

HIGHEST-SCORING SERIES

The highest-scoring series in the history of the NHL playoffs was the six-game 1985 Campbell Conference Final between the Chicago Blackhawks and Edmonton Oilers. The Oilers won 11-2, 7-3, 10-5, and 8-2 en route to a record total of 44 goals in the six-game set. The Blackhawks scored 25 times for a record 69 goals by the two teams. Jari Kurri led the way with a single-series record 12 goals for the Oilers.

OTHER 1985 HIGHLIGHTS

Before losing to the Oilers, the Blackhawks had been involved in two other record-setting series in the 1985 playoffs. Chicago outscored Detroit 9-5, 6-1, and 8-2 to set a three-game series record with 23 goals in the opening round. In their second-round series, the Blackhawks outscored the Minnesota North Stars 33-29 for a combined total of 62 goals, setting an NHL record that lasted until Chicago met Edmonton in the next round!

LOWEST-SCORING SERIES

Two times in NHL history the two teams playing in a playoff series have combined to score just one goal! In a two-game, total goal quarterfinal series in 1929 it took until 29:50 of overtime in the second game before Butch Keeling finally gave the New York Rangers a 1-0 victory over the New York Americans. It only took 4:02 of overtime in 1935 for Baldy Northcott to give the Montreal Maroons a 1-0 win over the Chicago Blackhawks.

▶ *Jean-Sebastien Giguere was the fourth goalie in NHL history to post three straight shutouts in one playoff series.*

FOUR-GAME SWEEPS

The Boston Bruins set a playoff record for a four-game series in 1972 when they scored 28 goals in a sweep of the St. Louis Blues. The Bruins won by scores of 6-1, 10-2, 7-2, and 5-3. In 2003, the Mighty Ducks of Anaheim held the Minnesota Wild to just one goal in a four-game series. Ducks goalie Jean-Sebastien Giguere tied a playoff record with three straight shutouts before the Wild finally scored in game four.

SHUTOUT RECORD

The record for most shutouts by both teams in a playoff series is five. Maple Leafs rookie Frank McCool blanked the Red Wings three straight times to open the 1945 Stanley Cup Finals. After Detroit stayed alive in game four, Red Wings rookie Harry Lumley posted back-to-back shutouts to force a seventh game, which Toronto won 2-1. The two teams scored just nine goals each in the series, the fewest ever in a seven-game set.

TEAM PENALTIES

The 1945 Stanley Cup Finals between Toronto and Detroit set two other playoff records. The Maple Leafs received only nine penalties in the entire series, setting a record for the fewest penalties in a seven-game set. The Red Wings were sent to the box only 10 times, giving the two teams the combined record as well. On April 6, 1980, the Minnesota North Stars were penalized a record 34 times in a single playoff game!

MOST GOALS, ONE GAME

On April 9, 1987, the Edmonton Oilers set a playoff record with 13 goals in a 13-3 drubbing of the Los Angeles Kings. Jari Kurri scored four times while Wayne Gretzky had a goal and six assists and surpassed Jean Beliveau as the leading scorer in playoff history. Back on April 7, 1982, the Kings had beaten the Oilers 10-8 in a game that set the record for most goals by both teams in one playoff game.

ONE-SIDED WIN

On March 30, 1944, the Montreal Canadiens beat the Toronto Maple Leafs 11-0 to wrap up their semifinal series in five games. The 11-goal outburst would be a single-game NHL playoff high for more than 40 years and remains the highest scored playoff win by shutout. The Canadiens scored seven goals in the third period, including five in a span of just 3:36, to set two other records that have never been broken.

POWERPLAY & SHORTHAND RECORDS

The Boston Bruins scored six powerplay goals in a brawl-filled 10-0 win over the Toronto Maple Leafs on April 2, 1969. Phil Esposito had four goals in the game, including three with the man advantage to tie an individual record. On April 11, 1981, the Bruins set another record with three shorthanded goals in one playoff game. That mark would later be tied by the New York Islanders in 1983 and the Toronto Maple Leafs in 1994.

Phil Esposito was the first player in 20 years to score three powerplay goals in a single playoff game, and just the second in 30 years.

LONGEST OVERTIME

At 2:25 a.m. on the morning after the game had begun on March 24, 1936, Mud Bruneteau of the Detroit Red Wings ended the longest game in NHL history. Hec Kilrea set up the play, but it was Brunteau who batted a rolling puck past Montreal Maroons goalie Lorne Chabot to give the Red Wings a 1-0 victory. The goal came at 16:30 of the sixth overtime period. Normie Smith stopped 90 shots to earn the shutout.

SHORTEST OVERTIME

Nine seconds into overtime on May 18, 1986, Mike McPhee faked a shot on goal and instead sent a pass to Brian Skrudland who redirected the puck past Calgary Flames goalie Mike Vernon. The goal gave the Montreal Canadiens a 3-2 victory in the shortest overtime game in NHL history. The previous record of 11 seconds was set in 1975 when J.P. Parise gave the New York Islanders a 4-3 win over the New York Rangers.

Brian Skrudland scored just 15 goals in 164 career playoff games, but two of them were overtime winners for the Montreal Canadiens.

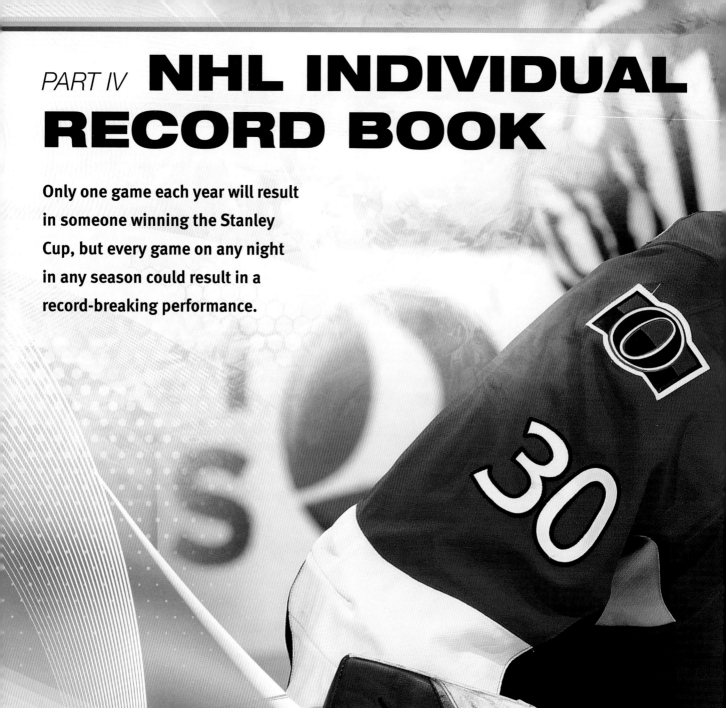

PART IV NHL INDIVIDUAL RECORD BOOK

Only one game each year will result in someone winning the Stanley Cup, but every game on any night in any season could result in a record-breaking performance.

"The Hamburglar" stole the show in the latter half of the 2014–15 season as Andrew Hammond posted a sizzling 20-1-2 mark to send Ottawa into the postseason.

INTRODUCTION: ALL-TIME SCORING RECORDS HISTORY

Though it's often been said that offense sells tickets but defense wins championships, the greatest scorers in hockey's history have managed to secure more than their share of Stanley Cups, too. And while winning the Cup remains the ultimate goal, the stories of the men who set scoring records are part of what makes the game great. Six individual scoring records stand as benchmarks in the history of hockey: most goals (single-season and career), most assists (single-season and career), and most points (single-season and career). The evolution of these six records is traced here, beginning with 1917–18, the NHL's first season.

MALONE SETS THE MARK

On the first night in NHL history (December 19, 1917), Joe Malone scored five goals to lead the Montreal Canadiens to a 7-4 win over the Ottawa Senators. Malone, who previously led the NHA with 43 goals in 20 games in 1912–13 and 41 goals in 19 games in 1916–17, finished the season with 44 goals in 20 games for a comfortable lead over Cy Denneny, who scored 36 goals for Ottawa that season.

TAKING AIM

It would take 12 years before anyone in the NHL reached the 40-goal plateau again. During the first season in which forward passing was allowed in all three zones (offensive, defensive, and neutral) in 1929–30, Montreal's Howie Morenz (40), Boston's Dit Clapper (41), and Bruins' teammate Cooney Weiland (43) all approached Malone's mark in a 44-game schedule, but couldn't beat it. However, Weiland did set a new record with 73 points, shattering Morenz' previous mark of 51.

50 IN 50

After scoring only five goals in 16 games during an injury-shortened rookie season, Maurice Richard finished among the league leaders with 32 goals the next year. In his third season of 1944–45, he set a new league record when he scored 50 goals during the 50-game schedule. He surpassed Joe Malone with his 45th goal in his 42nd game on February 25, 1945 and reached 50 on the final night of the season on March 18.

◀ *Maurice Richard was the first player in NHL history to score 50 goals in a season and 500 in a career.*

CLOSE CALLS

Though the season had grown to 70 games by 1949–50 and Gordie Howe scored 49 goals in 1952–53, no one had matched Maurice Richard's record of 50 goals heading into 1960–61. Toronto's Frank Mahovlich got off to a fast start that season, but finished the year with 48 goals. Montreal's Bernie Geoffrion went on a late role and reached 50 goals with two games to go in the season but couldn't break the record.

TO 51 & BEYOND

Bobby Hull became hockey's third 50-goal scorer during the 1961–62 season and was first to finally break the record, four seasons later. Hull scored his 50th goal of the 1965–66 season on March 2, 1966, but he and the Chicago Blackhawks were shut out for three straight games before Hull finally scored his 51st against Cesar Maniago of the New York Rangers on March 12. Hull finished the season with 54 goals and a record 97 points.

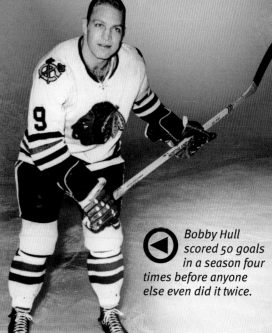

◀ *Bobby Hull scored 50 goals in a season four times before anyone else even did it twice.*

SETTING THEM UP

The NHL did not keep track of assists during the 1917–18 season, and players would not begin to put up impressive numbers until modern passing rules were introduced in 1929–30. That season, the Rangers' Frank Boucher doubled Dick Irvin's previous record of 18 with 36 assists. Montreal's Elmer Lach was first to top 50 assists (54) during the 1944–45 season, with Chicago's Stan Mikita becoming the first to top 60 (62) in 1966–67.

THE GREAT ONE

In just his second season in the NHL in 1980–81, Wayne Gretzky set new NHL records with 109 assists and 164 points. In 1981–82, Gretzky scored 50 goals in just 39 games to start the season and finished the year with 92 goals. He also added 120 assists for an astounding 212 points. Gretzky would continue setting new assist records, pushing the mark to 163 in 1985–86 when he also broke his own record with 215 points.

ALL-TIME GOAL SCORING

Maurice Richard scored his first career goal on November 8, 1942. Ten years to the day later, Richard scored the 325th goal of his career to surpass Nels Stewart as the NHL's all-time leader. Richard would push his career total to 544 on his retirement in 1960, but Gordie Howe was to break that mark on November 10, 1963. Howe would push his career total to 801, which now ranks him second all-time to Wayne Gretzky's 894.

ESPO & ORR

Scoring records began to soar after NHL expansion in 1967. Boston's Phil Esposito became the first player in history to top 100 points with 49 goals and 77 assists in 1968–69. Gordie Howe and Bobby Hull each topped 100 as well that season, with Hull setting a new record with 58 goals. Esposito broke both scoring marks with 76 goals and 152 points in 1970–71. Teammate Bobby Orr set a new record with 102 assists that season.

Phil Esposito's 76 goals and 152 points in 1970–71 set single-season records that seemed unbreakable.

Gordie Howe's career totals of 801 goals, 1,049 assists and 1,850 points now rank him second, eighth, and third all-time in those scoring categories.

ALL-TIME ASSISTS

Bill Cowley of the Boston Bruins broke Frank Boucher's career assist record with his 264th in 1943–44. Cowley pushed the record to 353, which was later broken by Elmer Lach, whose career total of 408 when he retired in 1954 was soon broken by Gordie Howe. Howe was the NHL's career assist leader for 30 years, pushing his total to 1,049. Wayne Gretzky broke the record on March 1, 1988 en route to 1,963 assists in his career.

ALL-TIME POINTS

Joe Malone was the first player in NHL history with 100 career points. Cy Denneny was first to reach 200 and 300, with Howie Morenz the first to hit 400. Nels Stewart, Syd Howe, and Bill Cowley all topped 500 before Elmer Lach reached 600. Maurice Richard pushed the career scoring mark over 900, with Gordie Howe reaching 1,000 on November 29, 1960. Wayne Gretzky, with 2,857 points, is the only player in history to top 2,000.

GOALS

Putting the puck in the net is what hockey is all about, and the players who score the most goals are the ones most celebrated. Players such as Joe Malone, Maurice Richard, and Mike Bossy were all noted as "natural" goal scorers, though the player who holds the NHL records for most goals in a season and most goals in a career was usually regarded as a playmaker first. Wayne Gretzky's 92 goals in a single season has been approached on a couple of occasions, but no one other than Gordie Howe is anywhere close to his career totals.

MOST GOALS, ONE GAME

7	Joe Malone, Que, January 31, 1920 at Quebec	Quebec 10, Toronto 6
6	Newsy Lalonde, Mtl, January 10, 1920 at Montreal	Montreal 14, Toronto 7
	Joe Malone, Que, March 10, 1920 at Quebec	Quebec 10, Ottawa 4
	Corb Denneny, Tor, January 26, 1921 at Toronto	Toronto 10, Hamilton 3
	Cy Denneny, Ott, March 7, 1921 at Ottawa	Ottawa 12, Hamilton 5
	Syd Howe, Det, February 3, 1944 at Detroit	Detroit 12, NY Rangers 2
	Red Berenson, St.L, November 7, 1968 at Philadelphia	St. Louis 8, Philadelphia 0
	Darryl Sittler, Tor, February 7, 1976 at Toronto	Toronto 11, Boston 4

◀ *Joe Malone's seven goals in an NHL game may never be surpassed, but he once scored nine goals in a single Stanley Cup game in 1913.*

SIX THE HARD WAY

A fringe player at best over his first six NHL seasons, expansion gave Red Berenson a chance to star with the St. Louis Blues. On November 7, 1968, Berenson became the first player in 24 years to score six goals in a game, and the only one in history to do this while playing on the road. He finished the 1968–69 season the first player from an NHL expansion team to crack the top 10 in scoring.

SEVEN IN ONE BLOW

Very little notice was taken at the time when Joe Malone scored seven goals in a game on January 31, 1920 to set a record that still stands. At the time, the NHL was in only its third season and there was little to differentiate it from its predecessor, the NHA. Malone had scored eight goals in an NHA game in 1917 and might have scored eight in the game in 1920, if not for a goal that was called back.

MOST GOALS, ONE PERIOD

Red Berenson and 10 other players have scored four goals in one period. The others are: Busher Jackson, Toronto, November 20, 1934; Max Bentley, Chicago, January 28, 1943; Clint Smith, Chicago, March 4, 1945; Wayne Gretzky, Edmonton, February 18, 1981; Grant Mulvey, Chicago, February 3, 1982; Bryan Trottier, Islanders, February 13, 1982; Al Secord, Chicago, January 7, 1987; Joe Nieuwendyk, Calgary, January 11, 1989; Petr Bondra, Washington, February 5, 1994; and Mario Lemieux, Pittsburgh, January 26, 1997.

STEENS MAKE HISTORY

St. Louis Blues forward Alex Steen joined an exclusive club after scoring his 30th goal of the season on March 15, 2014. Steen's one-timer from the top of the right circle was one for the record books as he and his father became the third such combination to score at least 30 goals in an NHL season. Thomas netted 30 during the 1984–85 campaign as the Steens joined Bobby and Brett Hull and Ken Hodge and Ken Hodge Jr. as the only father-son tandems in league history to each reach that plateau.

MAGNIFICENT MARLEAU

San Jose Sharks forward Patrick Marleau bolted out of the blocks to begin the 2012–13 season. He scored two goals in each of the team's first four games to become just the second player to open a campaign with four multi-goal performances. Ottawa's Cy Denneny also accomplished the feat to begin the 1917–18 season. Marleau was "held" to just a goal in his next contest, but tallied just eight more times in the final 43 games to end the lockout-shortened season.

MOST GOALS, ONE SEASON

92	Wayne Gretzky, Edm, 1981–82	80GP	80-game schedule
87	Wayne Gretzky, Edm, 1983–84	74GP	80-game schedule
86	Brett Hull, St.L, 1990–91	78GP	80-game schedule
85	Mario Lemieux, Pit, 1988–89	76GP	80-game schedule
76	Phil Esposito, Bos, 1970–71	78GP	78-game schedule
	Alexander Mogilny, Buf, 1992–93	77GP	84-game schedule
	Teemu Selanne, Wpg, 1992–93	84GP	84-game schedule
73	Wayne Gretzky, Edm, 1984–85	80GP	80-game schedule
72	Brett Hull, St.L, 1989–90	80GP	80-game schedule
71	Wayne Gretzky, Edm, 1982–83	80GP	80-game schedule
	Jari Kurri, Edm, 1984–85	73GP	80-game schedule
70	Mario Lemieux, Pit, 1987–88	77GP	80-game schedule
	Bernie Nicholls, L.A., 1988–89	79GP	80-game schedule
	Brett Hull, St.L, 1991–92	73GP	80-game schedule

▶ *Only Wayne Gretzky has scored more goals in a single season than Brett Hull (pictured).*

THE CENTURY MARK

Wayne Gretzky is the only player in NHL's history to score 100 goals in a single season when the regular schedule and playoffs are combined. In addition to the 87 goals he scored during the 1983–84 season, Gretzky scored 13 more in the playoffs that year. After his 92-goal effort in 1981–82, he scored just five more in five playoff games. Mario Lemieux and Brett Hull both had 97 goals combined in their best seasons.

50 IN 50

By the start of the 1980–81 season there had been 23 other players who had scored 50 goals since Maurice Richard first reached that milestone in 1944–45. The single-season record had grown to 76, but no one had matched Richard's feat of scoring 50 goals in 50 games. Mike Bossy of the New York Islanders finally achieved 50 in 50 that season, only to see Wayne Gretzky score 50 goals in just 39 games in 1981–82.

▼ *Wayne Gretzky makes nice with Phil Esposito after breaking his single-season goal-scoring record.*

MOST GOALS, CAREER

894	Wayne Gretzky, Edm, L.A., St.L, NYR in 20 seasons	1,487GP
801	Gordie Howe, Det, Hfd. in 26 seasons	1,767GP
741	Brett Hull, Cgy, St.L, Dal, Det, Phx in 19 seasons	1,269GP
731	Marcel Dionne, Det, L.A., NYR in 18 seasons	1,348GP
722	Jaromir Jagr, eight teams in 21 seasons	1,550 GP
717	Phil Esposito, Chi, Bos, NYR in 18 seasons	1,282GP

MOST GOALS IN 50 GAMES

The NHL does not officially track a record for the fastest 50 goals from the start of the season. It does, however, keep track of the most goals scored in 50 games from the start of a season. So, while Wayne Gretzky's mark of 50 goals in 39 games in 1981–82 is not an official NHL record, his 61 goals in 50 games that year are counted as such. Gretzky also scored 61 goals in the first 50 games of 1983–84.

A GRAND TOTAL

Wayne Gretzky is the only player in NHL history to score more than 1,000 goals in the regular season and the playoffs combined. His total of 894 regular-season goals and 122 playoff goals adds up to 1,016 overall. Only Gordie Howe (801 + 68 = 869), Brett Hull (741 + 103 = 844), and Mark Messier (694 + 109 = 803) top 800: Phil Esposito comes next, with 717 and 61 for a total of 778.

MOST GOALS, NHL & WHA COMBINED

Wayne Gretzky scored the final goal of his career on March 29, 1999. Combining his NHL totals of 1,016 goals with his 46 regular-season and 10 playoff goals during his one season in the World Hockey Association, Gretzky achieved a total of 1,072 goals in his entire career – one more than Gordie Howe, his childhood idol. During his six years in the WHA, Howe had scored 174 regular-season and 28 playoff goals for a total of 1,071.

ASSISTS

Following the 1910–11 season of the National Hockey Association, Martin Rosenthal (secretary of the Ottawa Senators) expressed the belief that the presentation of a trophy to the player with the most assists would go a long way toward improving team play. Though there is still no such trophy in the NHL today, if one were ever created, it might well be named after Wayne Gretzky, whose domination of the NHL record book is most apparent in the assist category. Not only does he hold almost every significant single-game and career record, his supremacy among the single-season leaders is staggering.

MORE IS BETTER

In his rookie season of 1979–80, Wayne Gretzky tied Marcel Dionne for the NHL scoring title with 137 points, but did not receive the Art Ross Trophy because Dionne had scored more goals (53 to Greztky's 51). Three times in later years, Gretzky would have more assists than anyone else in the NHL had points! Gretzky's career total of 1,963 also gives him more assists than anyone else's career points total.

MOST ASSISTS, CAREER

1,963	Wayne Gretzky, Edm, L.A., St.L, NYR in 20 seasons	1,487GP
1,249	Ron Francis, Hfd, Pit, Car, Tor in 23 seasons	1,731GP
1,193	Mark Messier, Edm, NYR, Van in 25 seasons	1,756GP
1,169	Raymond Bourque, Bos, Col in 22 seasons	1,612GP
1,135	Paul Coffey, nine teams in 21 seasons	1,409GP
1,080	Jaromir Jagr, eight teams in 21 seasons	1,550 GP

THE CENTURY MARK

Only three players in NHL history have ever topped 100 assists in a single season. Bobby Orr achieved this first with 102 assists in 1970–71 and Mario Lemieux did it with 114 assists in 1988–89. Those were the only times in their careers that Orr and Lemieux topped the century mark, but Wayne Gretzky managed it 11 times. He holds the seven top spots on the single-season assist list.

MOST ASSISTS, ONE SEASON

163	Wayne Gretzky, Edm, 1985–86	80GP – 80-game schedule
135	Wayne Gretzky, Edm, 1984–85	80GP – 80-game schedule
125	Wayne Gretzky, Edm, 1982–83	80GP – 80-game schedule
122	Wayne Gretzky, L.A., 1990–91	78GP – 80-game schedule
121	Wayne Gretzky, Edm, 1986–87	79GP – 80-game schedule
120	Wayne Gretzky, Edm, 1981–82	80GP – 80-game schedule
118	Wayne Gretzky, Edm, 1983–84	74GP – 80-game schedule
114	Mario Lemieux, Pit, 1988–89	76GP – 80-game schedule
	Wayne Gretzky, L.A., 1988–89	78GP – 80-game schedule
109	Wayne Gretzky, Edm, 1980–81	80GP – 80-game schedule
	Wayne Gretzky, Edm, 1987–88	64GP – 80-game schedule
102	Bobby Orr, Bos, 1970–71	78GP – 78-game schedule
	Wayne Gretzky, L.A., 1989–90	73GP – 80-game schedule

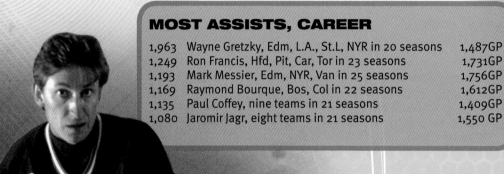

⬆ *Though Wayne Gretzky is the NHL's all-time goal-scoring leader, most fans will remember him best as hockey's premier playmaker.*

▶ *Joe Primeau (center) was the playmaker on the Maple Leafs Kid Line with Charlie Conacher and Busher Jackson.*

BILLY'S BIG NIGHT

On March 16, 1947, Billy Taylor of the Detroit Red Wings set a new NHL record with seven assists in a single game. Taylor set up Roy Conacher three times in the first 12 minutes and fed him for a fourth goal late in the second period. He also set up Sid Abel, Jack Stewart, and Mud Bruneteau in a 10-6 win over Chicago. Wayne Gretzky equaled Taylor's mark three times, but no one has ever surpassed this.

DALE DELIVERS

One of the few assist records that Wayne Gretzky does not hold is the record for most assists in a single period. Dale Hawerchuk established that mark with five assists in the second period of a game on March 6, 1984 to lead the Winnipeg Jets to a 7-3 win over the Kings in Los Angeles. Hawerchuk set up Wade Campbell once and Paul MacLean and Morris Lukowich twice each during the Jets' five-goal outburst.

MOST ASSISTS, ONE GAME

7	Billy Taylor, Det, March 16, 1947 at Chicago	Detroit 10, Chicago 6
	Wayne Gretzky, Edm, February 15, 1980 at Edmonton	Edm 8, Washington 2
	Wayne Gretzky, Edm, December 11, 1985 at Chicago	Edm 12, Chicago 9
	Wayne Gretzky, Edm, February 14, 1986, at Edmonton	Edm 8, Quebec 2

6   Six assists have been recorded in one game on 24 occasions since Elmer Lach of Montreal first accomplished this feat vs. Boston on February 6, 1943. The most recent player is Eric Lindros of Philadelphia on February 26, 1997.

Montreal's Petr Svoboda tries to contain Winnipeg Jets star Dale Hawerchuk.

REGULAR-SEASON AND PLAYOFFS

When Wayne Gretzky's 260 assists in 208 playoff games are added to his regular-season total, his all-time NHL total of 2,223 gives him a lead of 844 over runner-up Mark Messier's 1,379 assists. Gretzky had 11 playoff assists in 1986, which, when added to his regular-season record of 163 assists in 1985–86, gives him a combined total of 174. Gretzky holds down the top nine places in the single-season combined category. Mario Lemieux lies tenth.

FOUR ON ONE

From 1930–31 until 1935–36, NHL rules allowed for up to three assists to be counted on a single goal, though it rarely happened. The current system of two assists per goal was introduced in 1936–37. In one rare instance on January 10, 1935, the official scorer in New York awarded assists to Charlie Conacher, Baldy Cotton, Andy Blair, and Busher Jackson on a single goal by Joe Primeau of the Toronto Maple Leafs.

GOALS VS. ASSISTS

The 1935–36 season marked the first time in NHL history that the League's scoring leader had more assists than goals scored. Dave "Sweeney" Schriner of the New York Americans led the NHL with 19 goals and 26 assists for 45 points during the 48-game schedule. When Alex Ovechkin led the NHL in scoring, in 2007–08, he became the first player since Bobby Hull (1965–66) to do so with more goals than assists.

LEADER AMONG LEADERS

Wayne Gretzky's record-setting season of 163 assists in 80 games in 1985–86 makes him the only player in NHL history to average more than two assists per game over the course of an entire season. Gretzky led the NHL, or shared the lead, in assists 16 times in his 20-year career. Bobby Orr is the only other player in league history to have managed this feat five times.

POINTS

It was not until the 1947–48 season that the NHL-scoring leader received a special award (the Art Ross Trophy), but the game's top points producers have always been hockey's biggest stars. Goalscorers tended to get most of the glory, and often still do, while legendary set-up men such as Frank Boucher, Elmer Lach, and Stan Mikita often took a back seat to their teammates who put the puck in the net. Wayne Gretzky would finally prove beyond a shadow of a doubt just how valuable those perfect passes were.

MOST POINTS, ONE GAME

The Toronto Maple Leafs were slumping and owner Harold Ballard had blasted captain Darryl Sittler in the press when the Boston Bruins came to town on February 7, 1976. That night, Sittler exploded for a record 10 points (six goals, four assists) to lead the Leafs to an 11-4 victory. Edmonton's Sam Gagner came close to challenging Sittler with an eight-point effort (four goals, four assists) versus Chicago on February 2, 2012, becoming the 13th NHL player to amass that many points in a game.

EIGHT BY TEN

At the time of Darryl Sittler's 10-point game, the previous NHL single-game record had been eight points, first accomplished by Maurice Richard in 1944 and equaled by Bert Olmstead in 1954. Others since then to score eight points in one game are: Tom Bladon (Philadelphia), Bryan Trottier (New York Islanders), Peter Stastny (Quebec), Anton Stastny (also Quebec), Wayne Gretzky (twice for Edmonton), Paul Coffey (also Edmonton), Mario Lemieux (twice for Pittsburgh), and Bernie Nicholls (Los Angeles).

Youngest brother Anton Stastny stands behind his two older brothers, Peter (left) and Marian.

SITTLER IN '76

Darryl Sittler's 10-point night began a remarkable streak of records and milestones. Sittler finished 1975–76 with 41 goals and 59 assists to become the first player in the Leafs' history with a 100-point season. On April 22, 1976, he became just the third player to score five goals in a single playoff game. Then, on September 15, 1976, he scored the winning goal in the first Canada Cup international tournament.

Toronto's Darryl Sittler established himself as a top-rank NHL star during the 1975–76 season.

EIGHT TIMES TWO

Czechoslovakian brothers Peter and Anton Stastny (Marian came on board the following year) joined the Quebec Nordiques in 1980–81 and quickly transformed the second-year NHL club into a playoff team. Peter's four goals and four assists plus Anton's three goals and five assists in an 11-7 win over Washington on February 22, 1981 gave them a combined 16 points, breaking the single-game record for two brothers of 13 points set by Max and Doug Bentley on January 28, 1943.

MOST POINTS, ONE SEASON

215	Wayne Gretzky, Edm, 1985–86	80GP – 52 goals, 163 assists
212	Wayne Gretzky, Edm, 1981–82	80GP – 92 goals, 120 assists
208	Wayne Gretzky, Edm, 1984–85	80GP – 73 goals, 135 assists
205	Wayne Gretzky, Edm, 1983–84	74GP – 87 goals, 118 assists
199	Mario Lemieux, Pit, 1988–89	76GP – 85 goals, 114 assists
196	Wayne Gretzky, Edm, 1982–83	80GP – 71 goals, 125 assists
183	Wayne Gretzky, Edm, 1986–87	79GP – 62 goals, 121 assists
168	Mario Lemieux, Pit, 1987–88	77GP – 70 goals, 98 assists
	Wayne Gretzky, L.A., 1988–89	78GP – 54 goals, 114 assists
164	Wayne Gretzky, Edm, 1980–81	80GP – 55 goals, 109 assists
163	Wayne Gretzky, L.A., 1990–91	78GP – 41 goals, 122 assists
161	Mario Lemieux, Pit, 1995–96	70GP – 69 goals, 92 assists
160	Mario Lemieux, Pit, 1992–93	60GP – 69 goals, 91 assists

POINTS PROGRESSION

When modern NHL passing rules were introduced in 1929–30, Boston's Cooney Weiland compiled 73 points during the 44-game season to break Howie Morenz's previous record of 51. As the schedule grew to 70 games over the next 37 years, the single-season record grew by only 24 points to 97. NHL expansion quickly saw the record grow by 55 points to Phil Esposito's 152 in 1970–71, before Wayne Gretzky pushed the scoring record to more than 200 points.

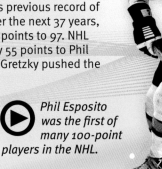

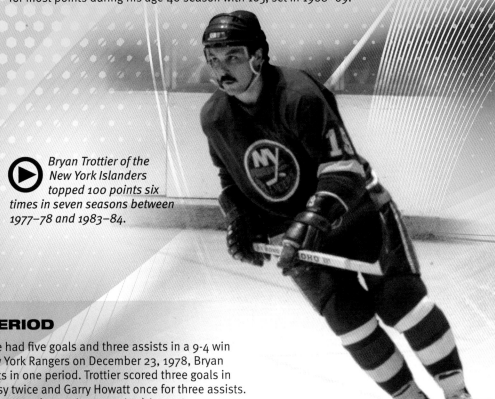

Phil Esposito was the first of many 100-point players in the NHL.

TOPPING 200

Through 75 games of his astounding 1981–82 season, Wayne Gretzky accumulated 199 points on 88 goals and 111 assists. He broke the 200-point barrier on March 25, 1982, with a pair of first-period assists on goals by Edmonton teammates Pat Hughes and Dave Semenko. In the second period, Gretzky scored a pair of shorthanded goals 27 seconds apart to hit the 90-goal plateau, too, as the Oilers downed the Calgary Flames 7-2.

BARRASSO, BRODEUR MAKE THEIR POINTS

Although the goaltender's primary job is to stop the puck, he's also free to contribute on the offensive end. Two-time Stanley Cup winner Tom Barrasso leads all netminders with 48 points (all assists), highlighted by an eight-point performance during the 1992–93 season with Pittsburgh. New Jersey goaltender Martin Brodeur moved into second place after picking up his 47th point – and 45th career assist – on Adam Henrique's goal against Phoenix on March 27, 2014. Former Edmonton netminder Grant Fuhr has 46 points and owns the single-season mark for goalies with 14 assists in 1983–84.

HITTING 100

The pre-expansion NHL record of 97 points was shared by Chicago teammates Bobby Hull (1965–66) and Stan Mikita (1966–67). On March 1, 1969, Phil Esposito had a goal and an assist in Boston's 8-5 win over the Rangers to give him 99 points on the season and break the record. The following night, Esposito's first of two goals in a 4-0 win over Pittsburgh made him the first player in NHL history to reach 100 points.

MOST POINTS, CAREER

2,857	Wayne Gretzky, Edm, L.A., St.L, NYR in 20 seasons	1,487GP (894G–1,963A)
1,887	Mark Messier, Edm, NYR, Van in 25 seasons	1,756GP (694G–1,193A)
1,850	Gordie Howe, Det, Hfd in 26 seasons	1,767GP (801G–1,049A)
1,802	Jaromir Jagr, eight teams in 21 seasons	1,550 GP (722G–1,080A)
1,798	Ron Francis, Hfd, Pit, Car, Tor in 23 seasons	1,731GP (549G–1,249A)
1,771	Marcel Dionne, Det, L.A., NYR in 18 seasons	1,348GP (731G–1,040A)

WHAT'S IN A NUMBER?

Jaromir Jagr proved age is but a number during the 2013–14 season, seizing a pair of impressive records. At 42 years and 20 days, Jagr became the second-oldest player to reach the 20-goal plateau with a tally on March 7 against Detroit – "trailing" only Gordie Howe (42 years, 324 days). Two weeks later, Jagr became the oldest player to reach the 60-point plateau in a season when he scored versus Minnesota. Howe holds the record for most points during his age-40 season with 103, set in 1968–69.

Bryan Trottier of the New York Islanders topped 100 points six times in seven seasons between 1977–78 and 1983–84.

MOST POINTS, ONE PERIOD

During an eight-point game in which he had five goals and three assists in a 9-4 win by the New York Islanders over the New York Rangers on December 23, 1978, Bryan Trottier set an NHL record with six points in one period. Trottier scored three goals in the second frame and set up Mike Bossy twice and Garry Howatt once for three assists. He also led the NHL in scoring with 134 points (47 goals, 87 assists) in 1978–79.

50-GOAL SEASONS

Ever since Maurice Richard scored his 50th in the 50th and final game of the 1944–45 season, 50 goals has been the single-season milestone all great scorers aspire to achieve. It took 16 years and a 20-game increase in the schedule before Bernie "Boom Boom" Geoffrion finally equaled Richard's record in 1960–61 and another five seasons after that before Bobby Hull surpassed it. Even with Wayne Gretzky having almost doubled the single-season record to 92 goals in 1981–82, there is still something about the 50-goal plateau that bespeaks greatness.

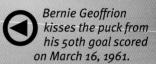

Bernie Geoffrion kisses the puck from his 50th goal scored on March 16, 1961.

RACING AFTER THE ROCKET

Toronto's Frank Mahovlich and Montreal's Bernie Geoffrion battled to become hockey's second 50-goal scorer in 1960–61. Mahovlich scored 36 times through 41 games, which had him on pace to score 60 during the 70-game season until he was slowed down by injuries. He finished the year with 48. Shaking off his own injuries, Geoffrion scored 19 goals in a 12-game stretch late into the season to reach 49 before netting #50 against Mahovlich's Maple Leafs.

MOST 50-OR-MORE GOAL SEASONS

9   Mike Bossy, NY Islanders, in 10 seasons
    Wayne Gretzky, Edmonton, Los Angeles, St. Louis, NY Rangers in 20 seasons
6   Guy Lafleur, Montreal, NY Rangers, Quebec in 17 seasons
    Marcel Dionne, Detroit, Los Angeles, NY Rangers in 18 seasons
    Mario Lemieux, Pittsburgh in 17 seasons
    Alex Ovechkin, Washington in 10 seasons
5   Bobby Hull, Chicago, Winnipeg, Hartford in 16 seasons
    Phil Esposito, Chicago, Boston, NY Rangers in 18 seasons
    Brett Hull, Calgary, St. Louis, Dallas, Detroit, Phoenix in 19 seasons
    Steve Yzerman, Detroit in 22 seasons
    Pavel Bure, Vancouver, Florida, NY Rangers in 12 seasons

OLDEST TO SCORE 50

The 1970–71 season marked the first time in NHL history when two players reached the 50-goal plateau in the same season. Both were members of the Boston Bruins. Phil Esposito established a new single-season mark with 76 goals that year, while John Bucyk finished with 51. At 35 years and 10 months of age, Bucyk was, and still remains, the oldest player in NHL history to score 50 goals in a season.

JOY OF SIX FOR OVECHKIN

Captain Alex Ovechkin reached the 50-goal plateau for the sixth time in his career and tied the franchise mark with his 472nd tally in Washington's 4-2 victory over Carolina on March 31, 2015. Ovechkin reached the half-century mark in goals for the second straight season and joined elite company by doing so on six different occasions. "Every year is harder and harder, but it's a huge (accomplishment) being with the names up there," said Ovechkin, who joined Wayne Gretzky (nine), Mike Bossy (nine), Mario Lemieux (six), Marcel Dionne (six) and Guy Lafleur (six). Playing in his 755th game, Ovechkin's second tally matched Peter Bondra for the franchise record - although the latter needed 961 games to accomplish the feat.

YOUNGEST TO SCORE 50

Wayne Gretzky scored 50 goals for the first time on April 2, 1980, in the 79th game of his first NHL season. He was just 19 years and two months old, making him the youngest player in history ever to reach the plateau. The only other teenager to score 50 goals in the NHL is Jimmy Carson of the Los Angeles Kings, who hit the mark at age 19 years, eight months on March 26, 1988.

John Bucyk's 51 goals and 116 points in 1970–71 were both career highs for the future Hall of Famer.

LUCKY PIERRE

Prior to Wayne Gretzky, the youngest player to score 50 goals in a single season had been Pierre Larouche, who was 20 years and five months old when he scored his 50th goal for the Pittsburgh Penguins in 1975–76. Four years later, Larouche reached the half-century mark for the Montreal Canadiens, making him the first player in NHL history to score 50 goals for two different teams … a feat later matched by Wayne Gretzky.

KIDS THESE DAYS …

Alex Ovechkin was 20 years and six months old when he scored 50 goals as a rookie with the Washington Capitals in 2005–06. Steven Stamkos of the Tampa Bay Lightning hit the 50-goal plateau in his second season of 2009–10, but he was still just 20 years and two months old, making him the third-youngest 50-goal scorer in NHL history. Sidney Crosby also scored 50 goals for the first time that season, but the Pittsburgh star was 22.

FIFTY-GOAL ROOKIES

Although Wayne Gretzky scored 51 goals during his first NHL season in 1979–80, he was not considered a rookie because of the year he spent in the World Hockey Association. Due to this ruling, the only four rookies in NHL history to score 50 goals are: Mike Bossy, New York Islanders (53 in 1977–78), Joe Nieuwendyk, Calgary (51 goals in 1987–88), Teemu Selanne, Winnipeg (76 goals in 1992–93), and Alex Ovechkin, Washington (52 goals in 2005–06).

◀ *Steven Stamkos became the third-youngest player in NHL history to score 50 goals in a season in 2009–10.*

▲ *On April 1, 1978, Mike Bossy became the first rookie in NHL history to score 50 goals. Only Bossy and Guy Lafleur topped 50 in 1977–78.*

MOST AND LEAST

Since the 1970–71 season, there have only been two complete NHL seasons (1998–99 and 2003–04) in which no player scored 50 goals. The busiest 50-goal season was 1992–93, when 14 players hit the magic mark: Alexander Mogilny (76), Teemu Selanne (76), Mario Lemieux (69), Luc Robitaille (63), Pavel Bure (60), Steve Yzerman (58), Pierre Turgeon (58), Kevin Stevens (55), Brett Hull (54), Dave Andreychuk (54), Pat Lafontaine (53), Mark Recchi (53), Brendan Shanahan (51), and Jeremy Roenick (50).

LIKE FATHER, LIKE SON

Only one father and son have each scored 50 goals in the NHL as both Bobby and Brett Hull topped the mark five times. With his father watching from a private box at the St. Louis Arena, Brett reached 50 for the first time on February 6, 1990, beating Jeff Reese of Toronto early in the third period of a 6-4 Blues victory. With his 59th goal on February 25, Brett surpassed Bobby's top single-season NHL mark.

MOST CONSECUTIVE 50-OR-MORE GOAL SEASONS

9   Mike Bossy, NY Islanders (1977–78, 1985–86)
8   Wayne Gretzky, Edmonton (1979–80, 1986–87)
6   Guy Lafleur, Montreal (1974–75, 1979–80)
5   Phil Esposito, Boston (1970–71, 1974–75)
    Marcel Dionne, Los Angeles (1978–79, 1982–83)
    Brett Hull, St. Louis (1989–90, 1993–94)

◀ *Bobby and Brett Hull pose with the Hart Trophy after Brett won it in 1991. Bobby had won it in 1965 and 1966, making them the only father-and-son NHL MVPs.*

100-POINT SEASONS

"Whoever thought," asked Bobby Hull at the end of the 1968–69 season, "that anyone would score 100 or more points and not win the scoring title?" Until that season, no one had ever scored 100 points in the NHL, but Hull scored 107 that year and still finished 19 points behind Phil Esposito in the race for the Art Ross Trophy. Since then, of course, literally hundreds of players have topped 100 points without winning a scoring title, and a few of those have finished more than 100 points behind the leader! Even so, like 50 goals, 100 points in a season remains a milestone that defines the game's greatest players.

HOWE ABOUT THAT?

Gordie Howe twice set single-season records for points in the 1950s, first with 86 in 1950–51 and then with 95 in 1952–53. By 1968–69, Howe was in his 23rd NHL season yet he'd reached a career high with 99 points heading into the final night of March 30, 1969. He collected two goals and two assists to shatter the 100-point mark and join Phil Esposito and Bobby Hull as charter members of the 100-point club.

THE FIRST TIME

The 1968–69 season marked the first time anyone had topped 100 points. Here's a look at the top scorers that year:

		GP	G	A	PTS	PIM
Phil Esposito	Boston	74	49	77	126	79
Bobby Hull	Chicago	74	58	49	107	48
Gordie Howe	Detroit	76	44	59	103	58
Stan Mikita	Chicago	74	30	67	97	52
Ken Hodge	Boston	75	45	45	90	75
Yvan Cournoyer	Montreal	76	43	44	87	31
Alex Delvecchio	Detroit	72	25	58	83	8
Red Berenson	St. Louis	76	35	47	82	43
Jean Béliveau	Montreal	69	33	49	82	55
Frank Mahovlich	Detroit	76	49	29	78	38
Jean Ratelle	NY Rangers	75	32	46	78	26

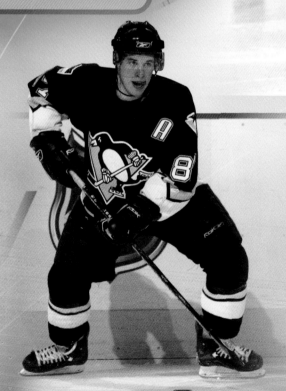

YOUNGEST TO 100

Wayne Gretzky, Peter Stastny, Dale Hawerchuk, Mario Lemieux, Teemu Selanne, Joe Juneau, Alex Ovechkin, and Sidney Crosby all reached 100 points in their first NHL season, but only Gretzky, Hawerchuk, Lemieux, Jimmy Carson (in his second year), and Crosby have done so as teenagers. With his August birthday, Crosby was the youngest ever at 18 years and eight months in 2005–06. A year later, he became the only player to twice top 100 points as a teenager.

▶ *Sidney Crosby won the Art Ross Trophy at age 19 in 2006–07. He was the first teenager to win a scoring title in any major professional sport.*

▲ *Gordie Howe finished among the NHL's top 10 scorers 21 times in his 26-year career.*

OLDEST TO 100

Gordie Howe celebrated his 41st birthday the day after he topped the 100-point mark in 1969. He was nearly 11 years older than Bobby Hull and 14 years senior to Phil Esposito. No other player in NHL history has produced a 100-point season after the age of 40. The second-oldest 100-point player behind Gordie Howe is Joe Sakic, who reached the mark for the sixth and final time in his career with the Colorado Avalanche at age 37 in 2006–07.

DEAL OR NO DEAL

Six NHL players have been traded during a 100-point season, including Joe Thornton, who led the league with 125 points for Boston and San Jose in 2005–06. The five other traded players are: Jean Ratelle (105 with the Bruins and Rangers, 1975–76), Bernie Nicholls (112 with the Kings and Rangers, 1989–90), John Cullen (110 with the Penguins and Whalers, 1990–91), Teemu Selanne (108 with the Jets and Ducks, 1995–96), and Wayne Gretzky (102 with the Kings and Blues, 1995–96).

◄ *Jean Ratelle was traded from the Rangers to the Bruins with Brad Park and Joe Zanussi for Phil Esposito and Carol Vadnais in a blockbuster deal on November 7, 1975.*

THE BEST DEFENSE IS A GOOD OFFENSE

Only five defensemen in NHL history have topped the 100-point plateau, led by Bobby Orr who did it six times and is the only defenseman to lead the NHL in scoring, which he achieved twice. The four others are: Denis Potvin (101 points with the Islanders, 1978–79), Al MacInnis (103 with the Flames, 1990–91), Brian Leetch (102 with the Rangers, 1991–92), and Paul Coffey, who did it three times with Edmonton and twice with Pittsburgh.

HIGHS & LOWS

Since 1968–69, there have been four seasons played in which no players reached 100 points. The first was 1994–95, when a labor dispute reduced the schedule to just 48 games; the other years were 1999–2000, 2001–02, and 2003–04. The 1992–93 season featured a record 21 players topping 100 points, while the 1984–85 season saw 16 players score 100 points or more, including league-leader Wayne Gretzky who had 208 points that year.

QUICK OFF THE MARK

On December 18, 1983, Wayne Gretzky collected two goals and two assists to lead the Edmonton Oilers past the Winnipeg Jets 7-5. The four points gave Gretzky 100 on the season in just 34 games, the quickest anyone has ever reached the milestone. Gretzky wound up missing six games due to injuries in 1983–84, but finished the year with 87 goals and 118 assists for 205 points and a record average of 2.77 points per game.

► *Wayne Gretzky averaged more than two points per game 10 times in his NHL career.*

MARIO'S MAGIC

In all, Wayne Gretzky reached the 100-point plateau in fewer than 40 games four times in his career. The only other player to score 100 points so quickly is Mario Lemieux, who reached 100 in his 36th game in 1988–89, when he went on to score 199 points. He also recorded 100 in 38 games in 1992–93, when he led the League with 160 points despite being limited to just 60 games played due to cancer treatments.

► *Mario Lemieux averaged more than two points a game six times in his career.*

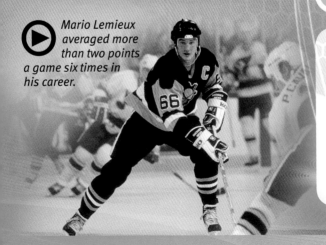

MOST 100-OR-MORE POINT SEASONS

15	Wayne Gretzky, Edmonton, Los Angeles, St. Louis, NY Rangers in 20 seasons
10	Mario Lemieux, Pittsburgh in 17 seasons
8	Marcel Dionne, Detroit, Los Angeles, NY Rangers in 18 seasons
7	Mike Bossy, NY Islanders in 10 seasons
	Peter Stastny, Quebec, New Jersey, St. Louis in 15 seasons

MOST CONSECUTIVE 100-OR-MORE POINT SEASONS

13	Wayne Gretzky, Edmonton, Los Angeles (1979–80, 1991–92)
6	Bobby Orr, Boston (1969–70, 1974–75)
	Guy Lafleur, Montreal (1974–75, 1979–80)
	Mike Bossy, NY Islanders (1980–81, 1985–86)
	Peter Stastny, Quebec (1980–81, 1985–86)
	Mario Lemieux, Pittsburgh (1984–85, 1989–90)
	Steve Yzerman, Detroit (1987–88, 1992–93)

GAMES, SEASONS, STREAKS, & SHOTS

▽ Gordie Howe played 80 games for the Hartford Whalers at the age of 51 in 1979–80.

Some stars shine brightly, if briefly, but others go on and on. Imagine if Bobby Orr or Mario Lemieux had had the longevity of Gordie Howe? What kind of numbers might they have put up? Playing day in and day out, year after year doesn't necessarily make a player great (though Doug Jarvis was an effective role player who helped the Montreal Canadiens win four straight Stanley Cups), but there's much to be said for putting up big numbers season after season after season.

MOST GAMES

1,767 Gordie Howe, Detroit, 1946–47 to 1970–71; Hartford, 1979–80
1,756 Mark Messier, Edmonton, NY Rangers, Vancouver, 1979–80 to 2003–04
1,731 Ron Francis, Hartford, Pittsburgh, Carolina, Toronto, 1981–82 to 2003–04
1,652 Mark Recchi, Pittsburgh, Philadelphia, Montreal, Carolina, Atlanta, Tampa Bay, Boston, 1987–88 to 2010–2011
1,651 Chris Chelios, Montreal, Chicago, Detroit, Atlanta, 1983–84 to 2003–04; 2005–06 to 2009–10
1,639 Dave Andreychuk, Buffalo, Toronto, New Jersey, Boston, Colorado, Tampa Bay, 1982–83 to 2003–04; 2005–06
1,635 Scott Stevens, Washington, St. Louis, New Jersey, 1982–83 to 2003–04

MOST GAMES, INCLUDING PLAYOFFS

1,992 Mark Messier, Edmonton, NY Rangers, Vancouver, 1,756 regular-season games, 236 playoff games

1,924 Gordie Howe, Detroit, Hartford, 1,767 regular-season games, 157 playoff games

1,917 Chris Chelios, Montreal, Chicago, Detroit, Atlanta, 1,651 regular-season games, 266 playoff games

1,902 Ron Francis, Hartford, Pittsburgh, Carolina, Toronto, 1,731 regular-season games, 171 playoff games

1,868 Scott Stevens, Washington, St. Louis, New Jersey, 1,635 regular-season games, 233 playoff games

FIRST TO PLAY 20

Dit Clapper was the first man to play 20 seasons in the NHL, spending them all with the Boston Bruins between 1927–28 and 1946–47. At 6'2" (1.9m) and 195 pounds (88 kilos), Clapper was among the biggest men of his era. He was one of the game's top-scoring forwards during his first 10 years, and then became a star defenseman. When he retired as a player on February 12, 1947, Clapper was immediately inducted into the Hockey Hall of Fame.

HOWE HE DID IT

Gordie Howe broke into the NHL with the Detroit Red Wings in 1946–47 and starred for 25 years, setting records that, at the time, seemed unbreakable. He had an effortless skating style, tremendous strength, and a powerful shot. Howe retired in 1971 at age 42, but made a comeback two years later and spent six seasons in the World Hockey Association before returning for a final NHL campaign with the Hartford Whalers in 1979–80.

MARTIN: HITTING MACHINE

New York Islanders left wing Matt Martin set an NHL record with 374 hits during the 2011–12 season. Martin's mark eclipsed the previous record of 356, set by Minnesota's Cal Clutterbuck during his rookie campaign in 2008–09. Martin lowered the boom on Boston captain Zdeno Chara for the record-breaking hit on March 31. The statistic has been kept only since the 2005–06 season.

◀ Boston's Dit Clapper was an All-Star at right wing twice in his career, and an All-Star defenseman on four occasions.

CAN'T MATCH THAT

Though Chris Chelios has equaled Gordie Howe's 26 seasons in the NHL, and Mark Messier tops him when playoff and regular-season games are combined, Howe's six seasons in the WHA leave his "major league" career unmatched. In all, he played 32 seasons and 2,186 regular-season games (2,421 when playoffs are counted) before retiring at age 51. He played alongside sons Mark and Marty in the WHA and the NHL, and was also active as a grandfather.

Doug Jarvis went to Washington from Montreal with Rod Langway in 1982 and helped turn the Capitals into contenders.

GOAL-SCORING STREAKS

Punch Broadbent of the original Ottawa Senators set an NHL record that still stands when he scored in 16 consecutive games during the 1921–22 season. Altogether, he totaled 27 goals during the streak, and led the NHL with 32 goals and 14 assists. During the 1979–80 campaign, Charlie Simmer of the Los Angeles Kings scored in 13 consecutive games, netting 17 goals during a streak that ranks as the longest of the modern era.

Charlie Simmer scored 56 goals in both 1979–80 and 1980–81.

IMPRESSIVE RUNS BY BOUWMEESTER, JARVIS

Although St. Louis' Jay Bouwmeester holds the NHL record for most consecutive games played by a defenseman, his quest to supplant Doug Jarvis for the overall mark came to an end on November 23, 2014. Bouwmeester was felled by a lower-body injury in the Blues' 3-2 win in Ottawa on the previous night, and was unable to answer the bell against Winnipeg to end his consecutive games streak at 737. The missed contest was Bouwmeester's first since March 3, 2004, while Jarvis did not sit out a game in his entire career while playing with Montreal, Hartford and Washington from 1975-87.

POINT STREAK

Beginning with the first game of the 1983–84 season, Wayne Gretzky collected at least one point (a goal or an assist) in 51 consecutive games for the Edmonton Oilers in a streak that earned comparisons to Joe DiMaggio's legendary 56-game hitting streak in baseball. Gretzky accumulated 61 goals and 92 assists for 153 points during his run. The streak finally ended on January 28, 1984, when Markus Mattsson and the Los Angeles Kings blanked Gretzky in a 4-2 victory.

ASSIST STREAKS

During his scoring streak in 1983–84, Wayne Gretzky set a separate record with at least one assist in 17 straight games. He tied that record in Los Angeles in 1989–90, but broke it when he had assists in 23 straight games for the Kings in the 1990–91 season. Gretzky collected 48 assists during the streak. When Adam Oates had assists in 18 straight games for the Boston Bruins in 1992–93, he had 28 assists during his streak.

OTHER SCORING STREAKS

Paul Coffey of the Edmonton Oilers set a record for defensemen with points in 28 straight games during the 1985–86 season. Coffey had 16 goals and 39 assists during his streak. In 2006–07, Paul Stastny of the Colorado Avalanche set a rookie record by collecting a point in 20 straight games. Stastny had 11 goals and 18 assists for 29 points in those 20 games. His father Peter enjoyed a 16-game rookie scoring streak in 1980–81.

Alex Ovechkin is one of just two players in NHL history to fire more than 500 shots on goal in a single season.

MOST SHOTS ON GOAL, ONE SEASON

550	Phil Esposito, Boston, 1970–71	78GP	78-game schedule
528	Alex Ovechkin, Washington, 2008–09	79GP	82-game schedule
446	Alex Ovechkin, Washington, 2007–08	82GP	82-game schedule
429	Paul Kariya, Anaheim, 1998–99	82GP	82-game schedule
426	Phil Esposito, Boston, 1971–72	76GP	78-game schedule

PENALTIES, POWERPLAYS, & SHORTHAND GOALS

Penalties have always been a part of hockey. In the early days, players could be sent off the ice for one, two, or three minutes, and multiple penalties were often met with fines instead of more time in the box. At various points in history, teams did not play shorthanded during a penalty but at other times, teams were not permitted to replace anyone who was penalized and occasionally had to play with only a skater or two on the ice. Though the NHL has always tracked penalty minutes, the League did not officially track powerplay or shorthand goals until the 1963–64 season.

ALL-TIME ANDREYCHUK

Dave Andreychuk played 23 seasons in the NHL between 1982 and 2006 and scored 640 goals. He was a powerplay specialist who scored nearly half his goals (42.8 percent) with the man advantage. His total of 274 career powerplay goals is an NHL record, which ranks him ahead of Brett Hull (265) and Phil Esposito (249) on the all-time list. Andreychuk's best total of 32 powerplay goals in 1992–93 ranks him second to Tim Kerr on the single-season list.

▶ Of the 370 goals Tim Kerr scored in his career, 150 (40.5 percent) were scored with a man advantage.

◀ Dave Andreychuk's 250th career powerplay goal on November 15, 2002 moved him past Phil Esposito into top spot in NHL history.

KERR'S BIG SEASON

Though often injured throughout his career, Tim Kerr was a prolific scorer who topped 50 goals in four straight seasons with the Philadelphia Flyers from 1983–84 to 1986–87. Parking his big body (6'3"/1.9m, 230 pounds/104 kilos) in front of the net, Kerr was especially dangerous on the powerplay. On March 8, 1986, he scored his 29th powerplay goal of the season to surpass Phil Esposito and Mike Bossy's previous record. Kerr was to push the single-season record to 34.

POWERPLAY GOALS IN A GAME

Though the NHL did not officially track powerplay and shorthand goals as a league statistic until the 1963–64 season, Camille Henry of the New York Rangers set a record with four powerplay goals in one game on March 13, 1954. Montreal's Bernie Geoffrion matched the record a year later. Others to score four powerplay goals in one game are: Bryan Trottier, Chris Valentine, Dave Andreychuk, Mario Lemieux, Luc Robitaille, and Scott Mellanby.

MOST POWERPLAY GOALS, ONE SEASON

34	Tim Kerr, Philadelphia, 1985–86	76GP – 80-game schedule
32	Dave Andreychuk, Buffalo, Toronto, 1992–93	83GP – 84-game schedule
31	Joe Nieuwendyk, Calgary, 1987–88	75GP – 80-game schedule
	Mario Lemieux, Pittsburgh, 1988–89	76GP – 80-game schedule
	Mario Lemieux, Pittsburgh, 1995–96	70GP – 82-game schedule
29	Michel Goulet, Quebec, 1987–88	80GP – 80-game schedule
	Brett Hull, St. Louis, 1990–91	78GP – 80-game schedule
	Brett Hull, St. Louis, 1992–93	80GP – 84-game schedule

SHORTHAND GOALS IN ONE SEASON

Mario Lemieux set a single-season record for shorthand goals when he scored 13 times while the Pittsburgh Penguins were a man short in 1988–89. Lemieux broke the previous record of 12 shorthand goals set by Wayne Gretzky in 1983–84. Other all-time leaders in this category include Gretzky with 11 in 1984–85 and Lemieux with 10 in 1987–88. Marcel Dionne (1974–75) and Dirk Graham (1988–89) are the only other players with 10 shorthand goals in one season.

THREE OF A KIND

Three is the record for shorthand goals by one player in a single game by Theo Fleury of the Calgary Flames in an 8-4 win over St. Louis on March 9, 1991. Fleury opened the scoring with a shorthand goal at 5:52 of the first period. He scored again with the Flames a man short 24 seconds into the third period and completed his unique hat trick with the final goal of the game, with just 2:25 remaining.

◀ *Theo Fleury's 35 career shorthand goals rank him among the NHL's best.*

MOST PENALTY MINUTES, CAREER

3,966	Tiger Williams, Toronto, Vancouver, Detroit, Los Angeles, Hartford in 14 seasons	962GP
3,565	Dale Hunter, Quebec, Washington, Colorado in 19 seasons	1,407GP
3,515	Tie Domi, Toronto, NY Rangers, Winnipeg in 16 seasons	1,020GP
3,381	Marty McSorley, Pittsburgh, Edmonton Los Angeles, NY Rangers, San Jose, Boston in 17 seasons	961GP
3,300	Bob Probert, Detroit, Chicago in 17 seasons	935GP

MOST PENALTY MINUTES, ONE SEASON

472	Dave Schultz, Philadelphia, 1974–75
409	Paul Baxter, Pittsburgh, 1981–82
408	Mike Peluso, Chicago, 1991–92
405	Dave Schultz, Los Angeles, Pittsburgh, 1977–78

PENALTIES IN ONE GAME

On March 31, 1991, Chris Nilan of the Boston Bruins received a record 10 penalties in one game versus the Hartford Whalers. Nilan received six minors, two majors, a 10-minute misconduct, and a game misconduct. Randy Holt of the Los Angeles Kings received nine penalties in a single period versus the Philadelphia Flyers on March 11, 1979. Holt had a minor, three majors, two 10-minute misconducts, and three game-misconducts for a record 67 penalty minutes in all.

▶ *Mark Messier's 63 career shorthand goals rank him second all-time among the single-season leaders behind Wayne Gretzky's 73.*

PLAYOFF POWERPLAYS

Brett Hull holds the career record for most powerplay goals in the playoffs with 38 in 202 career games, three more than Mike Bossy, who scored 35 in just 129 games. Bossy and Cam Neely share the record for most powerplay goals in the playoffs in one year. In the 1981 playoffs, Bossy had nine for the New York Islanders in 18 games, while Neely achieved nine for the Boston Bruins in 19 games in 1991.

PLAYOFF SHORTHAND

Mark Messier holds the career record for shorthand goals in the playoffs with 14, three more than his longtime teammate Wayne Gretzky and four more than another Oilers great, Jari Kurri. Gretzky (1983) is one of six players to share the record of three shorthand goals in a single playoff year, the others being Boston's Derek Sanderson (1969), Philadelphia's Bill Barber (1980), the Islanders' Lorne Henning (1980), Chicago's Wayne Presley (1989), and Edmonton's Todd Marchant (1997).

SCORING BY FORWARDS, SCORING BY DEFENSEMEN

Given that Wayne Gretzky holds the NHL career and single-season records for goals, assists, and points, it should come as no surprise that he holds these records for centers as well. Scoring records among both left and right wingers, however, are shared by several names, as are the scoring records held by defenseman. Many of the greatest players in NHL history can be found among the scoring leaders by position, but there are a few surprising names on these lists as well.

LEFT WING

Alexander the Great

In 2006–07, Alex Ovechkin of the Washington Capitals led the NHL with 65 goals and broke the single-season record for goals by a left winger of 63, set by Luc Robitaille of the Los Angeles Kings in 1992–93. Robitaille's 125 points during an 84-game schedule that season remain the record ahead of Pittsburgh's Kevin Stevens (123 in 1992–93) and Quebec's Michel Goulet (121 in 1983–84). Ovechkin's 112 points in 2006–07 have him tied for fifth.

More Than Just Lucky

Luc Robitaille holds the career records for both goals and points by a left winger. Robitaille scored 668 goals during his 19-year career with Los Angeles, Pittsburgh, Detroit, and the Rangers, and collected 1,394 points. Brendan Shanahan is next up with 656 goals. Robitaille's 726 career assists trail only John Bucyk among NHL left wingers. Bucyk had 813 assists in a 23-year career with Boston and Detroit, and ranks second to Robitaille with 1,369 points.

Luc Robitaille leads all left wingers in career scoring.

Juneau Who

Washington's Joe Juneau set the single-season NHL record for assists by a left winger with 70 during an 84-game season in 1992–93. Juneau broke the record of 69 assists established by Pittsburgh's Kevin Stevens during an 80-game season just one year before. Montreal's Mats Naslund (67 in 1985–86), Boston's John Bucyk (65 in 1970–71), Quebec's Michel Goulet (65 in 1983–84), and Edmonton's Mark Messier (64 in 1983–84) round out the leader board.

RIGHT WING

All Right

Gordie Howe's 801 goals, 1,049 assists, and 1,850 points during his 25 seasons with Detroit and one year with the Hartford Whalers each make him the all-time career leader among NHL right wingers. Brett Hull is second in the goal-scoring category with 741, while Mike Gartner lies third with 708. Jaromir Jagr ranks second to Howe with 953 assists and 1,599 points. Jagr's 149 points for Pittsburgh in 1995–96 make him the single-season leader.

The Golden Brett

Brett Hull's 86 goals for the St. Louis Blues in 1990–91 established the single-season record for a right winger. Alexander Mogilny (who scored 76 goals for Buffalo in 1992–93) and Teemu Selanne (who scored 76 for Winnipeg that same season) are second on the list, followed by Hull again, with 72 in 1989–90, Jari Kurri (who had 71 for Edmonton in 1984–85), and Hull a third time, with 70 goals in 1991–92.

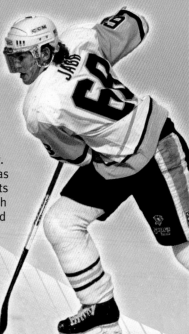

It's Better to Give ...

Though both are better remembered for their goals than assists, the Islanders' Mike Bossy and Montreal's Guy Lafleur hold down three of the top five places among the single-season assist leaders at right wing. Pittsburgh's Jaromir Jagr has the top spot, with 87 assists in 1995–96, and is tied with Bossy (1981–82) for second place, with 83 assists in 1998–99. Guy Lafleur had 80 assists in 1976–77, then 77 in 1978–79 to round out the top five.

Sprague Cleghorn scored a career-high 17 goals for Montreal in 1921–22 during a season that was just 24 games long.

DEFENSEMEN

Five for Five

Though he had 20 goals for the Maple Leafs in 1975–76 and had scored 11 more during the first two months of 1976–77, Ian Turnbull had not scored a goal in 30 games heading into Toronto's game with the Detroit Red Wings on February 2, 1977. That night, he fired five shots on goal and scored on each one, setting a new NHL record for goals by a defenseman in a 9-1 Leafs victory.

Four by Four

Seven NHL defensemen have scored four goals in a single game. One of those seven is Sprague Cleghorn. Though mainly recalled as one of the toughest players in NHL history, Cleghorn was a high-scoring defenseman who netted four goals for the Montreal Canadiens in a 10-6 win over the Hamilton Tigers on January 14, 1922. His younger brother, Odie Cleghorn, was a center for the Canadiens, who also scored four goals for Montreal in the same game.

Crazy Eights

On December 11, 1977, defenseman Tom Bladon of the Philadelphia Flyers collected four goals and four assists in an 11-1 win over the Cleveland Barons. Bladon's eight points in the game set a new record for defensemen, eclipsing Bobby Orr's three-goal, four-assist performance against the New York Rangers in 1973. On March 14, 1986, Paul Coffey tied the mark with two goals and six assists in Edmonton's 12-3 win over Detroit.

Six Times Six

Paul Coffey's six assists in his eight-point game gave him a share of another NHL record for defensemen. The five other defensemen who have had six assists in a single game are: Babe Pratt, January 8, 1944, Toronto 12, Boston 3; Pat Stapleton, March 30, 1969, Chicago 9, Detroit 5; Bobby Orr, January 1, 1973, Boston 9, Vancouver 2; Ron Stackhouse, March 8, 1975, Pittsburgh 8, Philadelphia 2, and Gary Suter, April 4, 1986, Calgary 9, Edmonton 3.

Ian Turnbull played 10+ seasons in the NHL and reached double digits in goals seven times.

Tom Bladon was Philadelphia's top scoring defenseman three times in six seasons in the mid-1970s.

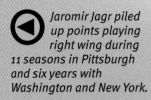

Jaromir Jagr piled up points playing right wing during 11 seasons in Pittsburgh and six years with Washington and New York.

DEFENSEMEN SCORING LEADERS

Goals, Career, & Single Season
410	Raymond Bourque, Boston, Colorado in 22 seasons	1,612 GP
48	Paul Coffey, Edmonton, 1985–86	79 GP – 80-game schedule

Assists, Career, & Single Season
1,169	Raymond Bourque, Boston, Colorado in 22 seasons	1,612 GP
102	Bobby Orr, Boston, 1970–71	78 GP – 78-game schedule

Points, Career, & Single Season:
1,579	Raymond Bourque, Boston, Colorado in 22 seasons	1,612 GP
139	Bobby Orr, Boston, 1970–71	78 GP – 78-game schedule

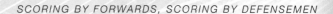

ROOKIE RECORDS

There's always something exciting about a young player making his NHL debut. Whether it's somebody that everyone's been hyping as a star since childhood or a late-round draft pick known only by his team's most diehard fans, they've all got the same chance to make their mark once they crack the lineup. A fast start certainly doesn't guarantee a long and brilliant career, but achievements earned as a rookie can bring some measure of immortality. Only one rookie each year gets to win the Calder Trophy but everyone has a chance to get their name in the record book.

ROOKIE SCORING LEADER

Nels Stewart is the only rookie in NHL history to lead the League in scoring. Stewart joined the Montreal Maroons in 1925–26 and topped the League with 34 goals and 42 points during the 36-game season. In 1979–80, rookie Wayne Gretzky tied Marcel Dionne for the NHL point-scoring title but lost the Art Ross Trophy because his 51 goals were two fewer than Dionne's. Gretzky wasn't considered a rookie because he had played previously in the World Hockey Association.

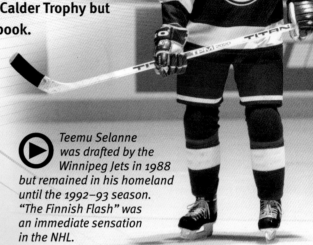

▶ *Teemu Selanne was drafted by the Winnipeg Jets in 1988 but remained in his homeland until the 1992–93 season. "The Finnish Flash" was an immediate sensation in the NHL.*

ROOKIE ASSIST RECORD

Because he was not considered a rookie, neither Wayne Gretzky's 86 assists nor his 137 points in 1979–80 stand as NHL rookie records. Instead, the rookie record for assists is shared between Quebec's Peter Stastny (1980–81) and Washington's Joe Juneau (1992–93), who both had 70 assists in their first year in the NHL. Teemu Selanne's 132 points for the Winnipeg Jets in 1992–93 stands as the rookie record in that category.

A FAST 50

Mike Bossy was the first rookie in NHL history to reach the 50-goal plateau when he scored 53 times for the New York Islanders in 1977–78. Calgary's Joe Nieuwendyk was the next rookie 50-goal scorer, with 51 goals in 1987–88. In 1992–93, Teemu Selanne shattered Bossy's rookie record when he scored 76 goals for the Winnipeg Jets. The only other rookie to top 50 goals is Alex Ovechkin, who scored 52 for Washington in 2005–06.

MOST POINTS BY A ROOKIE, ONE SEASON

132	Teemu Selanne, Winnipeg, 1992–93	84GP – 84-game schedule
109	Peter Stastny, Quebec, 1980–81	77GP – 80-game schedule
106	Alex Ovechkin, Washington, 2005–06	81GP – 82-game schedule
103	Dale Hawerchuk, Winnipeg, 1981–82	80GP – 80-game schedule
102	Joe Juneau, Boston, 1992–93	84GP – 84-game schedule
	Sidney Crosby, Pittsburgh, 2005–06	81GP – 82-game schedule
100	Mario Lemieux, Pittsburgh, 1984–85	73GP – 80-game schedule

KREIDER COMES TO PLAY

After helping Boston College to win the NCAA title, Chris Kreider joined the New York Rangers during their 2012 playoff run. Kreider, 21, collected five goals as the top-seeded Rangers advanced to the Eastern Conference finals before being bested in six games by the New Jersey Devils. The scoring outburst broke a 59-year-old NHL record for most playoff goals before having played in a single regular season game. Montreal's Eddie Mazur held the previous mark of four goals, set in parts of three postseasons between 1950 and 1953. He officially played in his first NHL game during the 1953–54 campaign.

▲ *In 2005–06, Alex Ovechkin joined Teemu Selanne as the only NHL rookies to top 50 goals and 100 points.*

BIG NIGHTS

The NHL began play December 19, 1917. On that first night, Joe Malone scored five goals for the Montreal Canadiens in a 7-4 win over Ottawa and Harry Hyland scored five for the Montreal Wanderers in a 10-9 win over Toronto. However, both Malone and Hyland were long-time veterans of the earlier National Hockey Association. Mickey Roach (Toronto, March 6, 1920), Howie Meeker (Toronto, January 8, 1947), and Don Murdoch (Rangers, October 12, 1976) all scored five goals in a game as true NHL rookies.

FOUR TIMES THREE

Excluding Joe Malone and Harry Hyland, Alex Smart set a record on January 14, 1943, with three goals in his first NHL game. Smart was called up to the Canadiens from the Quebec Senior Hockey League and led Montreal to a 5-1 win over Chicago. On October 10, 1979, WHA veteran Real Cloutier scored a hat trick in his first NHL game. Fabian Brunnstrom of the Dallas Stars and Derek Stepan of the New York Rangers would later score three in their respective NHL debuts on October 15, 2008 and Oct. 9, 2010.

HILL OF AN EFFORT

On February 14, 1977, Al Hill was called up from Springfield to play his first NHL game for Philadelphia Flyers. Hill scored on each of his first two shots on goal and later added three assists for five points in the game. He is the only true rookie in history to collect five points in his first NHL game, a feat matched only by Joe Malone and Harry Hyland in their five-goal games on December 19, 1917.

MORE BIG NIGHTS

On February 15, 1980, Wayne Gretzky set up seven goals in Edmonton's 8-2 win over Washington to establish a record for most assists by a player in one game during his first NHL season. When brothers Peter (four goals, four assists) and Anton Stastny (three goals, five assists) both collected eight points in Quebec's 11-7 win over Washington on February 22, 1981, they set a new record for most points by a rookie player in one game.

FOUR FOR FOUR

After a solid 1952–53 campaign with Edmonton in the Western Hockey League, Earl "Dutch" Reibel earned an NHL job with Detroit the following year. He made his debut in the season opener on October 8, 1953 and set up all four goals in a 4-1 win over the New York Rangers. The only other rookie to collect four assists in his first NHL game is Roland Eriksson with the Minnesota North Stars on October 6, 1976.

BUBBA & BRIAN

Selected second overall behind Dale McCourt in the 1977 NHL Draft, Barry "Bubba" Beck joined the Colorado Rockies directly out of junior hockey and became the first rookie defenseman in NHL history to reach the 20-goal plateau when he scored 22 times in 1977–78. Brian Leetch broke his record in 1988–89, with 23 goals for the New York Rangers during his first full NHL season. Dion Phaneuf is the only other rookie defenseman to score 20 goals, reaching this milestone while with the Calgary Flames in 2005–06.

LUCKY NO. 13 FOR MACKINNON

Colorado Avalanche forward Nathan MacKinnon highlighted his rookie season by besting one of Wayne Gretzky's records. The Calder Trophy winner extended his point streak to 13 games – the longest such stretch by an 18-year-old – and he did so in thrilling fashion. MacKinnon set up defenseman Andre Benoit for the winning goal 4:28 into overtime as Colorado skated to a 3-2 victory over Detroit on March 6, 2014. Gretzky recorded his 12-game stretch during the 1979-80 season.

THREE OF THE BEST

Raymond Bourque set a rookie record for defensemen with 65 points in his first season with the Boston Bruins in 1979–80. The record lasted just one season before Larry Murphy broke it. Murphy joined the Los Angeles Kings in 1980–81 and promptly set new records for a rookie defenseman, with 60 assists and 76 points. Brian Leetch is the only other rookie defenseman to collect over 70 points, with 71 for the Rangers in 1988–89.

KING KEEPS THRONE

Martin Jones enjoyed quite the start to his NHL career in the 2013-14 season. The 23-year-old was summoned from Manchester of the American Hockey League when Los Angeles Kings stud goaltender Jonathan Quick and backup Ben Scrivens went down to injury. Jones hit the ground running, winning his first eight starts to tie an NHL record for the best in-season career beginning. Jones was so dominant in that stretch that he recorded a .966 save percentage and 0.98 goals-against average.

◀ *After launching his career in Los Angeles, Larry Murphy would collect 1,216 points, ranking him fifth all-time among defensemen behind Raymond Bourque, Paul Coffey, Al MacInnis, and Phil Housley.*

THREE-GOAL GAMES & FASTEST GOALS

You can get it done fast, or you can get it done right ... but sometimes you can achieve both. And often in hockey, when the goals start to come, they come in bunches. Not surprisingly, the greatest-scoring seasons in NHL history have resulted in a record number of hat tricks, too. From Joe Malone to Phil Esposito, to Mike Bossy and Wayne Gretzky, the single-season record for scoring three or more goals in a game has grown very little since the dawn of the NHL. Likewise, many different records for fastest goals have been spread evenly throughout the League's entire history.

BOSSY, THEN GRETZKY

Mike Bossy of the New York Islanders set a new record with nine hat tricks (six three-goal games, three four-goal games) during the 1980–81 season, when he also became the first player to equal Maurice Richard's feat of 50 goals in 50 games. Bossy's new record lasted just one year before Wayne Gretzky had 10 hat tricks in 1981–82, when he scored 50 goals in 39 games and set a new NHL-scoring record with 92 goals.

GRETZKY AGAIN

Wayne Gretzky's 10 hat tricks in 1981–82 included six three-goal games, three four-goal games, and a five-goal game on December 30, 1981 that saw him reach 50 goals in his 39th game. Gretzky equaled the hat-trick record with 10 again (six three-goal games, four four-goal games) during his 87-goal season in 1983–84. Mario Lemieux approached the record when he scored 85 goals in 1988–89, recording seven three-goal games, one four-goal game, and one five-goal game.

MALONE SETS THE MARK

Though he played just 20 games in 1917–18, Joe Malone scored 44 goals during the NHL's first season and had three or more goals in a game seven times. His goal-scoring record was surpassed for the first of many times when Maurice Richard scored 50 goals in 50 games in 1944–45, but it was not until the 1970–71 season that anyone matched Malone's hat-trick record. Phil Esposito had seven three-goal games as part of his record-breaking 76-goal season.

TAYLOR-MADE IN EIGHT SECONDS

In a span of eight seconds, Taylor Hall inserted his name into the record books – at the expense of Wayne Gretzky. The current Edmonton Oiler scored two goals in that span against the New York Islanders on October 17, 2013. Hall deposited a brilliant feed from Justin Schultz to draw first blood in the contest at 15:52 of the first period – and cleaned up a rebound of a shot by Mark Arcobello shortly thereafter. The outburst was one second better than the two-goal performance by Gretzky, who set his mark on February 18, 1981.

 Taylor Hall, right, has reason to celebrate with defenseman Ladislav Smid after scoring his second goal in eight seconds.

MOST THREE-OR-MORE GOAL GAMES, CAREER

50 Wayne Gretzky, Edmonton, Los Angeles, St. Louis, NY Rangers, in 20 seasons, 37 three-goal games, 9 four-goal games, 4 five-goal games

40 Mario Lemieux, Pittsburgh, in 17 seasons, 27 three-goal games, 10 four-goal games, 3 five-goal games

39 Mike Bossy, NY Islanders, in 10 seasons, 30 three-goal games, 9 four-goal games

33 Brett Hull, Calgary, St. Louis, Dallas, Detroit, Phoenix, in 19 seasons, 30 three-goal games, 3 four-goal games

32 Phil Esposito, Chicago, Boston, NY Rangers, in 18 seasons, 27 three-goal games, 5 four-goal games

FAST OFF THE FACE-OFF

Three players in NHL history have scored a goal just five seconds after the game's opening face-off: Doug Smail, who scored for the Winnipeg Jets against the St. Louis Blues on December 20, 1981; Bryan Trottier of the New York Islanders versus Boston on March 22, 1984; and Buffalo's Alexander Mogilny versus Toronto on December 21, 1991. On February 14, 2003, Boston's Mike Knuble set a record when he scored twice in the first 27 seconds versus Florida.

FOUR GOALS, 49 SECONDS

The Dallas Stars and St. Louis Blues set an NHL record by combining for four goals in 49 seconds on April 3, 2015 - and it all started innocently enough. Stars forward Travis Moen scored on a penalty shot at 19:49 of the first period, but the Blues answered as Patrik Berglund netted his second of the contest 15 ticks into the second and Jaden Schwartz netted the first of his three just 17 seconds later. Dallas captain Jamie Benn answered at the 38-second mark for the first of his two in the period, but St. Louis had the last laugh by recording a 7-5 victory.

JAGR STILL HAS IT

Jaromir Jagr became the oldest player to record a hat trick, doing so at the tender age of 42 years, 322 days on January 3, 2015. The veteran forward surpassed Gordie Howe (41, November 2, 1969) for the honor by scoring three times to lead New Jersey to a 5-2 triumph over rival Philadelphia. Jagr scored twice in the first period before poking home a loose puck in the slot midway into the second to complete his 15th career hat trick - and first since March 26, 2006, which also came at the expense of the Flyers.

TWO-BY-FOUR

Trailing Boston 3-2 early in the third period on January 4, 1931, Nels Stewart banged the rebound from a Hooley Smith shot past Bruins goalie Tiny Thompson to give the Montreal Maroons the tying goal at 5:55. On the ensuing face-off, Stewart won the draw over to Smith, who quickly got the puck back to Stewart, who then blasted another shot past Thompson after just four seconds. Later, the Maroons would add another goal for a 5-3 victory.

TWO-BY-FOUR X TWO

Nels Stewart's record for the two fastest goals was not equaled for nearly 65 years. Then, on December 15, 1995, Winnipeg Jets rookie defenseman Deron Quint bounced a shot off the stick of an Oilers player and into the net on a powerplay at 7:51 of the second period. After Alexei Zhamnov won the ensuing face-off, Quint fired a shot from center that bounced off a metal glass partition and into the net, four seconds later.

HIS FIRST CAME FAST

With many NHL veterans in the Armed Forces, 20-year-old Gus Bodnar was one of several newcomers trying out for Toronto in the fall of 1943. Bodnar earned a roster spot and was on the ice to start the season when the Maple Leafs hosted the Rangers on October 30, 1943. He scored just 15 seconds after the opening face-off, setting a record that still stands for the fastest goal by a player in his first NHL game.

◀ *Nels Stewart scored fast and often. In his best season of 1929–30, Stewart scored 39 goals for the Montreal Maroons during a 44-game schedule.*

FAST TRICK

On March 23, 1952, the New York Rangers hosted Chicago in a battle of the NHL's two worst teams on the final night of the season. Only 3,254 fans were there, but they witnessed history being made when the Blackhawks' Bill Mosienko scored at 6:09, 6:20, and 6:30 of the third period to complete a hat trick in just 21 seconds. Gus Bodnar set up each of Mosienko's goals, giving him hockey's three fastest assists.

TIME FOR A CHANGE

Bill Mosienko's hat-trick record has never seriously been threatened, although Jean Beliveau scored three goals for the Montreal Canadiens in a span of just 44 seconds on November 5, 1955. All three Beliveau goals were scored while the Detroit Red Wings were two men short. Prior to the start of the next season, the NHL passed a rule allowing players serving a minor penalty to return to the ice if a powerplay goal was scored.

▶ *Bill Mosienko's three goals in 21 seconds obliterated the previous record of 1:52 for the fastest hat trick set by Detroit's Carl Liscombe on March 13, 1938.*

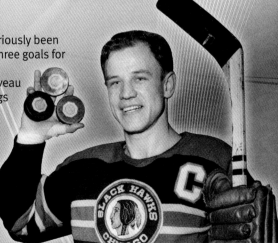

500 GOALS, 1,000 POINTS, & SCORING PLATEAUS

Scoring 500 goals and collecting 1,000 points are the career milestones that define a great scorer. Maurice Richard was the first player to score 500 goals, and his career total of 544 became its own milestone for many years. Even though Gordie Howe had pushed the career mark well past 700 by then, much was still made of the fact when Bobby Hull passed Maurice Richard in 1971 and when Phil Esposito passed him in 1976. Howe was first to collect 1,000 points and even though Wayne Gretzky has pushed the career record to 2,857, the 1,000-point mark remains significant.

FIRST TO 1,000

On November 27, 1960, Gordie Howe got an assist in a 2-0 win over Toronto for the 1,000th point in his career. The first player to reach this milestone, he had done so in 938 regular-season games. On March 14, 1962, Howe became second to Maurice Richard to score 500 goals when he beat Gump Worsley of the New York Rangers for the milestone marker. It took Howe 1,045 games compared to Richard's 863.

HAT TRICKS & EMPTY NETS

Jean Beliveau was the second player in NHL history to record 1,000 career points and the fourth (after Richard, Howe, and Bobby Hull) to score 500 goals. Beliveau scored three goals on February 11, 1971 to reach 500. Wayne Gretzky, Mario Lemieux, Mark Messier, Brett Hull, Jaromir Jagr, and Mats Sundin also scored hat tricks to hit 500. Mike Bossy, Gretzky, Jari Kurri, and Keith Tkachuk each scored their 500th goal into an empty net.

FIRST TO 500

From the time he surpassed Nels Stewart with his 325th career goal in 1952, Maurice Richard set a new scoring record every time he put the puck in the net. Entering the 1957–58 season, Richard had scored 493 goals and the countdown was on to 500. He scored six goals in the first five games of the new season en route to scoring his 500th against Glenn Hall of the Chicago Blackhawks on October 19, 1957.

FAST FIGURES

Wayne Gretzky hit the 1,000-point plateau in just 424 games. At the time, only Guy Lafleur (720), Marcel Dionne (740), and Phil Esposito (745) had scored 1,000 points in fewer than 800 games. Since Gretzky, only Mario Lemieux (513), Mike Bossy (656), and Peter Stastny (682) have done so in under 700 games. Only Gretzky (575), Lemieux (605), Bossy (647), and Brett Hull (693) have managed to score 500 goals in fewer than 800 games.

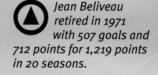

Jean Beliveau retired in 1971 with 507 goals and 712 points for 1,219 points in 20 seasons.

FACTS & FIGURES

Toronto's Mats Sundin was the first player to score his 500th career goal in overtime. Sundin, Gordie Howe, and Keith Tkachuk are the only players to score their 500th goals shorthanded. Thirteen players got their 500th on the powerplay. Fourteen have scored 500 goals with the same franchise: Maurice Richard, Gordie Howe, Bobby Hull, Jean Beliveau, Stan Mikita, Guy Lafleur, Mike Bossy, Gilbert Perreault, Wayne Gretzky, Bryan Trottier, Mario Lemieux, Steve Yzerman, Joe Sakic, and Mike Modano.

Mats Sundin's 564 goals and 1,349 points in 18 seasons are tops all-time among NHL players from Sweden.

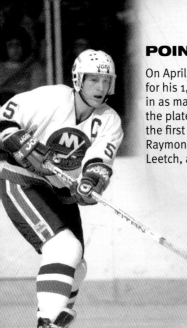

POINTS FROM THE POINT

On April 4, 1987, Denis Potvin of the New York Islanders scored a goal for his 1,000th career point. Potvin was the third Islanders player in as many years, joining Bryan Trottier and Mike Bossy to reach the plateau and the 21st player in NHL history to do so, but he was the first defenseman. Since then, fellow defensemen Paul Coffey, Raymond Bourque, Larry Murphy, Phil Housley, Al MacInnis, Brian Leetch, and Nicklas Lidstrom have all topped 1,000 points.

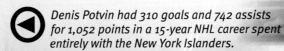

Denis Potvin had 310 goals and 742 assists for 1,052 points in a 15-year NHL career spent entirely with the New York Islanders.

Mike Gartner only scored 50 goals once in his career, but his remarkable consistency over 19 seasons resulted in 708 career goals.

JAGR'S MEMORABLE NIGHT

Aesthetically pleasing it was not, but Jaromir Jagr scored his milestone 700th goal on March 1, 2014. The veteran became the seventh member of the exclusive club after skating in from the right circle and wristing a shot that caromed off the skate of New York Islanders defenseman Andrew MacDonald and past Evgeni Nabokov at 3:31 of the second period. He also notched his 1,040th assist on defenseman Marek Zidlicky's goal.

OVER 40

Wayne Gretzky scored 40 goals or more a record 12 times in his career, doing it from his rookie year in 1979–80 through 1990–91. Marcel Dionne and Mario Lemieux both scored 40 goals or more 10 times. Gretzky is also the only player in history to top 60 goals four years in a row, which he did from 1981–82 to 1984–85. Both Mike Bossy and Brett Hull topped 60 goals for three straight seasons during their careers.

HE'S THE BOSS

Mike Bossy played just 10 seasons in the NHL, but he topped 50 goals nine times in his career and only fell short in his final year when injuries limited him to 38 goals in 63 games. Bossy's goals-per-game average of .762 is unmatched and only Wayne Gretzky equals his career total of five seasons with 60 or more goals. Phil Esposito and Mario Lemieux both scored 60 goals or more four times in their careers.

When Maurice Richard scored his 500th goal in 1957, only Gordie Howe, Nels Stewart, and Ted Lindsay had even scored as many as 300.

RETIRED PLAYERS CLOSEST TO 500 GOALS

	Seasons	Games	Goals
Glenn Anderson, Edm, Tor, NYR, St.L	16	1,129	498
Jean Ratelle, NYR, Bos	21	1,281	491
Norm Ullman, Det, Tor	20	1,410	490
Brian Bellows, Min, Mtl, T.B., Ana, Wsh	17	1,188	485
Darryl Sittler, Tor, Phi, Det	15	1,096	484
Sergei Fedorov, Det, Ana, CBJ, Wsh	18	1,248	483
Bernie Nicholls, L.A., NYR, Edm, N.J., Chi, S.J.	18	1,127	475
Alexander Mogilny, Buf, Van, N.J., Tor	16	990	473
Denis Savard, Chi, Mtl, T.B.	17	1,196	473
Pat LaFontaine, NYI, Buf, NYR	15	865	468

RETIRED PLAYERS CLOSEST TO 1,000 POINTS

	Seasons	Games	G	A	Points
Paul Kariya, Ana, Col, Nash, StL	15	989	402	587	989
Rick Middleton, NYR, Bos	14	1,005	448	540	988
Dave Keon, Tor, Hfd	18	1,296	396	590	986
Andy Bathgate, NYR, Tor, Det, Pit	17	1,069	349	624	973
Maurice Richard, Mtl	18	978	544	421	965
Kirk Muller, N.J., Mtl, NYI, Tor, Fla, Dal	19	1,349	357	602	959
Larry Robinson, Mtl, L.A.	20	1,384	208	750	958
Rick Tocchet, Phi, Pit, L.A., Bos, Wsh, Phx	18	1,144	440	512	952
Chris Chelios, Mtl, Chi, Det, Atl	26	1,651	185	763	948
Jason Arnott, Edm, NJ, Dal, Nas, Was, StL	18	1,244	417	521	938
Steve Thomas, Tor, Chi, NYI, N.J., Ana, Det	20	1,235	421	512	933
Neal Broten, Min, Dal, N.J., L.A	17	1,099	289	634	923

GOALTENDING RECORDS

Goaltenders once played barefaced, wearing equipment that, despite its weight, could only blunt the pain of a puck. Even some of the all-time greats had trouble in dealing with the pressure of the position. "How would you like it," Jacques Plante once said, "if you were out on your job or in your office and you made a little mistake? Suddenly a bright red light flashed on behind you and then 18,000 people started screaming ..." Better equipment and better coaching have taken away much of the pressure goalies face today, but it still takes guts to stand in front of a puck traveling nearly 100 miles per hour!

▶ *Martin Brodeur is one of only two goalies in NHL history to reach double digits in shutouts four times. The other one is Terry Sawchuk.*

TERRY TERRIFIC

For years, Terry Sawchuk dominated goaltending statistics. His 971 games played, 447 wins, and 103 shutouts were all considered unattainable career records and his single-season total of 44 wins (accomplished with Detroit in 1950–51 and 1951–52) remained unbroken until 1973–74, when Bernie Parent won 47 games for Philadelphia. Sawchuk surpassed Harry Lumley's career win total of 330 during the 1961–62 season and stood as the all-time leader until Patrick Roy won his 448th game on October 17, 2000.

◀ *Ben Scrivens had every reason to be tired after stopping all 59 shots in a 3-0 win against San Jose.*

BIG BEN STANDS TALL

Ben Scrivens endeared himself to his new team by setting an NHL record for saves in a regular-season shutout with 59 in Edmonton's 3-0 triumph over San Jose on January 29, 2014. Acquired from Los Angeles just two weeks prior, Scrivens' performance was the most in a blanking since the NHL began tracking this statistic in 1956. The previous-best mark in a shutout was set by Phoenix's Mike Smith on April 3, 2012 and Scrivens' save total was the most since Quebec's Ron Tugnutt stopped an amazing 70 shots in a 3-3 tie versus Boston on March 21, 1991.

PERFECT DOZEN FOR EMERY

Ray Emery became the first NHL goaltender to begin a season with 12 consecutive victories. He turned aside all 16 shots he faced en route to a 2-0 shutout against Calgary on March 26, 2013. The blanking was the first in over three years for Emery, who suffered his first and only loss of the lockout-shortened campaign with a 2-1 setback to Anaheim three nights later. Emery finished the season with a 17-1-0 mark and a stingy 1.94 goals against average.

SINGLE-SEASON RECORD

By the 2006–07 season, Bernie Parent's record of 47 wins in 1973–74 had lasted 23 years ... the same time as it had taken until Parent surpassed Terry Sawchuk. On April 3, 2007, Martin Brodeur tied Parent's single-season record with a 2-1 shootout victory over the Ottawa Senators. Three days later, he secured his 48th win with a 3-2 win against Parent's old team in Philadelphia. Parent, though, had not enjoyed the benefit of overtime or shootout wins.

◀ *Ray Emery began the 2012–13 season with 12 straight victories and ended the impressive campaign with just one regulation loss.*

SHUTOUT RECORD #1

In 2008–09, Martin Brodeur sat out for 16 weeks with his first major injury (a torn biceps tendon), but returned to action on February 26, 2009 and posted his 99th career shutout. Two games later, he got #100 on March 1 and ended the season with 101. On December 21, 2009, Brodeur made 35 saves in a 4-0 win over Pittsburgh to break Terry Sawchuk's NHL record with his 104th career shutout.

SHUTOUT RECORD #2

Though Martin Brodeur had broken Terry Sawchuk's NHL shutout record, there was still one mark on the horizon. George Hainsworth had recorded 94 shutouts in his NHL career with Montreal and Toronto in the 1920s and 30s, but he had also posted 10 while playing for Saskatoon in the rival Western Hockey League for a major professional total of 104. Brodeur got his 105th shutout on December 30, 2009, once again blanking Pittsburgh in a 2-0 victory.

▶ *Patrick Roy only led the NHL in wins twice … but he did win the Stanley Cup four times.*

SHUTOUT STREAKS

During the 1927–28 season, when forward passing was not yet permitted in the offensive zone, Alec Connell of the Ottawa Senators set an all-time record when he posted shutouts in six consecutive games and did not allow a goal in 416 minutes and 29 seconds of playing time. During the 2003–04 season, Brian Boucher of the Phoenix Coyotes set a modern record with five consecutive shutouts and went 332:01 without allowing a goal.

CONSISTENT LUNDQVIST

New York Rangers goaltender Henrik Lundqvist overcame a seven-week absence due to a vascular injury to record his ninth 30-win season in 2014–15, joining Martin Brodeur (14), Patrick Roy (13) and Ed Belfour (nine) as the only netminders to reach that feat. Lundqvist recorded his 30th victory on the last game of the campaign, turning aside 22 shots in a 4-2 triumph over Washington on April 11.

MOST SHUTOUTS, ONE SEASON (ALL-TIME)

22	George Hainsworth, Montreal, 1928–29	44 GP
15	Alec Connell, Ottawa, 1925–26	36 GP
	Alec Connell, Ottawa, 1927–28	44 GP
	Hal Winkler, Boston, 1927–28	44 GP
	Tony Esposito, Chicago, 1969–70	63 GP
14	George Hainsworth, Montreal, 1926–27	44 GP

◀ *No one is ever likely to surpass the 22 shutouts George Hainsworth posted in 1928–29, nor better his 0.92 goals-against average from that year.*

MOST SHUTOUTS, ONE SEASON (SINCE CENTER ICE RED LINE IN 1943–44)

15	Tony Esposito, Chicago, 1969–70	76 GP
13	Harry Lumley, Toronto, 1953–54	70 GP
	Dominik Hasek, Buffalo, 1997–98	82 GP
12	Terry Sawchuk, Detroit, 1951–52	70 GP
	Terry Sawchuk, Detroit, 1953–54	70 GP
	Terry Sawchuk, Detroit, 1954–55	70 GP
	Glenn Hall, Detroit, 1955–56	70 GP
	Bernie Parent, Philadelphia, 1973–74	78 GP
	Bernie Parent, Philadelphia, 1974–75	80 GP
	Martin Brodeur, New Jersey, 2006–07	82 GP

ST. PATRICK

Patrick Roy became the first goalie in history with 500 wins in the regular season by posting a 2-0 victory over the Dallas Stars on December 27, 2001. Roy, who pushed his total to 551 wins, played in 1,029 games to break Terry Sawchuk's record. Roy also holds many career playoff records – including most games by a goaltender (247), most minutes (15,209) and most wins (151). His 23 postseason shutouts trail only Martin Brodeur's 24.

PART V

NHL AWARDS/ ALL-STAR/ENTRY DRAFT

For the vast majority of players, it all starts at the NHL Entry Draft. The best of them will go on to win major individual awards and earn selection to All-Star and All-Rookie teams.

▶ *Goaltender Carey Price was Montreal's shining light during the 2014–15 season, setting a franchise record in wins (44) while leading the league in goals-against average (1.96) and save percentage (.933) en route to claiming both the Hart and Vezina trophies.*

INDIVIDUAL AWARDS I — MOST VALUABLE PLAYER

The Hart Trophy was accepted by the directors of the NHL at a special Governors meeting on February 9, 1924. Dr. David Hart, father of Cecil Hart (a Montreal sports administrator and future coach of the Canadiens), donated the trophy, which would be given to the player voted to be the "most useful" to his team. It was the first individual award in NHL history. In 1960 a new Hart Memorial Trophy was donated to replace the original. The winner is selected by the members of the Professional Hockey Writers Association and voting takes place at the end of the regular season.

Elmer Lach, the NHL's MVP in 1944–45, poses with the original Hart Trophy.

THE FIRST WINNER

Frank Nighbor of the Ottawa Senators was the first winner of the Hart Trophy for the 1923–24 season. Nighbor, considered the NHL's best defensive forward, received a total of 38 points in the balloting to edge out Montreal Canadiens defenseman Sprague Cleghorn, who had 37 points. He was presented with the trophy by NHL president Frank Calder and Governor-General Lord Julian Byng on the ice in Ottawa before a playoff game against Montreal on March 11, 1924.

THE OTHER ROOKIE

Wayne Gretzky was the only other rookie in NHL history to win the Hart Trophy and he won it for the first of a record nine times in 1979–80. Technically, Gretzky was not considered a rookie because he had spent the previous season as a professional player in the World Hockey Association at age 17. He was ineligible for the Calder Trophy as Rookie of the Year, but won the Hart and the Lady Byng Trophy.

THE STRATFORD STREAK

According to stories, Howie Morenz had begged the Montreal Canadiens to tear up his first pro contract because he wasn't sure he could play in the NHL. But he needn't have worried! Morenz led the Canadiens to the Stanley Cup as a rookie in 1923–24 and was soon considered the game's top star. He won the Hart Trophy for the first time in 1928 and became the first player to win it back-to-back in 1931 and 1932.

CAMPBELL'S RARE FEAT

Brian Campbell became the third defenseman since 1954 to win the Lady Byng Trophy when he accomplished the feat after the 2011–12 season. The Florida Panthers blueliner collected just three minor penalties while logging a league-high 26 minutes, 53 seconds of ice time per game. Red Kelly was the last defenseman to claim the award – also he also won it for the fourth time while playing center in 1961

ROOKIE WINNERS

Nels Stewart was a rookie with the Montreal Maroons in 1925–26. He promptly led the NHL in scoring that season and led the Maroons to a Stanley Cup championship in just their second season. Stewart was also rewarded with the Hart Trophy as league MVP. A year later, the Canadiens' Herb Gardiner won the Hart after his first season in the NHL, although Gardiner was a veteran of five professional seasons in the Western Canada Hockey League.

A SHORE THING

There was no Norris Trophy to recognize the NHL's top defenseman in his day, but there can be little doubt that Eddie Shore was hockey's best blueliner. As tough as he was talented, Shore could score goals, too. He won the Hart Trophy for the first time in 1933, then won it back-to-back in 1935 and 1936. When he won it again in 1938, Shore became the first four-time MVP in NHL history.

WORST COMES IN FIRST

Tom Anderson had been a forward for seven NHL seasons before being converted to defense by the Brooklyn Americans in 1941–42. Despite his team's last-place finish in the NHL standings, Anderson established a career high in points and won the Hart Trophy. The only other person to be named league MVP while a member of a last-place team was Chicago Blackhawks goalie Al Rollins in 1954, who won despite his team's dismal 12-51-7 record.

THE MEN IN THE NETS

Chicago's Al Rollins (1954) is one of just seven goalies to have won the Hart Trophy, including Dominik Hasek, who is the only goalie to receive it twice. Hasek claimed the Hart in back-to-back seasons with the Buffalo Sabres in 1997 and 1998. The other goalies to have won the award are: Roy Worters, New York Americans, 1928; Chuck Rayner, New York Rangers, 1950; Jacques Plante, Montreal Canadiens, 1962; Jose Theodore, Montreal Canadiens, 2002; and Carey Price, Montreal Canadiens, 2015.

 Dominik Hasek is the only goalie to win the Hart Trophy twice. He also won the Vezina Trophy on six occasions.

CROSBY SHOW

Pittsburgh Penguins captain Sidney Crosby claimed his second Hart Trophy in impressive fashion, seizing 128 of 137 first-place votes in 2014. Crosby, who also won the award in 2007 when he was 19, scored 36 goals and set up a league-best 68 others to surpass the 100-point plateau for the fifth time in his career. "You look back, at 19 I probably took it for granted a little bit," he said. "When you win [the Hart Trophy] that young, you probably expect to win it maybe sooner and you might think it's a little easier than it actually is."

TWO CLOSE TO CALL

Jose Theodore's Hart Trophy win in 2002 was the result of the closest vote in history. In fact, Theodore and Calgary's Jarome Iginla finished tied in the balloting with 483 points apiece, but the Canadiens netminder was declared the winner because he had received 26 first-place votes to Iginla's 23. Theodore edged out Colorado's Patrick Roy for the Vezina Trophy in similar fashion, as both players finished tied in points, but Theodore received more first-place votes.

A CASE FOR THE DEFENSE

Bobby Orr became the first player in history to win the Hart Trophy three years in a row when he was named NHL MVP in 1970, 1971, and 1972. Orr was the first defenseman to win the Hart since the creation of the Norris Trophy in 1954. The only other defenseman to win since then is Chris Pronger, who won the Hart as a member of the St. Louis Blues in 2000.

Chris Pronger won both the Hart Trophy and the Norris Trophy with the St. Louis Blues for the 1999–2000 season.

THE PLAYERS' CHOICE

Created as the Lester Pearson Award in 1971 and renamed the Ted Lindsay Award in 2010, this trophy is presented to the "most outstanding player" as voted on by the members of the NHL Players Association. Fifteen players have won the Hart Trophy and Lindsay Award in the same season: Guy Lafleur, Wayne Gretzky, Mario Lemieux, Mark Messier, Brett Hull, Sergei Fedorov, Eric Lindros, Dominik Hasek, Jaromir Jagr, Joe Sakic, Martin St. Louis, Sidney Crosby, Alex Ovechkin, Evgeni Malkin and Carey Price.

Washington's Alex Ovechkin won the Hart Trophy in 2008, 2009 and 2013.

Pittsburgh's Sidney Crosby poses with the Hart Trophy, which he won along with the Art Ross Trophy and NHL Players Association MVP award in 2007.

MOST HART TROPHY WINS

9	Wayne Gretzky
6	Gordie Howe
4	Eddie Shore
3	Mario Lemieux
	Bobby Clarke
	Bobby Orr
	Howie Morenz
	Alex Ovechkin

INDIVIDUAL AWARDS II — GOALIE AWARDS

On May 14, 1927, the NHL formally accepted the donation of the Vezina Trophy at a league meeting. The owners of the Montreal Canadiens donated the trophy in memory of goaltender Georges Vezina, who died of tuberculosis on May 27, 1926. Before the 1981–82 season, the Vezina Trophy went to the goalie (or goalies) on the team allowing the fewest goals during the regular season. Since then, the trophy has gone to the goaltender adjudged to be the best at his position, as voted by the NHL general managers. The Jennings Trophy was presented to the NHL on December 8, 1981 to honor the goalies on the team that allows the fewest goals.

GEORGE FOR GEORGES

The Montreal Canadiens had struggled in 1925–26 while Georges Vezina was too sick to play. They signed George Hainsworth for the 1926–27 season on the recommendation of former Canadiens star Newsy Lalonde, who had played with the Western Hockey League star for three seasons in Saskatoon. Hainsworth played every minute of every game for the Canadiens over the next three seasons and won the Vezina Trophy in each of the first three years it was presented.

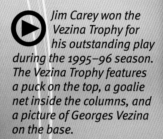

Jim Carey won the Vezina Trophy for his outstanding play during the 1995–96 season. The Vezina Trophy features a puck on the top, a goalie net inside the columns, and a picture of Georges Vezina on the base.

TINY THOMPSON COMES UP BIG

In an era when most goalies were small, Cecil "Tiny" Thompson stood 5'10" (177m). His nickname likely came about because of the minuscule size of his goals-against average. Thompson posted a 1.15 average in his first NHL season with the Boston Bruins in 1928–29. When forward passing rules were modernized in 1929–30, Thompson's average rose to 2.19, which was easily the best in the League and earned him the Vezina Trophy. He would go on to win the award on four occasions.

DURNAN DELIVERS

Bill Durnan entered the NHL as a 27-year-old rookie with the Montreal Canadiens in 1943–44. He played only seven years in the NHL, but won the Vezina Trophy six times. Durnan was ambidextrous: he was able to use his stick or catch the puck equally well with either hand and had special gloves designed to allow him to do this. Despite his stardom, the pressure of the game's most difficult position forced his retirement in 1950.

Montreal's Bill Durnan won the Vezina Trophy six times in seven seasons between 1943–44 and 1949–50.

TWO GOALIES, ONE WINNER

Though NHL teams were only required to dress one goaltender until the 1965–66 season, the 1950–51 Maple Leafs split their netminding duties between Turk Broda and Al Rollins. Combined, the two Toronto goalies allowed one less goal (139–138) than Terry Sawchuk, who played all 70 games for Detroit. Rule changes in the 1960s would have allowed both Toronto goalies to share the award, but Rollins received the Vezina Trophy alone because he played more games than Broda.

TWO GOALIES, TWO WINNERS

In 1964–65, another pair of Toronto goalies edged out Detroit for the NHL's best defensive record. Terry Sawchuk was now a Maple Leaf and played 36 games in goal to Johnny Bower's 34. At first, the NHL announced only Sawchuk's name would be engraved on the Vezina Trophy, but at a league meeting in June, the NHL decided that there could be joint winners so long as each goalie had played at least 25 games.

TWO TEAMS, TWO WINNERS

Only once in NHL history have two teams tied for the fewest goals against. In 1973–74, both Philadelphia and Chicago allowed 164 goals during the 78-game season. As a result, the Vezina Trophy was shared by the Flyers' Bernie Parent and the Blackhawks' Tony Esposito, who were their teams' only goalies to have played at least 25 games. Each goalie got his name engraved on the trophy and both received the $1,500 cash prize.

 Tony Esposito won the Vezina Trophy three times: once by himself, once with Chicago teammate Gary Smith, and once in a tie with Philadelphia's Bernie Parent.

WILLIAM JENNINGS

Bill Jennings began his association with hockey in 1959 as the legal counsel for the Graham-Paige Corporation when it acquired controlling interest in Madison Square Garden Corporation, owner of the New York Rangers. Jennings took an active role in the Rangers, becoming club president in 1962, and was an ardent advocate of NHL expansion. The William M. Jennings Trophy, awarded annually to the goaltender(s) of the team allowing the fewest goals, is named in his honor.

SEVENTH HEAVEN

During their run of five straight Stanley Cup championships from 1956 to 1960, the Montreal Canadiens led the NHL in goals for and goals against in each season, giving Jacques Plante five straight Vezina Trophy wins. Plante won the Vezina a sixth time in 1961–62, when his brilliant play was also rewarded with the Hart Trophy, and combined with Glenn Hall to win the Vezina for a record seventh time with the St. Louis Blues in 1968–69.

CLEAN SWEEP FOR PRICE

Montreal goaltender Carey Price certainly cleaned up at the 2015 NHL Awards, winning the Hart and Vezina trophies and Ted Lindsay Award before picking up a share of the William Jennings Trophy (with Chicago's Corey Crawford). The first player in NHL history to sweep those four awards, Price became the first goaltender to win the Hart since Jose Theodore of the Canadiens in 2001–02.

THE DOMINATOR

Since 1981–82 when NHL general managers began voting for the winner of the Vezina Trophy, no one has won it more often than Dominik Hasek. A star in Europe who was used sparingly in his first few NHL seasons, "The Dominator" established himself as a star with the Buffalo Sabres in 1994–95. He won the Vezina Trophy for the first time that year and was to do so again five more times over the next seven seasons.

MOST VEZINA TROPHY WINS

7	Jacques Plante
6	Dominik Hasek
	Bill Durnan
5	Ken Dryden
4	Martin Brodeur
	Michel Larocque
	Terry Sawchuk
	Tiny Thompson

MOST JENNINGS TROPHY WINS

5	Martin Brodeur
	Patrick Roy
4	Ed Belfour
3	Dominik Hasek
	Brian Hayward
2	Corey Crawford
	Roman Turek

New Jersey's Martin Brodeur, the NHL's all-time leader in wins and shutouts, also ranks among the top winners of both the Vezina and Jennings trophies.

INDIVIDUAL AWARDS III — OTHER TROPHIES

Since the donation of the Hart Trophy in 1924, the NHL has assembled an impressive array of silverware that is handed out annually to the top performers in the game. Some are awarded based on statistics compiled during the regular season, but most are voted on by members of the Professional Hockey Writers Association or other groups involved in the game. Most awards are presented based on performance in the regular season but are handed out a few days after the Stanley Cup Final in a lavish ceremony that has become a popular television event.

CALDER TROPHY

In 1933, the Canadian Press began conducting a poll to name the NHL's top rookie. From 1937 until his death in 1943, NHL President Frank Calder bought a new trophy each year for the top rookie. After his death, the NHL created the Calder Memorial Trophy. To be eligible, a player cannot have played more than 25 games in any single preceding season nor in six or more games in each of any two preceding seasons.

ART ROSS TROPHY

The Art Ross Trophy was presented to the NHL in 1947 to honor the League's top scorer. If two or more players are tied for the scoring lead (as has happened three times), the trophy goes to the player with the most goals, or who played in fewer games. Elmer Lach of the Montreal Canadiens was the first recipient in 1947–48. Wayne Gretzky has won the Art Ross Trophy a record 10 times.

◄ *Elmer Lach was the NHL's scoring leader twice: first in 1944–45 before the creation of the Art Ross Trophy and again in 1947-48.*

NORRIS TROPHY

The James Norris Memorial Trophy was presented to the NHL in 1953 by the four children of the late James Norris in memory of the former owner-president of the Detroit Red Wings. It is presented annually to the defense player who demonstrates throughout the season the greatest all-around ability in the position. Detroit's Red Kelly was the first recipient in 1953–54. Boston Bruins' superstar Bobby Orr won the Norris Trophy a record eight times.

► *Frank Boucher won the Lady Byng Trophy seven times in eight seasons from 1927–28 through 1934–35. He was given the original trophy to keep.*

► *Bobby Orr won the Norris Trophy as the NHL's best defenseman for eight straight seasons from 1967–68 through 1974–75.*

LADY BYNG TROPHY

In 1925, the wife of Canada's Governor-General at the time, Lady Evelyn Byng, presented a trophy for sportsmanship. The first winner for the 1924–25 season was Frank Nighbor of the Ottawa Senators. Lady Byng donated a new trophy in 1936, when Frank Boucher of the New York Rangers was allowed to keep the original after winning it seven times in eight seasons. After her death in 1949, the NHL presented a new Lady Byng Memorial Trophy.

SELKE TROPHY

The Selke Trophy is awarded to the NHL's best defensive forward. It was presented in 1977 by the Board of Governors of the NHL to honor Frank J. Selke, one of the great architects of championship teams in Toronto and Montreal. Canadiens great Bob Gainey won the award in each of the first four seasons it was presented and it has since been won three times by Montreal's Guy Carbonneau, Jere Lehtinen of Dallas and Detroit's Pavel Datsyuk. Boston's Patrice Bergeron won the award in 2012, 2014 and 2015.

MASTERTON TROPHY

The Bill Masterton Memorial Trophy was presented by the Professional Hockey Writers Association in 1968 to commemorate the late Bill Masterton, a player with the Minnesota North Stars who died January 15, 1968 following an injury sustained in an NHL game. It is presented annually to the NHL player who best exemplifies the qualities of perseverance, sportsmanship, and dedication to hockey. The winner is determined from among nominees representing each NHL team.

▲ Bob Gainey won the Selke Trophy every season from 1977–78 through 1980–81.

▶ Pat Burns is the only three-time recipient of the Jack Adams Award, winning it with Montreal in 1989, Toronto in 1993, and Boston in 1998.

JACK ADAMS AWARD

The Jack Adams Award is presented annually to the NHL coach adjudged to have contributed the most to his team's success. At the end of the regular season, the winner is selected by a poll of members of the NHL Broadcasters' Association. The award was presented in 1974 by the NHL Broadcasters' Association to commemorate the late Jack Adams, longtime coach and general manager of the Detroit Red Wings. The late Pat Burns is the only three-time winner, while Bob Hartley won the first for the Calgary Flames' franchise in 2015.

KING CLANCY TROPHY

The King Clancy Memorial Trophy is presented annually to the player who best exemplifies leadership qualities, on and off the ice, and has made a noteworthy humanitarian contribution in his community. It was presented to the NHL by the Board of Governors in 1988 to honor the late King Clancy. One of the most popular figures in professional hockey, Francis Michael "King" Clancy's career spanned over 60 years, including roles as NHL player, coach, and manager.

MAURICE RICHARD TROPHY

The Maurice "Rocket" Richard Trophy is awarded to the player finishing the regular season as the NHL's goal-scoring leader. Unlike the Art Ross Trophy, there is no provision for breaking ties. In 1999, the Trophy was presented to the NHL by the Montreal Canadiens to honor Maurice Richard, who led the League in goals five times and was the first player in history to score 50 goals in one season and 500 in his career.

GENERAL MANAGER OF THE YEAR

The NHL General Manager of the Year Award was created in 2009–10 to recognize the work of the League's general managers. Voting for this award is conducted among the 30 club General Managers and a panel of NHL executives, print, and broadcast media at the conclusion of the regular season. The inaugural award was presented to Don Maloney of the Phoenix Coyotes during the 2010 Stanley Cup Final.

MARK MESSIER LEADERSHIP AWARD

The Mark Messier NHL Leadership Award was first presented in 2007. It honors an individual who leads by positive example through on-ice performance, motivation of team members, and a dedication to community activities and charitable causes. Mark Messier, who is considered to be one of the greatest sports leaders of all time, solicits suggestions from club and League personnel and NHL fans, but the selection of the three finalists and the ultimate winner is Messier's alone.

FOUNDATION PLAYER AWARD

The NHL Foundation Award is presented to the player who best applies commitment, perseverance and teamwork to enrich the lives of the people in his community. St. Louis Blues forward Kelly Chase won the inaugural award in 1998 and no player has won it on more than one occasion. Hall of Famers Ron Francis and Joe Sakic received the honor in 2002 and 2007, respectively, and San Jose's Brent Burns won the award in 2015.

ALL-STAR TEAMS
(INCLUDING ALL-ROOKIE TEAM)

At the conclusion of every season since 1930–31, the NHL has listed a set of First-Team and Second-Team All-Stars. Though these lists have sometimes been used to help make up the teams for the annual NHL All-Star Game, being named to the First or Second All-Star Team is a separate honor. Voting for the NHL All-Star Team is conducted among the representatives of the Professional Hockey Writers Association at the end of the season. Raymond Bourque had a record 13 selections to the First-All-Star Team, though Gordie Howe's total of 21 selections (12 to the First-Team, nine to the Second) is the highest overall total.

THE FIRST TIME

Nearing the final month of the 1930–31 season, the Canadian Press asked 37 sports editors of newspapers in NHL cities to vote on a selection of First- and Second-Team All-Stars. The results were:

First Team		Second Team
Charlie Gardiner, Chi	G	Tiny Thompson, Bos
Eddie Shore, Bos	D	Sylvio Mantha, Mtl
King Clancy, Tor	D	Ching Johnson, NYR
Howie Morenz, Mtl	C	Frank Boucher, NYR
Bill Cook, NYR	RW	Dit Clapper, Bos
Aurel Joliat, Mtl	LW	Bun Cook, NYR

FAST START

Montreal Canadiens goalie Bill Durnan was named a First-Team All-Star in each of his first four seasons in the NHL, beginning with his rookie year of 1943–44. This feat remained unmatched until the 2008–09 season, when Alex Ovechkin of the Washington Capitals earned his fourth straight selection as a First-Team All-Star at left wing since his rookie season in 2005–06. Ovechkin made it five in a row to establish a new record in 2009–10.

Alex Ovechkin was a First-Team All-Star in each of his first five NHL seasons.

ALL-STAR COACHES

From 1930–31 to 1945–46, the selection of First- and Second-Team All-Stars included a coach. Lester Patrick of the New York Rangers took First-Team honors in each of the first six seasons and again in 1937–38. Dick Irvin earned First-Team honors three years in a row with Montreal, from 1943–44 to 1945–46, while Jack Adams earned First-Team honors with Detroit in 1936–37 and 1942–43. Art Ross, Paul Thompson, Cooney Weiland, and Frank Boucher were each selected once.

ALL-STAR TIE

In 1937–38, Gord Drillon of the Toronto Maple Leafs and Cecil Dillon of the New York Rangers are both listed at right wing for the First All-Star Team. (Many lists show them tied for the Second Team as well.) In actual fact, Dillon received 16 first-place votes (worth three points apiece) to Drillon's 15 among the 31 ballots cast, but Drillon received 14 second-place votes to Dillon's 11 and so they both ended up with 59 points.

GOALTENDER LEADERS IN ALL-STAR SELECTIONS THROUGH 2015

Player	Total	First Team	Second Team	Seasons
Glenn Hall	11	7	4	18
Frank Brimsek	8	2	6	10
Martin Brodeur	7	3	4	20
Jacques Plante	7	3	4	18
Terry Sawchuk	7	3	4	21
Bill Durnan	6	6	0	7
Dominik Hasek	6	6	0	15
Ken Dryden	6	5	1	8
Patrick Roy	6	4	2	18

DEFENSE LEADERS IN ALL-STAR SELECTIONS THROUGH 2015

Player	Total	First Team	Second Team	Seasons
Raymond Bourque	19	13	6	22
Nicklas Lidstrom	12	10	2	19
Doug Harvey	11	10	1	20
Earl Seibert	10	4	6	15
Bobby Orr	9	8	1	12
Eddie Shore	8	7	1	14
Red Kelly	8	6	2	20
Pierre Pilote	8	5	3	14
Paul Coffey	8	4	4	21

Raymond Bourque's 13 selections to the First All-Star Team not only lead all defensemen, but all players in NHL history.

Bobby Hull was a First-Team All-Star for seven straight seasons from 1963–64 to 1969–70, second only to Bobby Orr's string of eight straight through 1974–75.

CENTER LEADERS IN ALL-STAR SELECTIONS THROUGH 2015

Player	Total	First Team	Second Team	Seasons
Wayne Gretzky	15	8	7	20
Jean Beliveau	10	6	4	20
Mario Lemieux	9	5	4	18
Phil Esposito	8	6	2	18
Stan Mikita	8	6	2	22

LEFT WING LEADERS IN ALL-STAR SELECTIONS THROUGH 2015

Player	Total	First Team	Second Team	Seasons
Bobby Hull	12	10	2	16
Alex Ovechin	10	7	3	10
Ted Lindsay	9	8	1	17
Frank Mahovlich	9	3	6	18

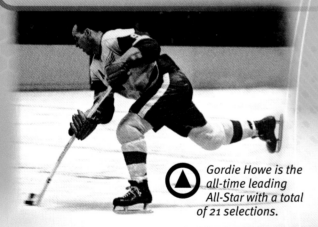

Gordie Howe is the all-time leading All-Star with a total of 21 selections.

ALL-ROOKIE TEAM

The NHL named an All-Rookie Team for the first time for the 1982–83 season. Voting is conducted by the Professional Hockey Writers Association after the regular season. Pavel Bure (1992) is the only Calder Trophy winner not to be named to the All-Rookie Team because his vote was split between left and right wing. Since then, the team has honored a goalie, two defensemen, and three forwards regardless of which position the forwards play.

DOUBLE HONORS

Goalies Tom Barrasso (Buffalo Sabres, 1983–84), Ron Hextall (Philadelphia Flyers, 1986–87), and Ed Belfour (Chicago Blackhawks, 1990–91) were all named to the All-Rookie Team and selected as NHL First-Team All-Stars in the same season. Forwards Teemu Selanne (Winnipeg Jets, 1992–93) and Alex Ovechkin (Washington Capitals, 2005–06) also achieved this rare double honor. Goalie Jamie Storr of the Los Angeles Kings is the only player to be chosen to the All-Rookie Team twice: in 1997–98 and 1998–99.

RIGHT WING LEADERS IN ALL STAR SELECTIONS THROUGH 2015

Player	Total	First Team	Second Team	Seasons
Gordie Howe	21	12	9	26
Maurice Richard	14	8	6	18
Jaromir Jagr	8	7	1	20
Mike Bossy	8	5	3	10
Guy Lafleur	6	6	0	17

With more All-Star selections than any other netminder, Glenn Hall is truly worthy of the nickname "Mr. Goalie."

ALL-STAR GAMES TO 1968

Hockey All-Star and/or benefit games date back to at least 1900 when games were held to aid Canadian soldiers fighting in the Boer War. The first All-Star game played at the sport's highest level was a 1908 benefit to aid the family of the late Hod Stuart, a future Hockey Hall of Famer. Three NHL benefit games were held in the 1930s prior to the first official All-Star Game in 1947. Until 1965, the NHL All-Star Game was held in the preseason and until 1968, it usually pitted the defending Stanley Cup champions against a team of All-Stars. There was no fan voting for All-Stars in this era.

PORTAGE LAKE HOCKEY TEAM.

HOD STUART BENEFIT

Hod Stuart was a star player who died in a diving accident in the summer of 1907, a few months after helping the Montreal Wanderers win the Stanley Cup. On January 2, 1908, a crowd of about 3,800 fans helped to raise just over $2,000 for Stuart's family at a game between the Wanderers and a group of All-Stars at the Montreal Arena. The game featured seven future Hall of Famers including Art Ross and Frank Patrick.

◭ Hod Stuart sits second from the right in the middle row in this photo of the 1903–04 Portage Lake hockey team of Houghton, Michigan.

THE ACE BAILEY GAME

The NHL held its first All-Star Game at Maple Leaf Gardens in Toronto on February 14, 1934. It was a benefit for Ace Bailey, a Maple Leafs star whose career (and nearly his life) had ended when he suffered a fractured skull after being hit from behind by Boston's Eddie Shore. Nevertheless, Shore and Bailey shook hands prior to the All-Star Game in which the Maple Leafs defeated a team of NHL stars 7-3.

MORENZ & SEIBERT

A second NHL All-Star Game was held at the Montreal Forum on November 2, 1938 to benefit the family of Canadiens superstar Howie Morenz, who had died in the hospital on March 8, 1937 while recovering from a badly broken leg. A third benefit was held on October 29, 1939 to aid the family of Babe Seibert, a longtime NHL star who had drowned that summer, shortly after being named coach of the Canadiens.

THE FIRST ANNUAL GAME

At the NHL meetings on September 4, 1946, a letter was read from John Carmichael of the *Chicago Daily News* in which he asked for permission to stage a charity game between the NHL champions and an All-Star team, with 25 percent of the receipts going to the Players' Emergency Fund. No game was held that year, but on October 13, 1947, the first annual NHL All-Star Game was held in Toronto for the benefit of the players' pension fund.

◄ Ace Bailey shakes the hand of Boston's Eddie Shore prior to the NHL's first All-Star benefit game. Shore and several other Bruins players donned helmets after Bailey's injury.

DETROIT STARS BEAT ALL-STARS

In each of the first three games, the NHL All-Stars defeated the defending Stanley Cup champions, who had been the Toronto Maple Leafs for three straight years. Then, in 1950, the newly crowned champion Detroit Red Wings ended the streak with a convincing 7-1 victory. Detroit's Ted Lindsay scored just 19 seconds into the game and ended up with a hat trick, while rookie goalie Terry Sawchuk came within 1:33 of posting a shutout.

UNPOPULAR NEW FORMAT

The format of the game changed in 1951 and 1952, with a team made up of the NHL's First-Team All-Stars, augmented by players from the four American-based teams facing the NHL's Second-All Stars filled out with additional Leafs and Canadiens. The games were close but boring, with both ending in ties, and the format proved unpopular. In 1953, the Stanley Cup champions would once again oppose the All-Stars, something that would remain the format through 1968.

HE AIN'T HEAVY

Max and Doug Bentley were the first brothers to play as teammates in the All-Star Game, when the two Chicago Blackhawks stars took part in the first game of 1947. A year later, after Max had been traded to Toronto, they appeared as opponents, with Max on the side of the Stanley Cup champion Maple Leafs while Doug was playing for the All-Stars. Brothers Charlie and Lionel Conacher had faced each other in 1934 in the Ace Bailey Game.

▶ *Brothers Max and Doug Bentley played in the NHL All-Star Game as teammates in 1947 and as opponents in 1948, 1949, and 1951.*

HOWE MANY?

After failing to earn a spot at the inaugural game in 1947, Gordie Howe made his first All-Star Game appearance in 1948. From that year until his first retirement in 1971, he played in 22 of 23 All-Star games, missing out only in 1956 because of an ankle injury. When he returned to the NHL for the 1979–80 season after six years in the World Hockey Association, Howe took part in his 23rd and final All-Star Game.

ALL-STAR RECORDS

Between 1947 and 1968, the NHL All-Stars met the defending Stanley Cup champions a total of 19 times. The All-Stars held a 10-7 advantage with two ties. During this time period, the lowest-scoring All-Star games in history were played, with both the 1952 and 1956 games ending tied at 1-1. In 1967, the Montreal Canadiens won 3-0 to mark the only shutout in All-Star Game history. Goalies Charlie Hodge and Gary Bauman shared the honors.

MOVING TO MID-SEASON

The All-Star Game in 1967 was played on January 18, marking the first time in NHL history that it was played mid-season instead of the middle of October. (For that reason, no All-Star Game was held in the calendar year of 1966.) It had long been thought that the preseason All-Star Games did not generate enough publicity in American cities because of conflicts with football and the World Series.

LAST OF ITS KIND

The NHL All-Star Game of 1968 marked the last time that the defending Stanley Cup champions took part. Although the Toronto Maple Leafs were without injured goalie Johnny Bower, youngsters Bruce Gamble and Al Smith outperformed All-Stars Ed Giacomin, Terry Sawchuk, and Glenn Hall to give Toronto a 4-3 victory. Smith preserved the win with a late stop on Bobby Hull. Bobby Orr made his All-Star debut and played brilliantly in a losing effort.

ALL-STAR GAMES SINCE 1969

In 1969, the format of the All-Star Game changed, with the top stars from the East Division facing those from the West Division. When the NHL was split into four divisions in 1974–75, the 1975 game pitted All-Stars from the two divisions within the Wales Conference against All-Stars from the Campbell Conference and would continue to do so until 1994, when the NHL reintroduced geographic names. In recognition of the NHL's participation in the Olympics, the 1998 All-Star Game featured North American and World Teams, as would be the case until the East-West format resumed in 2003. Fan voting has determined the starting lineups in the All-Star Game since 1986.

EAST VS. WEST

The first East-West All-Star Game in 1969 ended in a 3-3 tie, with Claude Larose of the Minnesota North Stars beating Ed Giacomin for the tying goal with just 2:53 remaining. Detroit's Frank Mahovlich scored twice to lead the East. Toe Blake came out of retirement to coach the East Division team, while Scotty Bowman coached the West Division in his first of a record 13 All-Star Game appearances behind the bench.

ALL-STAR MVPS

The All-Star Game of 1962 marked the first time that a Most Valuable Player was selected. Eddie Shack was the surprise winner, picking up a goal and an assist in the Toronto Maple Leafs' 4-1 win over the All-Stars. Frank Mahovlich was the first two-time winner with selections in 1963 and 1969. Both Wayne Gretzky (1983, 1989, and 1999) and Mario Lemieux (1985, 1988, and 1990) have been named All-Star MVP a record three times.

INTERNATIONAL EXHIBITIONS

In 1979, the NHL replaced the All-Star Game with a three-game Challenge Cup series between NHL stars and the Soviet Union at Madison Square Garden. After splitting two close games, the Soviets scored a 6-0 shocker in game three to win the series. A two-game exhibition series with the Soviets in Quebec City called Rendez-Vous '87 replaced the 1987 All-Star Game. The NHL won the first game 4-3, with the Soviets taking the second 5-3.

FASTEST GOALS

Rick Nash of the Columbus Blue Jackets set a record at the 2008 All-Star Game when he scored for the Western Conference 12 seconds after the opening faceoff, breaking Ted Lindsay's record of 19 seconds set in 1950. Owen Nolan holds the record for the two fastest goals by one player when he scored for the Western Conference just eight seconds apart late in the second period of the 1997 All-Star Game on his home ice in San Jose.

TAVARES JOINS ELITE COMPANY

John Tavares matched an NHL All-Star Game record by scoring four goals to lead Team Toews to a 17-12 victory over Team Foligno on Jan. 25, 2015. The New York Islanders captain joined Wayne Gretzky (1983), Mario Lemieux (1990), Mike Gartner (1991), Vincent Damphousse (1993) and Dany Heatley (2003) for the honor. "Yeah, I'll take it," Tavares said of his accomplishment. "(Gretzky and Lemieux) are two of the best to ever play, probably (Nos.) 1 and 2 - so yes, it's pretty cool."

 Detroit's Steve Yzerman was 18 in his first All-Star Game appearance in 1984. He was 34 when he played his eighth and final All-Star Game in 2000.

New York Islanders captain John Tavares found his scoring touch in the 2015 All-Star Game.

RECORD SCORES

Led by New York Islanders captain John Tavares' four goals, Team Toews skated to a 17-12 triumph over Team Foligno in the 2015 NHL All-Star Game. Team Toews' total set an All-Star Game record for most goals by one team, besting the 16 amassed by the Wales Conference in 1993. In addition, the 29-goal combination eclipsed the previous mark of 26, which was set in 2001 when the North America team skated to a 14-12 triumph over the World.

Rivals Sidney Crosby (left) and Alex Ovechkin appeared as teammates on the Eastern Conference team at the 2007 All-Star Game.

SUPERSKILLS COMPETITION

In 1990, the NHL introduced a skills competition to the All-Star Game festivities. Events have included hardest shot, shooting accuracy, fastest skater, and various styles of goaltending competition. Boston's Raymond Bourque was the first shooter to hit four targets in four shots in 1992, and he did so again in 1993. Bruins defenseman Zdeno Chara won his fifth consecutive hardest shot competition after unleashing a record 108.8 mph slap shot in 2012. As a result, Nashville's Shea Weber settled for second place for third straight year.

ONLY ALL-STAR SHOOTOUT

Four goals from Atlanta's Dany Heatley, plus another in the shootout, were not enough for the Eastern Conference in the 2003 All-Star Game. Heatley also set up the goal to tie the game at 5-5 midway through the third period, but Dallas goalie Marty Turco was the ultimate hero as he stopped three of four shots in the shootout while Markus Naslund, Bill Guerin, and Paul Kariya all scored on Patrick Lalime to give the West a 6-5 victory.

Dany Heatley's four goals in 2003 tied an All-Star record shared by Wayne Gretzky, Mario Lemieux, Vince Damphousse, Mike Gartner - and later John Tavares.

ALL-STAR SCORING LEADERS

Wayne Gretzky and Mario Lemieux share the record for most goals in the All-Star Game with 13. Joe Sakic is the all-time assist leader with 16 in 12 games. Points' leaders are:

25	Wayne Gretzky	(13G–12A in 18 GP)
23	Mario Lemieux	(13G–10A in 10 GP)
22	Joe Sakic	(6G–16A in 22 GP)
20	Mark Messier	(6G–14A in 15 GP)
19	Gordie Howe	(10G–9A in 23 GP)

THE ALL-STAR GAME RENEWED

The 2007 All-Star Game in Dallas was the NHL's 55th, but it was the first to be played since 2004. There was no game in 2005 because of a lockout and none in 2006 due to the break in the schedule required by the Winter Olympics in Turin, Italy. Sidney Crosby and Alex Ovechkin both made their All-Star debuts in the lineup of the Eastern Conference, but veteran Joe Sakic led the West to a 12-9 victory.

OLDEST & YOUNGEST ALL-STARS

A record crowd of 21,002 in Detroit saw Gordie Howe make his final All-Star appearance in 1980 at age 51. Fleming MacKell was just 18 years and five months old when he appeared in the 1947 Game with the Stanley Cup champion Toronto Maple Leafs. The youngest-ever player to suit up for an All-Star team is Steve Yzerman, who was 18 years and eight months old when he played for the Campbell Conference in 1984.

Mario Lemieux (left) and Wayne Gretzky were teammates for the first time at Rendez Vous '87 in February of 1987. They would team up more famously at the Canada Cup that September.

ENTRY DRAFT HISTORY

For decades, NHL teams developed players for their farm systems through a sponsorship system that allowed them to sponsor junior hockey teams and stock their rosters with top teenaged prospects. During the "Original Six" Era, each NHL club was allowed to sponsor two junior clubs. Each minor pro club affiliated with an NHL team could also sponsor two additional junior clubs. On each of these teams, the sponsoring pro club controlled the professional rights for a maximum of 18 players on the roster. The cost involved in sponsoring teams gave the wealthier NHL clubs an edge in obtaining top junior talent. In an effort to phase out the sponsorship system, the NHL introduced the Draft (originally called the Amateur Draft, but known as the Entry Draft since 1979) in 1963 as a new means of player recruitment.

AGE REQUIREMENTS

For the first NHL Draft in 1963, players were eligible if they turned 17 between August 1, 1963 and July 31, 1964. The age was increased to 18 in 1965 and then to 20 in 1967. When the rival World Hockey Association began signing underage talent, the NHL reduced the draft age to 18 in 1974 and has kept it there since 1980. Current rules state that a player must be 18 by September 15 of his draft year.

THE FIRST DRAFT

The first NHL Amateur Draft was held on June 5, 1963 at the Queen Elizabeth Hotel in Montreal. There were four rounds conducted according to a predetermined order and the six teams did not have to pick a player in every round. In all, only 21 players were selected in 1963. The first choice was Garry Monahan, whom the Montreal Canadiens selected from St. Michael's College in Toronto, where he played Junior B hockey.

THE CULTURAL OPTION

In order to protect the French-Canadian character of the Montreal Canadiens, it was agreed in 1963 that the team could select up to two players of French-Canadian heritage before other teams made their choices. By 1968, the Canadiens had not yet used this "cultural option." Through trades with Detroit and the Oakland Seals, Montreal already had the first two picks that year, but they used their extra pick beforehand to select goalie Michel Plasse first overall.

STATE YOUR CASE

Hockey's widespread growth was clearly on display during the 2013 NHL draft as players were selected from 22 different states, ranging from as far north as Alaska to the balmy confines of Florida. In total, 57 Americans were drafted – with traditional hot spot Minnesota being the birthplace of 11 of them, followed by Massachusetts (six), Michigan (five) and New York (five). As for some non-traditional locales, the states of Arizona, Idaho, Nebraska, South Carolina and Texas were all represented.

Michel Plasse played only 32 games for Montreal over two seasons. His 11-year NHL career saw him suit up with six different clubs.

DETERMINING DRAFT ORDER

The Amateur Draft of 1968 was the first to use division standings to determine the order of selection. Since 1969, the overall standings of the entire league have been used to determine Draft Order. Beginning in 1995, a weighted lottery among non-playoff teams has been used to finalize first-round selections. Teams can only improve by four places, so only the worst five teams in the standings have a chance to get the first overall pick.

LAFLEUR & DIONNE

Guy Lafleur and Marcel Dionne were the overwhelming consensus as the top two players available in the 1971 Amateur Draft. The Montreal Canadiens were no longer allowed to grab the top French-Canadian prospects, but a trade with the Oakland Seals made at the draft in 1970 wound up giving Montreal the first pick in 1971. The Canadiens selected Lafleur, with Dionne going second overall to the Detroit Red Wings and later starring with the Los Angeles Kings.

 Garry Monahan played only 14 games over two seasons for Montreal before moving on to Detroit, Los Angeles, Toronto and, finally, the Vancouver Canucks during the 1970s.

EUROPEAN FIRSTS

In 1989, the Quebec Nordiques made Mats Sundin from Nacka HK in Sweden the first European player to be chosen first overall in the NHL Entry Draft. Others since then are: Roman Hamrlik (Czech Republic), Tampa Bay, 1992; Patrick Stefan (Czech Republic), Atlanta, 1999; Ilya Kovalchuk (Russia), Atlanta, 2001; Alex Ovechkin (Russia), Washington, 2004 and Nail Yakupov (Russia), Edmonton, 2012. The first European player ever selected in the draft was Finland's Tommi Salmelainen, picked 66th by St. Louis in 1969.

 Mats Sundin (right) was the first European player to be selected first overall when the Quebec Nordiques chose him with the top pick in 1989.

L'AFFAIR LINDROS

The Quebec Nordiques are the only team in history to have the top pick in the NHL Draft three years in row. After selecting Mats Sundin in 1989, they chose Owen Nolan first overall in 1990 and Eric Lindros with the first choice in 1991. Lindros refused to report to Quebec, and just before the 1992 Entry Draft he was traded to the Philadelphia Flyers for six players (including Peter Forsberg), two draft picks, and $15 million.

THE ENTRY DRAFT

After the WHA disbanded in 1979 and four of its teams were absorbed into the NHL, many former WHA players were made available in the draft. Since these players had professional experience, it would be inaccurate to label them amateurs and so the name of the NHL Amateur Draft was officially changed to the NHL Entry Draft. Rob Ramage was selected first overall, though #4 pick Mike Gartner and #8 Raymond Bourque proved the biggest talents.

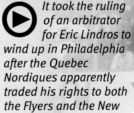 *After playing in the WHA in 1978–79, Rob Ramage went first overall to the Colorado Rockies in 1979 in the newly named NHL Entry Draft.*

THE CROSBY LOTTERY

With superstar prospect Sidney Crosby draft eligible and because a lockout had wiped out the 2004–05 season, there was a lot of talk about the fairest way to determine the order of selection for the 2005 Entry Draft. In the end, the NHL came up with a weighted lottery based on the results of the past three seasons that still gave each of the 30 teams a mathematical chance of winning the top pick. The Pittsburgh Penguins won and chose Crosby.

FIRST OVERALL DRAFT PICKS IN THE HOCKEY HALL OF FAME THROUGH 2014

1970	Gilbert Perreault	Buffalo Sabres
1971	Guy Lafleur	Montreal Canadiens
1973	Denis Potvin	New York Islanders
1981	Dale Hawerchuk	Winnipeg Jets
1984	Mario Lemieux	Pittsburgh Penguins
1988	Mike Modano	Minnesota North Stars
1989	Mats Sundin	Quebec Nordiques

  *It took the ruling of an arbitrator for Eric Lindros to wind up in Philadelphia after the Quebec Nordiques apparently traded his rights to both the Flyers and the New York Rangers.*

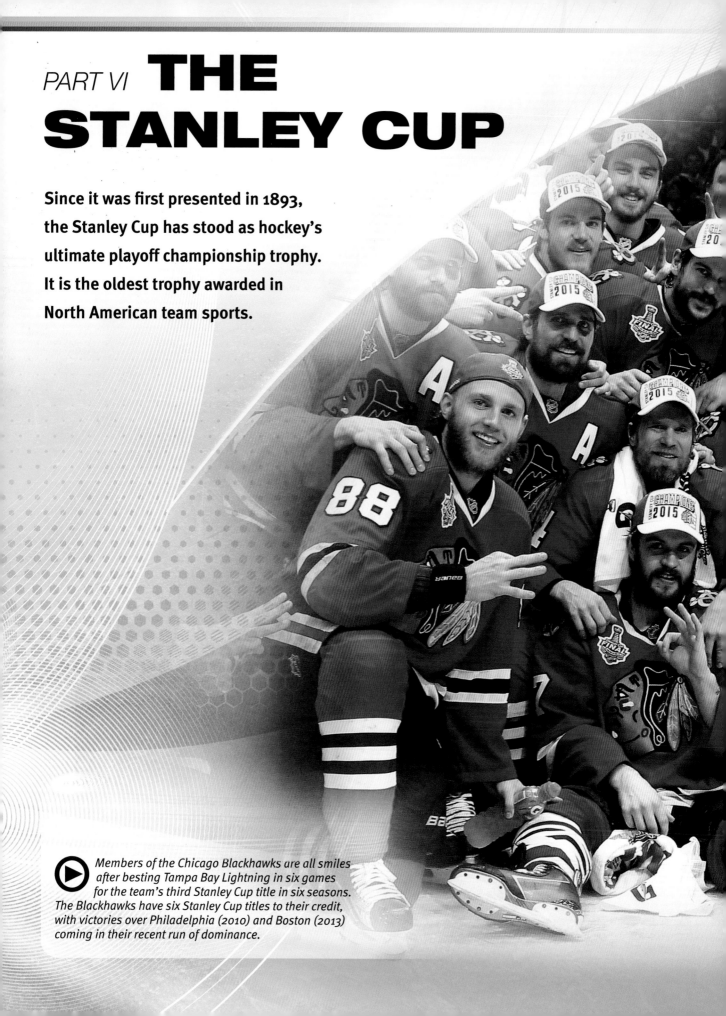

PART VI THE STANLEY CUP

Since it was first presented in 1893, the Stanley Cup has stood as hockey's ultimate playoff championship trophy. It is the oldest trophy awarded in North American team sports.

Members of the Chicago Blackhawks are all smiles after besting Tampa Bay Lightning in six games for the team's third Stanley Cup title in six seasons. The Blackhawks have six Stanley Cup titles to their credit, with victories over Philadelphia (2010) and Boston (2013) coming in their recent run of dominance.

HISTORY OF THE STANLEY CUP

On March 18, 1892, a plan was announced to donate a hockey trophy to symbolize the championship of Canada. Since 1888, Lord Stanley of Preston had been Governor-General of Canada and he and his family had all become fans of the rugged winter sport. At first, the Stanley Cup was a challenge trophy available to any of the top leagues across Canada but by 1914, it had developed into a rivalry between the two best professional leagues. Since 1926–27, when the National Hockey League emerged as the top league in hockey, the Stanley Cup has been awarded to the NHL's playoff champion.

THE FIRST CHAMPIONS

Though they preferred to call themselves the Montreal Hockey Club, most people recognize the team as the Montreal Amateur Athletic Association, or the Montreal AAA, because of the team's affiliation with what was once Canada's most prestigious sports organization. The Montreal AAA hockey club was presented with the Stanley Cup as its first champion in 1893 for having finished in first place in the Amateur Hockey Association of Canada. No playoffs were required.

◀ *The Montreal Wanderers were photographed in Winnipeg during their Stanley Cup challenge against the Kenora Thistles in March of 1907. The Wanderers won the Stanley Cup in 1906, 1907, and 1908.*

CHALLENGE THE CHAMPION

In the early days of hockey, no one league controlled the Stanley Cup in the way that the NHL does today. In an era when cold weather was necessary to create ice and train travel made road trips lengthy, there was only one way to ensure the national nature of the Stanley Cup. The champions of any top league could challenge the current Cup holder to a series, much in the same way as a boxer challenges for a world title.

WINNIPEG WINS IT

The first successful challengers to defeat the current champions for the Stanley Cup were the Winnipeg Victorias. On February 14, 1896, they defeated the Montreal Victorias 2-0 in a one-game Stanley Cup Final. Winnipeg's George "Whitey" Merritt was the first goalie to wear leg guards in a Stanley Cup game, utilizing cricket wicketkeepers' pads for this purpose. On December 30, 1896, the two "Victorias" played a rematch and Montreal beat Winnipeg 6-5 to win back the Stanley Cup.

THE CUP GOES PRO

Until the fall of 1906, hockey in Canada was strictly an amateur sport. It was then that the Ottawa "Silver Seven" and the Stanley Cup champion Montreal Wanderers led a movement allowing teams to openly pay their players. The two trustees who oversaw the Stanley Cup agreed to allow the trophy to become the top prize in professional hockey. Two years later, the Allan Cup was donated to become the top prize for amateur hockey.

END OF AN ERA

After 1906, several professional leagues existed in Canada and many of the new league's champions challenged for the Stanley Cup. Soon, two leagues emerged as a cut above the rest: the National Hockey Association (forerunner of the NHL) and the Pacific Coast Hockey Association. Beginning with the 1913–14 season, the champions of the NHA met the champions of the PCHA in a "World Series of hockey" for the Stanley Cup. The challenge era was over.

USA IS A-OK

As early as 1907, champion teams from American leagues began to enquire about Stanley Cup challenges but the trustees maintained that the trophy had been donated to honor a Canadian champion. In 1912, they refused even to allow two Canadian teams to play for the Stanley Cup in an American city. However, in 1915, the trustees announced that the trophy represented the "world's hockey honors" and that American teams would now be welcome to compete.

SICKNESS IN SEATTLE

The Portland Rosebuds of the PCHA were the first American team to compete for the Stanley Cup when they lost to the NHA champion Montreal Canadiens in 1916. A year later, the Seattle Metropolitans beat the Canadiens to become the first American Stanley Cup champions. In 1919, Seattle and Montreal met again, but that series was halted due to the worldwide Spanish influenza epidemic. Joe Hall of the Canadiens died of the flu on April 5, 1919.

THE NHL TAKES OVER

Though the NHL was formed in 1917, it would take the collapse of the rival western leagues in 1926 for NHL teams to become the only ones eligible to compete for the Stanley Cup. Champions of other leagues would occasionally make challenges, but none was ever accepted. On June 30, 1947, a formal agreement between the Stanley Cup trustees and NHL President Clarence Campbell finally gave the League full control over the playoffs for the Stanley Cup.

NHL FIRSTS

The first all-NHL Stanley Cup Final saw the Ottawa Senators beat the Boston Bruins in 1927. Then, in 1929, Boston beat the New York Rangers in the first all-American Finals. The first best-of-seven series for the Stanley Cup was played in 1939, when Boston beat the Toronto Maple Leafs. In 1941, Boston beat Detroit in the first sweep of a four-game series and a year later Toronto beat Detroit in the first seven-game series to go the distance.

SWEET 16

Expansion of the NHL in 1967 from six teams to 12 saw the playoffs also double from four teams to eight. Further expansion increased the playoffs to 12 teams by 1974–75, and then to 16 in 1979–80. It was not until the 1986–87 season that all four rounds of the playoffs became best-of-seven series. The first team to get 16 playoff victories en route to winning the Stanley Cup were the 1987 Edmonton Oilers.

NHL STANLEY CUP STANDINGS, 1918–2015

Montreal*	23
Toronto°	13
Detroit	11
Boston	6
Chicago	
Edmonton	5
NY Islanders	4
NY Rangers	
New Jersey	3
Pittsburgh	
Los Angeles	2
Philadelphia	
Colorado	
Dallas	1
Calgary	
Carolina	
Anaheim	
Tampa Bay	

* Montreal also won the Stanley Cup in 1916 for a total of 24

° Total includes victories by the Toronto Arenas in 1918 and Toronto St. Patricks in 1922. The Toronto Blueshirts also won the Stanley Cup in 1914.

The Montreal Canadiens celebrate after defeating the Los Angeles Kings for the Stanley Cup in 1993. The victory gave the Canadiens their 24th Cup championship.

STANLEY CUP DYNASTY TEAMS

There is probably no real consensus on what constitutes a sports dynasty, although the most basic criteria would seem to be winning three or more championships in a row. The term is also applied to those hockey teams who won the Stanley Cup four or five times in a six- or seven-year span. Today, the modern economics of sports have made it almost impossible to keep a team together long enough to accomplish these feats. As a result, the dynasty label is sometimes applied to contemporary teams with two or more championships within a decade or so of dominance, but the true era of hockey dynasties lasted from 1947 to 1990.

PRE-NHL DYNASTIES

Featuring future Hall of Famers Mike Grant and Graham Drinkwater, the Montreal Victorias were hockey's first dynasty. After winning the Stanley Cup in 1895, the Vics lost a challenge to the Winnipeg Victorias in 1896 but won the Cup back in a rematch and held it until 1899. The Ottawa Hockey Club, better known today as "the Silver Seven," won the Stanley Cup in 1903 and defeated numerous challengers before losing to the Montreal Wanderers in 1906.

OTTAWA SENATORS, 1920–27

The Ottawa Senators became the first team in NHL history to win back-to-back Stanley Cup titles in 1920 and 1921. They won the Cup again in 1923. At this time, the NHL champions played off against the champions of the Pacific Coast Hockey Association and/or the Western Canada Hockey League for the Stanley Cup. After the demise of the Western leagues, Ottawa won the first all-NHL Stanley Cup Final in 1927, when they defeated the Boston Bruins.

TORONTO MAPLE LEAFS, 1947–51

With victories in 1949, 1950, and 1951, the Toronto Maple Leafs were the first team in NHL history to win three straight Stanley Cup titles. Hall of Famers Turk Broda and Ted Kennedy, as well as Bill Barilko and Howie Meeker, were among eight Leafs players to win the Cup in 1947 and in each of those three years as well. Toronto's trade of five players for Max Bentley early in the 1947–48 season was key to their success.

DETROIT RED WINGS, 1950–55

Gordie Howe, Ted Lindsay, Red Kelly, and Marcel Pronovost were four future Hall of Famers who won the Stanley Cup four times in six years with the Detroit Red Wings and finished first overall in the NHL standings a record seven straight times, from 1948–49 to 1954–55. Goalie Harry Lumley won the Cup in 1950 but was traded to make room for Terry Sawchuk, who recorded four shutouts in eight playoff games to win the Cup in 1952.

MONTREAL CANADIENS, 1956–60 (I)

The only team in hockey history to win the Stanley Cup five years in a row, during their record run the Montreal Canadiens never trailed in a playoff series and were never pushed to a seventh game. Altogether, they posted 20 wins against just five losses during the Finals. The Canadiens' five straight Stanley Cup titles capped off a stretch in which they reached the Finals every year from 1951 to 1960. They also won the Cup in 1953.

MONTREAL CANADIENS, 1956–60 (II)

Twelve players were members of all five Canadiens Stanley Cup teams between 1956 and 1960, including future Hall of Famers Jean Beliveau, Bernie Geoffrion, Doug Harvey, Tom Johnson, Dickie Moore, Jacques Plante, Henri Richard, and Maurice Richard. Coach Toe Blake was also a future Hall of Famer. During the dynasty years, Canadiens players combined to win 15 NHL trophies and earn 15 selections to the First All-Star Team and 10 selections to the Second.

TORONTO MAPLE LEAFS, 1962–67

Coach and general manager Punch Imlach combined Leafs products with shrewd trades to put together a talented team who won the Stanley Cup three years in a row, from 1962 to 1964. Considered too old to win the Cup again in 1967, Toronto surprised Montreal in the Finals that year. Eleven players were members of all four Leafs Cup teams, including Red Kelly, whose eight Cups overall are the most ever won by a player who was not a member of the Montreal Canadiens.

MONTREAL CANADIENS, 1965-69

Often overlooked due to the great Montreal teams of the 1950s and 1970s, the Canadiens of the late 1960s won the Stanley Cup four times in five years despite unprecedented changes to the NHL. The Canadiens won their first two titles of this dynasty playing in a six-team league and the shrewd moves of general manager Sam Pollock allowed them to maintain their dominance and win two more Cups in the two years after expansion.

MONTREAL CANADIENS, 1976-79

Perhaps the greatest team in the history of hockey, the Montreal Canadiens averaged more than 57 wins and 125 points per year in the four seasons from 1975–76 and 1977–78, and posted a playoff record of 48-10 (including 16-3 in the Finals) in winning four straight championships. A total of 15 players were members of all four Cup-winning teams, including Hall of Famers Guy Lafleur, Steve Shutt, Bob Gainey, Larry Robinson, Guy Lapointe, and Ken Dryden.

 Canadiens captain Yvan Cournoyer carries the Stanley Cup after Montreal's victory over Philadelphia in 1976. It was the first of four straight titles for Montreal.

NEW YORK ISLANDERS, 1980-83

Led by stars Mike Bossy, Bryan Trottier, and Denis Potvin, the New York Islanders won the Stanley Cup four years in a row and reached the Finals a fifth straight time in 1984 before losing to the Edmonton Oilers, whom they had defeated in 1983. It took four rounds of playoff victories to win the Stanley Cup by the 1980s and no team in history has ever matched the Islanders' streak of winning 19 consecutive playoff series.

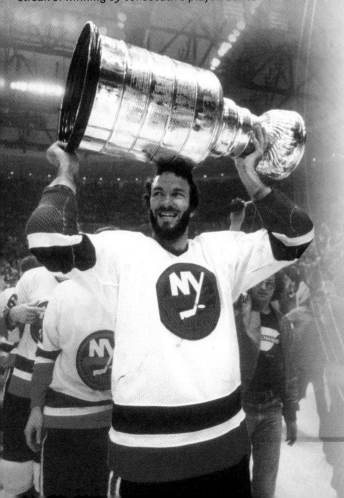

Oilers captain Mark Messier whoops it up after Edmonton's fifth Stanley Cup win in 1990. Adam Graves reaches up to touch the prized trophy.

Ken Morrow holds the Stanley Cup aloft. Morrow won a gold medal with the US Olympic team in 1980 three months before winning his first of four Cup titles.

EDMONTON OILERS, 1984-90

Led by Wayne Gretzky, the Edmonton Oilers reached the Stanley Cup Finals after just four seasons and won the Cup in their fifth year. Edmonton went on to win the Cup four times in five seasons. After Gretzky was traded to Los Angeles in 1988, Mark Messier led the Oilers to another Stanley Cup championship in 1990, giving himself, Glenn Anderson, Grant Fuhr, Randy Gregg, Charlie Huddy, Jari Kurri, and Kevin Lowe five titles in seven years.

THE STANLEY CUP RECORD BOOK

The stakes are raised in the Stanley Cup Final. Big moments take on even bigger meaning and mistakes become magnified, while reputations can be made or destroyed. Throughout the history of the Stanley Cup, the sport's truly great performers have always been able to raise their game when everything is on the line. No matter the era, superstars such as Frank McGee, Cyclone Taylor, Newsy Lalonde, Maurice Richard, Denis Potvin, and Wayne Gretzky have all made their mark in the Stanley Cup record book.

FRANK MCGEE – 1905

Though he had sight in only one eye, Frank McGee was a goal-scoring machine with the Ottawa "Silver Seven" in the early 1900s. During his career, McGee averaged nearly three goals per game but scored just once in a game-one victory over Dawson City in their 1905 challenge. Told the Dawson City players were unimpressed with his play, McGee exploded for 14 goals in a 23-2 victory in game two on January 16, 1905.

OTHER EARLY-ERA RECORDS

Both Frank McGee's 14 goals and Ottawa's 23 in one game in 1905 established Stanley Cup records that are not likely to be broken! With their 9-2 victory over Dawson City in the first game, Ottawa scored 32 goals in just two games. One year later, the Silver Seven beat Queen's University 16-7 and 12-7 in a Stanley Cup challenge, setting a combined record for the era of 42 goals in a single series.

MOST GOALS, ONE GAME

Four different NHL players have scored four goals in one game in the Stanley Cup Finals. Newsy Lalonde of the Montreal Canadiens was first to do so versus Seattle, back in 1919. Others to accomplish the feat are: Babe Dye of the Toronto St. Patricks versus Vancouver in 1922, Ted Lindsay of the Detroit Red Wings versus Montreal in 1955, and Maurice Richard of the Montreal Canadiens versus Boston in 1957.

MOST YEARS IN THE FINALS

Maurice Richard, Jean Beliveau, and Henri Richard of the Montreal Canadiens and Red Kelly of Detroit and Toronto all played in the Stanley Cup Final 12 times in their careers. Had Maurice Richard not been suspended for the 1955 playoffs after punching a linesman, he would have played in 13 finals overall and joined teammates Bernie Geoffrion, Doug Harvey, Tom Johnson, and Bert Olmstead in appearing in 10 straight finals, from 1951 to 1960.

Frank McGee stands at the top right of this 1905 team photo with his six main Ottawa teammates and the Stanley Cup.

HIGHEST-SCORING SERIES

The highest-scoring Stanley Cup series in the NHL era took place in 1973. Despite the presence of future Hall of Fame goalies Ken Dryden and Tony Esposito, the Montreal Canadiens scored 33 goals in winning the six-game series while the Chicago Blackhawks scored 23 times for a combined total of 56 goals. Montreal's 8-7 win over Chicago in game five on May 8, 1973 is the highest-scoring Stanley Cup game in NHL history.

Tony Esposito won the Stanley Cup as a part-time player in Montreal in 1969, but his Blackhawks were beaten by the Canadiens in the Finals in 1971 and 1973.

COACHING RECORDS

Dick Irvin appeared in the Finals 16 times in his coaching career with the Chicago Blackhawks, Toronto Maple Leafs, and Montreal Canadiens but won the Stanley Cup just four times. Scotty Bowman appeared in the Finals 13 times with the St. Louis Blues, Montreal Canadiens, Pittsburgh Penguins, and Detroit Red Wings and won the Cup a record nine times. Toe Blake won the Stanley Cup eight times in nine appearances in the Finals with the Montreal Canadiens.

GOING THE EXTRA MILE

Los Angeles traveled the longest path to win the Stanley Cup in NHL history in 2014. The Kings became the first team to win three consecutive Game 7s to reach the final before defeating the Rangers in five to claim their second title in three years. Philadelphia (1987) and Calgary (2004) also played in 26 contests, but both fell in Game 7 of the Stanley Cup final. Tampa Bay also played in 26 contests, but fell to Chicago in six games in the 2015 Stanley Cup final.

NEVER-SAY-DIE KINGS

Los Angeles showed its resiliency in the 2014 playoffs, becoming the first team to win three consecutive contests in either the conference or Stanley Cup final after facing two-goal deficits. The Kings began their impressive stretch by overcoming a 2-0 hole en route to a 5-4 overtime victory in Game 7 of the Western Conference final versus defending champion Chicago. Los Angeles was not done, however, as it erased a 2-0 deficit in Game 1 of the Stanley Cup final versus the New York Rangers before skating to a 3-2 overtime triumph. Game 2 saw more of the same as the Kings rallied from disadvantages of 2-0, 3-1 and 4-2 before posting a 5-4 win in double overtime.

▶ Jean Beliveau pours a drink into the Stanley Cup after his first championship as team captain in 1965.

MOST POINTS, ONE SERIES

Wayne Gretzky collected three goals and 10 assists for the Edmonton Oilers against the Boston Bruins in 1988 to set a record for the most points in the Stanley Cup Finals. Technically, the 1988 Final is considered a four-game sweep for the Oilers, but the points are also counted from the game on May 24, 1988, which was suspended late in the second period due to a power failure. Gretzky collected two assists in that game.

SCORING RECORDS BY DEFENSEMEN

Denis Potvin (New York Islanders, 1980, six games), Al MacInnis (Calgary Flames, 1989, six games), and Brian Leetch (New York Rangers, 1994, seven games) all share the record for defensemen of scoring five goals in a single Stanley Cup series. Larry Murphy set a record with nine assists for the Pittsburgh Penguins in six games in 1991, while Edmonton's Paul Coffey set the record for most points with 11 (three goals, eight assists) in just five games in 1985.

MOST GOALS, ONE STANLEY CUP SERIES (SINCE 1918)

9	Cyclone Taylor, Vancouver Millionaires (five games) in 1918	
	Frank Foyston, Seattle Metropolitans (five games) in 1919	
	Babe Dye, Toronto St. Patricks (five games) in 1922	
8	Alf Skinner, Toronto Arenas (five games) in 1918	
7	Jean Beliveau, Montreal (five games) in 1956	
	Mike Bossy, NY Islanders (four games) in 1982	
	Wayne Gretzky, Edmonton (five games) in 1985	

MOST GOALS SCORED IN STANLEY CUP FINALS (SINCE 1918)

34	Maurice Richard, Mtl.	59 games
30	Jean Beliveau, Mtl.	64 games
24	Bernie Geoffrion, Mtl.	53 games
21	Henri Richard, Mtl.	65 games
	Yvan Cournoyer, Mtl.	50 games

MOST CAREER ASSISTS IN STANLEY CUP FINALS (SINCE 1918)

35	Wayne Gretzky, Edm., LA	31 games
32	Gordie Howe, Det.	55 games
	Jean Beliveau, Mtl.	64 games
31	Doug Harvey, Mtl., Stl.	54 games
26	Henri Richard, Mtl	65 games

CRAZY EIGHT

By besting the New Jersey Devils in six games, the Los Angeles Kings became the first eighth-seeded team to win the Stanley Cup. Upon closer inspection, the Kings realistically weren't seriously challenged in any of the series – after all, they won the first three games of all four sets. The only other eighth seed to reach the Stanley Cup Finals was the 2005–06 Edmonton Oilers, who lost a seven-game series against the Carolina Hurricanes

STANLEY CUP WINNING/ OVERTIME GOALS

Few things in sports can match the excitement of an overtime goal in a Stanley Cup game. Future Hall of Famer Bill Cook was the first player in NHL history to win the Stanley Cup in overtime when he scored for the New York Rangers to defeat the Toronto Maple Leafs in 1933. Since then, only 15 other NHL players have scored the Stanley Cup-winning goal in overtime. Some of them, like Brett Hull in 1999 or Toe Blake in 1944, were among the greatest players of their day; others may well have been forgotten if not for their one shining moment of greatness.

CORB DENNENY, 1918

The NHL was formed in November of 1917 and its league champion, the Toronto "Arenas," played for the Stanley Cup for the first time in the spring of 1918, when they faced the Vancouver Millionaires in a seesaw series that went the full five games. However, the final was scoreless through two periods before Toronto went ahead 1-0 early in the third. Cyclone Taylor tied it up, but Corb Denneny scored just one minute later and Toronto held on for a 2-1 victory.

WINNIPEG VICTORIAS
Stanley Cup Champions–1901

Top Row—left to right: M. HOOPER E. B. WOOD J. MARSHALL J. C. G. ARMYTAGE G. A. CARRUTHERS
A. B. GINGRASS F. T. CADHAM

Bottom Row: W. E. ROBINSON G. W. JOHNSTONE R. M. FLETT D. BAIN M. L. FLETT A. BROWN W. PRATT

CHARLIE GARDINER, 1934

Many people rate Charlie Gardiner of the Chicago Black Hawks as the greatest goaltender of his day, while some consider him to be the greatest of all time. Though plagued by headaches, Gardiner was unbeatable in the last game of the 1934 Stanley Cup Final, shutting out the Detroit Red Wings until Mush March finally scored after 30:05 of overtime to give Chicago a 1-0 victory. Tragically, Gardiner died of a brain hemorrhage just two months later.

MOST CAREER GAME-WINNING GOALS IN THE FINALS

9   Jean Beliveau, Montreal
8   Maurice Richard, Montreal
6   Bernie Geoffrion, Montreal
    Yvan Cournoyer, Montreal

DAN BAIN, 1901

A talented all-around athlete who starred in many sports, Dan Bain earned his most lasting fame as a hockey player. After helping the Winnipeg Victorias win the Stanley Cup for the first time in 1896, Bain became the first player in history to score the Cup-winning goal in overtime in 1901. His goal after four minutes of extra play gave the Victorias a 2-1 win over the Montreal Shamrocks on January 31, 1901.

 Dan Bain sits just to the right of the Stanley Cup in this 1901 team photo of the Winnipeg Victorias.

PETE LANGELLE, 1942

The Toronto Maple Leafs were favored in the 1942 Stanley Cup Finals but they dropped the first three games of the best-of-seven series to the Detroit Red Wings. A shakeup to the lineup helped the Leafs win three straight, but they trailed game seven 1-0. After tying the score early in the third period, Pete Langelle put Toronto ahead. The Leafs went on to a 3-1 victory to cap the greatest comeback in hockey history.

PETE BABANDO, 1950

With the circus invading Madison Square Garden, the New York Rangers played the entire 1950 Stanley Cup Finals on the road. Still, they forced the Detroit Red Wings to a seventh game, only to lose in double overtime on a goal by Pete Babando. The only other time the seventh game of the Stanley Cup Final has been decided in overtime is in 1954, when Detroit beat the Montreal Canadiens on a goal by Tony Leswick.

BILL BARILKO, 1951

Though better known for his bruising body checks, Bill Barilko scored to give the Toronto Maple Leafs a 3-2 victory over Montreal in game five of the Stanley Cup Final. His goal ended the only series in hockey history in which every game was decided in overtime. Later that summer, Barilko was killed in a plane crash and the Leafs would not win the Stanley Cup again until 1962 – the same year that the wreckage was finally discovered.

BOBBY ORR, 1970

When Bobby Orr joined the Boston Bruins as an 18-year-old in 1966, they had not won the Stanley Cup since 1941; they had not even made the playoffs since 1959. But, with Orr and Phil Esposito leading the way, the Bruins quickly became a powerhouse. Orr capped a glorious run through the 1970 playoffs by scoring the Stanley Cup-winning goal in overtime – and celebrated with his stick held high while flying through the air.

BOB NYSTROM, 1980

The New York Islanders set records for futility as an expansion team in 1972–73, but poor finishes led to stellar draft picks such as Denis Potvin, Bryan Trottier, and Mike Bossy. By their fourth season, the Islanders were an elite club. Still, four more years of playoff disappointments followed. Finally, at 7:11 of overtime in game six of the 1980 Stanley Cup Final, Bob Nystrom redirected a John Tonelli pass past Flyers goalie Pete Peeters and the Islanders were champions.

BOB BAUN, 1964

With seven minutes to go in game six of the Stanley Cup Final, Toronto's Bob Baun blocked a shot by Detroit's Alex Delvecchio and was carried off the ice on a stretcher. He had his injured ankle taped and frozen, and returned to score the winning goal in overtime. Only after Toronto won the Stanley Cup in game seven did Baun agree to have his ankle x-rayed ... and learned that he had suffered a fractured fibula.

HENRI RICHARD, 1966

At 2:20 of overtime, Dave Balon of the Montreal Canadiens made a return pass to Henri Richard. Although Richard was hauled down before he could shoot, somehow the puck wound up in the Detroit net. Richard claimed the puck bounced in off his knee, though Red Wings goalie Roger Crozier insisted he had swiped it in with his glove. Despite Crozier's protest, referee Frank Udvari ruled it a goal and the Canadiens won the Stanley Cup.

MOST CAREER OVERTIME GOALS IN THE FINALS

3	Maurice Richard, Montreal	(one in 1946, one in 1951, one in 1958)
2	Don Raleigh, NY Rangers	(two in 1950)
	Jacques Lemaire, Montreal	(one in 1968, one in 1977)
	John LeClair, Montreal	(two in 1993)

ALEC MARTINEZ, 2014

After scoring the series-clinching goal to unseat defending champion Chicago in the Western Conference final, Los Angeles defenseman Alec Martinez picked a fine time to record his first goal of the 2014 Stanley Cup. Martinez tallied 14:43 into double overtime as the Kings posted a 3-2 victory over the New York Rangers in Game 5 to capture their second Stanley Cup title in three years. Rookie Tyler Toffoli's hard shot from above the right faceoff circle was kicked out by goaltender Henrik Lundqvist, but Martinez deposited the puck into the open left side of the net to ignite a wild celebration at Staples Center.

PATRICK KANE, 2010

It had been 49 years since Chicago's last Stanley Cup victory, so what did a few extra minutes matter? At 4:06 of overtime in game six, Patrick Kane slipped the puck past Philadelphia goalie Michael Leighton, but it disappeared under the white canvas skirt laced around the bottom of the net. Kane immediately began celebrating, although it took four more seconds for the clock to stop and several more minutes before video replays confirmed the Cup-winning goal.

Chicago's Patrick Kane scored one of the strangest Stanley Cup-winning goals against Philadelphia in the 2010 Finals.

NHL PLAYOFF RECORD BOOK

▶ Chris Chelios became the oldest player to win the Stanley Cup at age 46 as a member of the 2008 Detroit Red Wings.

Over the years, the format of the NHL playoffs has changed a lot. From the split-season setup of the first few seasons, where the top team from the first half met the second-half winners to decide the League Championships to the grueling four-round, 16-win setup first put in place in 1987, the playoffs are the true test of NHL greatness. Players don't earn a salary in the postseason and though there is a pool of bonus money, it's the chance to lift the Stanley Cup at the end of the tough marathon that pushes players to their limit and beyond.

ROOKIE RECORDS

Dino Ciccarelli of the Minnesota North Stars set a rookie playoff record with 14 goals in 1981. Jeremy Roenick (11) and Claude Lemieux (10) are the only other rookies to reach double digits. Ciccarelli's 21 playoff points in 1981 set another record that was tied in 2010 by Ville Leino of the Philadelphia Flyers. Leino reversed Ciccarelli's numbers, collecting seven goals and setting a new rookie record with 14 assists en route to his 21 points.

HAT TRICK HEROES

Jari Kurri set a scoring record when he collected three hat tricks in a single playoff series against the Chicago Blackhawks in the Conference Finals in 1985, including one four-goal game. Kurri set another record with four hat tricks in the playoffs overall that year. In all, he scored seven playoff hat tricks in his career, tying Maurice Richard for second place all-time behind Wayne Gretzky, who notched 10 playoff hat tricks.

MOST GOALS, ONE PLAYOFF YEAR

Back in 1919, in the NHL's second season, Montreal Canadiens star Newsy Lalonde scored 17 playoff goals to set a record that would remain unmatched for 57 years. Reggie Leach finally broke the record in 1976 when he scored 19 goals for the Philadelphia Flyers. Neither Newsy's Canadiens nor Leach's Flyers wound up winning the Stanley Cup, but Jari Kurri's Edmonton Oilers did so when he tied the record with 19 goals in 1985.

STINGY TIM

Boston Bruins goaltender Tim Thomas set an NHL record for most saves in a single postseason when he turned aside 798 of 849 shots in 2011. The two-time Vezina Trophy winner also made history after yielding just eight goals, the fewest allowed in a seven-game Stanley Cup Finals. Thomas' mark snapped former Toronto Maple Leafs netminder Frank McCool's long-standing record of nine, which was set in 1945.

GIBSON STANDS TALL

Anaheim's John Gibson and Boston's Tiny Thompson are the only goaltenders in NHL history to record a shutout in both their regular-season and playoff debuts. After blocking 18 shots in a 3-0 triumph over Vancouver on April 7, 2014, the 20-year-old played Game 4 of the Western Conference second-round series with Los Angeles on May 10. Recalled from Norfolk of the American Hockey League, Gibson made 28 saves to join Thompson, who accomplished the feat in November 1928 and March 1929.

 Jari Kurri won the Stanley Cup five times with the Oilers between 1984 and 1990 and was the playoffs' top goal-scorer on four occasions.

ONE-GOAL WONDERS

The New York Rangers competed in an NHL-record 15 consecutive one-goal games during a postseason stretch spanning from 2014–15. After playing nail-biters in the final two contests of the 2014 Stanley Cup versus Los Angeles, New York began the 2015 playoffs with 13 straight one-goal decisions – with nine of those resulting in a 2–1 final score.

OVERTIME RECORDS

Mel Hill of the New York Rangers set a record that has never been matched when he scored three overtime goals in a single series against the Boston Bruins in 1939. Maurice Richard is the only other player even to score three overtime goals in a single playoff year. Richard's six career overtime goals were a record until 2006, when Joe Sakic of the Colorado Avalanche scored his seventh overtime goal. Sakic got an eighth in 2008.

▶ Joe Sakic's eight career overtime goals for Colorado are two more than Montreal's Maurice Richard on the all-time playoff list.

GAMES & SEASONS

Chris Chelios holds the NHL record for most years in the playoffs, reaching the postseason 24 times in his 26-year career. Chelios also holds the record for most playoff games played with 266 for the Montreal Canadiens, Chicago Blackhawks, and Detroit Red Wings. Larry Robinson set a record for most consecutive years in the playoffs, reaching the postseason in every one of his 20 seasons with the Canadiens and the Los Angeles Kings from 1972–73 and 1991–92.

ASSIST RECORDS

Wayne Gretzky holds or shares the playoff records for assists in one game, one series, and one year. In 1985, Gretzky had 14 assists in one series to tie the record set by Rick Middleton two years before. On April 9, 1987, Gretzky had six assists versus Los Angeles to tie a record set by Mikko Leinonen in 1982. In 1988, Gretzky had 31 assists in the playoffs to break his own record of 30, set in 1985.

MOST GOALS, ONE GAME

Five different NHL players have scored five goals in one playoff game. Newsy Lalonde of the Montreal Canadiens was first to do so versus Ottawa in 1919. The others to accomplish the same feat are: Maurice Richard of the Canadiens versus Toronto in 1944, Darryl Sittler of the Maple Leafs versus Philadelphia in 1976, Reggie Leach of the Flyers versus Boston in 1976, and Mario Lemieux of Pittsburgh versus Philadelphia in 1989.

PLAYOFF POINTS

In 1983, Boston's Rick Middleton set a single series record with five goals and 14 assists for 19 points in seven games versus Buffalo. Patrick Sundstrom of New Jersey (1988) and Mario Lemieux (1989) share the record for most points in one playoff game with eight. Wayne Gretzky set the record for points in one playoff year with 17 goals and 30 assists for 47 points in 1985. Lemieux ranks second, with 44 points in 1991.

LONGEST PLAYOFF GAMES

1.	March 24, 1936	Detroit 1, Montreal 0	(Goal Scorer: Mud Bruneteau)	116:30 into overtime
2.	April 3, 1933	Toronto 1, Boston 0	(Goal Scorer: Ken Doraty)	104:46
3.	May 4, 2000	Philadelphia 2, Pittsburgh 1	(Goal Scorer: Keith Primeau)	92:01
4.	April 24, 2003	Anaheim 4, Dallas 3	(Goal Scorer: Petr Sykora)	80:48
5.	April 24, 1996	Pittsburgh 3, Washington 2	(Goal Scorer: Petr Nedved)	79:15
6.	April 7, 2007	Vancouver 5, Dallas 4	(Goal Scorer: Henrik Sedin)	78:06
7.	March 23, 1943	Toronto 3, Detroit 2	(Goal Scorer: Jack McLean)	70:18
8.	May 4, 2008	Dallas 2, San Jose 1	(Goal Scorer: Brenden Morrow)	69:03

MOST GOALS IN PLAYOFF CAREER

122	Wayne Gretzky, Edm, LA, Stl, NYR	208 games
109	Mark Messier, Edm, NYR	236 games
106	Jari Kurri, Edm, LA, NYR, Ana	200 games
103	Brett Hull, Cgy, Stl, Dal, Det	202 games
93	Glenn Anderson, Edm, Tor, NYR, Stl	225 games

Rick Middleton's 33 playoff points (11 goals, 22 assists) for Boston in 1983 are the most ever by a player on a team that didn't reach the Finals.

MOST ASSISTS IN PLAYOFF CAREER

260	Wayne Gretzky, Edm, LA, Stl, NYR	208 games
186	Mark Messier, Edm, NYR	236 games
139	Raymond Bourque, Bos, Col	214 games
137	Paul Coffey, nine teams	194 games
128	Doug Gilmour, seven teams	182 games

MOST POINTS IN PLAYOFF CAREER

382	Wayne Gretzky, Edm, LA, Stl, NYR	208 games
295	Mark Messier, Edm, NYR	236 games
233	Jari Kurri, Edm, LA, NYR, Ana	200 games
214	Glenn Anderson, Edm, Tor, NYR, Stl	225 games
137	Paul Coffey, nine teams	194 games

THE CONN SMYTHE TROPHY

The Conn Smythe Trophy is an annual award presented to the Most Valuable Player for his team in the playoffs. Since 1970, the winner has been selected in a vote by members of the Professional Hockey Writers Association at the conclusion of the last game in the Stanley Cup Finals. Unlike similar trophies in other sports, the Conn Smythe Trophy is based on performance in the entire playoffs, not just the championship round. The award was presented to the NHL in 1964 by Maple Leaf Gardens Limited to honor Conn Smythe, the longtime coach, general manager, president, and owner-governor of the Toronto Maple Leafs.

◄ *The trophy for NHL playoff MVP is adorned with maple leaves and features a silver replica of Maple Leaf Gardens in honor of Toronto's Conn Smythe.*

THE FIRST WIN

The Conn Smythe Trophy was awarded for the first time in 1965 to Canadiens captain Jean Beliveau after Montreal defeated the Chicago Blackhawks in seven games to win the Stanley Cup. Beliveau had eight goals and eight assists for 16 points in 13 playoff games, including five goals and five assists for 10 points in the Finals. Beliveau's goal, just 14 seconds into the seventh game, set the tone in a surprisingly easy 4-0 victory.

MOST WINS

Goalie Patrick Roy is the only three-time winner of the Conn Smythe Trophy. Roy won his first with the Montreal Canadiens in 1986, leading a rookie-laden team to a surprising victory. He was just 20 years old, making him the youngest player to receive the honor. In 1993, Roy won again with the Canadiens after a brilliant performance including 10 overtime victories. He won for the final time with the Colorado Avalanche in 2001.

A HOCKEY GRAND SLAM

Bobby Orr's overtime goal to win the Stanley Cup in 1970 was a fitting conclusion to a year which had seen him win not only the Norris Trophy as Best Defenseman and the Hart Trophy as MVP, but he also became the first defenseman to win the Art Ross Trophy as the League's scoring leader. The announcement that he had also won the Conn Smythe Trophy made him the first player to win four major awards in one season.

TWO IN A ROW

Bobby Orr won the Conn Smythe Trophy again after Boston's Stanley Cup victory in 1972, but the first player to win the award twice in a row was Philadelphia Flyers goalie Bernie Parent. He won the Conn Smythe Trophy after Philadelphia's Stanley Cup victories in 1974 and 1975. Wayne Gretzky would win the trophy in 1985 and 1988, but the only other player to do so twice in succession is Mario Lemieux, who won in 1991 and 1992.

▶ *The Islanders' acquisition of Butch Goring at the 1980 trade deadline helped turn a perennial playoff disappointment into a championship team.*

FIRST ... & LAST

Serge Savard of the Montreal Canadiens became the first defenseman to win the Conn Smythe Trophy in 1969. Savard beat out teammates Rogie Vachon (who took over for injured goalie Gump Worsley during the playoffs), Dick Duff (the top scorer in the Finals), and Jean Beliveau. Savard was the last player to win the trophy in a vote conducted by the NHL Governors. His win was not announced until three days after Montreal won the Stanley Cup.

FOUR IN A ROW

The New York Islanders are the only team to produce four consecutive Conn Smythe Trophy winners. Bryan Trottier took the honors in 1980 after leading the playoffs in scoring when the Islanders won their first of four straight championships. Butch Goring secured the Trophy for his two-way excellence in 1981; Mike Bossy won after scoring seven goals in four games in the 1982 Finals, while goalie Billy Smith won after shutting down Edmonton in 1983.

CONSOLATION PRIZE?

Four goalies have won the Conn Smythe Trophy despite playing for teams that did not win the Stanley Cup. Those goalies are: Roger Crozier, Detroit Red Wings, 1966; Glenn Hall, St. Louis Blues, 1968; Ron Hextall, Philadelphia Flyers, 1987; and Jean-Sebastien Giguere, Anaheim Ducks, 2003. The only position player to win the award for a losing team was Reggie Leach, who won it with Philadelphia in 1976, despite the Flyers' loss to the Montreal Canadiens.

MASTER BLASTER

With his booming slap shot, Al MacInnis was a defenseman who was always an offensive threat. He is one of only a few defenseman to top 100 points in a single season and trails only Raymond Bourque and Paul Coffey in career goals, assists, and points by a defenseman. Though several others had tied in the past, MacInnis became the first defenseman to lead the postseason in scoring in 1989 and earned the Conn Smythe Trophy when Calgary won the Stanley Cup.

▶ *Calgary's Al MacInnis had 31 points (seven goals, 24 assists) in 22 playoff games in 1989.*

◀ *Roger Crozier was considered a surprise winner of the Conn Smythe Trophy in 1966 when his Detroit Red Wings lost the Stanley Cup to Montreal.*

▼ *Jonathan Toews' Conn Smythe Trophy award in 2010 capped off a remarkable season for the Chicago Blackhawks captain.*

ONE SEASON, TWO MVPS

Boston's Bobby Orr (1970 and 1972), Montreal's Guy Lafleur (1977), and Edmonton's Wayne Gretzky (1985) are the only players to win both the Hart Trophy as regular-season MVP and the Conn Smythe Trophy as playoff MVP in the same year. Lafleur and Gretzky also won the Ted Lindsay Award (then known as the Lester Pearson Award) as the players' choice for MVP, giving them three such honors in a single season.

CLEARING CUSTOMS

In 1994, Brian Leetch became the first American to win the Conn Smythe Trophy. The defenseman led all players in postseason scoring to help the New York Rangers win the Stanley Cup for the first time since 1940. In 2002, Detroit's Nicklas Lidstrom became the first European-born player to win the Conn Smythe Trophy. That summer, Lidstrom brought the Stanley Cup, the Conn Smythe Trophy, and the Norris Trophy back to his hometown of Vasteras, Sweden.

SILVER & GOLD

In 2010, Chicago Blackhawks captain Jonathan Toews became the first player in hockey history to win an Olympic gold medal, the Stanley Cup, and the Conn Smythe Trophy all in the same season. Toews and teammates Duncan Keith and Brent Seabrook all won the Cup and a gold medal in 2010, joining Ken Morrow (1980), Brendan Shanahan (2002), and Steve Yzerman (2002) as the only six players to accomplish this rare double.

DANDY DUNCAN

Duncan Keith did it all en route to receiving the Conn Smythe Trophy at the conclusion of the 2015 playoffs, including scoring the eventual winning goal to lead the Chicago Blackhawks to a 2–0 victory over the Tampa Bay Lightning in Game 6 of the Stanley Cup final. Keith became only the second defenseman to net the Cup-clinching goal and secure the Conn Smythe Trophy since Boston's Bobby Orr accomplished the feat in both 1970 and 1972. A two-time Norris Trophy and Olympic gold-medal winner, Keith had three goals and 18 assists to tie Chris Chelios for the most points (21) by a Blackhawks blue-liner in a single postseason.

PART VII

MINOR PRO, JUNIOR, COLLEGE, & HIGH-SCHOOL HOCKEY

Since the 1920s, minor pro hockey leagues have been a proving ground for NHL players. Junior teams have fed top talent upward since the sport's earliest days, while college and high-school teams have been producing quality players for more than a generation.

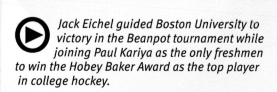

Jack Eichel guided Boston University to victory in the Beanpot tournament while joining Paul Kariya as the only freshmen to win the Hobey Baker Award as the top player in college hockey.

MINOR PRO LEAGUES & STARS

Even before hockey became a professional sport in the early 1900s, there had long been a hierarchy among the game's top leagues. Provincial amateur organizations in Quebec, Manitoba, and Ontario dominated the Stanley Cup competition in the beginning and all had junior and intermediate divisions preparing players for the senior ranks. Many professional hockey leagues came and went during the 1910s and into the 20s, and when the NHL emerged as the game's only "major" league in 1926–27, several new leagues were designated as minor-pro. Today, the American Hockey League is the top rung of minor-pro hockey, grooming both top prospects and long-shot hopefuls for the NHL.

THE USAHA

Though technically not a minor league or a professional hockey league, the United States Amateur Hockey Association proved a fertile training ground for the NHL in the early 1920s. Among the future stars to come out of this league were Nels Stewart, a scoring champion who won the Hart Trophy as MVP as an NHL rookie in 1925–26, and Roy Worters, who became the first goalie to win the Hart Trophy in 1928–29.

THE CAN-AM LEAGUE

The Canadian-American Hockey League was one of hockey's first minor-pro circuits when it began in 1926–27. Franchises were originally placed in New Haven, Springfield, Boston, Providence, and Quebec City. It would later have a team in Philadelphia and operate briefly in Newark and the Bronx as well. The League lasted through the 1935–36 season, extending the careers of many former NHL players and launching new stars, too. In 1936–37, the Can-Am merged with the International Hockey League to form what would become the American Hockey League.

CAN-AM AFFILIATES

Art Ross of the Boston Bruins was quick to see the benefits of aligning his NHL team with a minor-league squad. The Boston Tigers, and then the Boston Cubs, of the Can-Am league were directly affiliated with the Bruins. Future stars such as Dit Clapper, Woody Dumart, and Bobby Bauer all got their starts in professional hockey in this league. Dit Clapper went on to become the first player in history to play 20 years in the NHL.

THE CAN-PRO LEAGUE

The Canadian Professional Hockey League began in 1926–27, with teams in the Ontario cities of Stratford, London, Hamilton, Windsor, and Niagara Falls. It would soon expand to American cities as well and was renamed the International Hockey League in 1929–30. The Montreal Maroons, Toronto Maple Leafs, and Detroit Cougars (soon to be Red Wings) were all quick to form relationships with teams in this league. Perhaps the biggest star to come out of this loop was Turk Broda.

OTHER TEAMS, TOO

Lester Patrick of the New York Rangers also saw the benefits of minor league affiliation. Until 1932–33, the Rangers ran the Springfield Indians of the Can-Am League and then groomed prospects with the Philadelphia Arrows. Future Hall of Famer Earl Siebert was among many Rangers who got their pro starts in Springfield. The Montreal Canadiens established a long-lasting relationship with the Providence Reds, though Providence owned most of its own players.

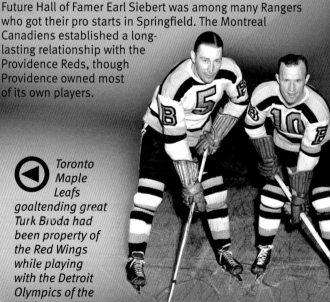

◀ *Toronto Maple Leafs goaltending great Turk Broda had been property of the Red Wings while playing with the Detroit Olympics of the IHL in 1935–36.*

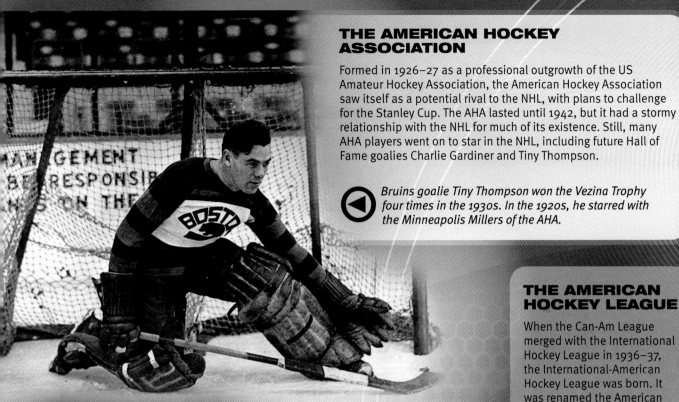

THE AMERICAN HOCKEY ASSOCIATION

Formed in 1926–27 as a professional outgrowth of the US Amateur Hockey Association, the American Hockey Association saw itself as a potential rival to the NHL, with plans to challenge for the Stanley Cup. The AHA lasted until 1942, but it had a stormy relationship with the NHL for much of its existence. Still, many AHA players went on to star in the NHL, including future Hall of Fame goalies Charlie Gardiner and Tiny Thompson.

◀ *Bruins goalie Tiny Thompson won the Vezina Trophy four times in the 1930s. In the 1920s, he starred with the Minneapolis Millers of the AHA.*

THE AMERICAN HOCKEY LEAGUE

When the Can-Am League merged with the International Hockey League in 1936–37, the International-American Hockey League was born. It was renamed the American Hockey League after the 1939–40 season. Over the years, the AHL would grow to become the primary development circuit for the NHL. While many NHL teams have had AHL affiliates over the years, the 2010–11 season marked the first time that each of the 30 NHL teams had its own individual AHL farm club.

THE INTERNATIONAL HOCKEY LEAGUE

Unrelated to the previous league of the same name, a new International Hockey League was formed in December 1945. It began with four teams, and though growth was slow in the 1950s, it picked up in the 1960s and the League was on a par with the AHL by the 1970s. Rapid expansion in the 1990s strained the IHL's relationship with the NHL and the League folded in 2001, when six IHL franchises were admitted into the AHL.

SUPER SOMMER

Roy Sommer coached in his American Hockey League-best 1,257th game on March 26, 2014, guiding Worcester to a 5-3 victory over Portland. The 56-year-old spent his entire coaching career with the San Jose Sharks' affiliate, beginning with the Kentucky Thoroughblades from 1998 to 2001. Leading the Cleveland Barons from 2001 to 2006, he has grown comfortable with Worcester en route to unseating Frank Mathers for the record.

MONARCHS RULE BEFORE REIGN

Adrian Kempe and Vincent LoVerde each scored in the first period and Patrick Bartosak made 31 saves as Manchester Monarchs claimed the Calder Cup after a 2–1 Game 5 triumph over the Utica Comets on June 14, 2015. Manchester was competing in its final season as the American Hockey League affiliate of the Los Angeles Kings and will be replaced by the Ontario Reign, who hold the designation as the current champion when the 2015–16 season begins.

THE CALDER CUP

The American Hockey League's championship trophy is named in honor of Frank Calder, the first president of the NHL. Twenty-seven members of the Hockey Hall of Fame have won the Calder Cup in their careers, including Johnny Bower, Terry Sawchuk, Gerry Cheevers, Larry Robinson, Doug Harvey, and Patrick Roy. The Springfield Indians, under the leadership of Hockey Hall of Famers Eddie Shore and Jack Butterfield, won a record three straight Calder Cup championships in 1960, 1961, and 1962.

THE ECHL

Billing itself as the "Premier AA Hockey League," the ECHL is the second tier of modern minors. Many teams in the ECHL have affiliate relationships with NHL teams and/or AHL teams. Founded in 1988, with just five teams and growing to a high of 31 in 2003, the "EC" originally stood for East Coast, but the League now has 19 teams spanning the entire United States, from Alaska to Florida, and is known only by its initials.

◀ *Boston's Dit Clapper (#5) spent the entire 1925–26 season with the Boston Tigers of the Can-Am League. Bill Cowley (#10) played just one game in the American Hockey Association in 1934–35 before making his NHL debut.*

JUNIOR HOCKEY IN NORTH AMERICA

The origins of junior hockey as a separate and distinct competitive level of the game for players age 20 and under began in the early 1890s. By the 1930s, most small towns across Canada had their own junior clubs, and it was not uncommon for more than 100 teams to be in competition for the national Memorial Cup championship. Before a decline after World War Two, there were 10 distinct regions (five in the East and five in the West) of junior hockey. By 1971, junior hockey had been reorganized and the groups that would become the Ontario Hockey League, the Western Hockey League, and the Quebec Major Junior Hockey League were established as the top rank.

THE MEMORIAL CUP

Captain James T. Sutherland of Kingston, Ontario was the man responsible for the Memorial Cup, which was created to honor Kingston hockey stars Allan "Scotty" Davidson and George Richardson, who had been killed in battle during World War One. From 1919 to 1971, the Memorial Cup featured an East-West championship final that followed lengthy playoffs all across Canada. Since 1972, the Memorial Cup has been a round-robin tournament featuring teams from the top three Major Junior leagues.

BIRTH OF JUNIOR HOCKEY

The Ontario Hockey Association was formed in Toronto on November 27, 1890. It originally consisted of 13 teams competing at the level that would become known as "senior hockey." A junior category was introduced for the winter of 1892–93. While many other provincial associations soon began to introduce junior hockey clubs too, it was not until the Canadian Amateur Hockey Association came into existence in 1914 that junior hockey began to make major strides.

NHL SPONSORSHIP

Shortly after taking over the Toronto Maple Leafs in 1927, Conn Smythe reached agreements with the Toronto Marlboros and St. Michael's College to make their junior clubs part of the Maple Leafs' farm system. For decades afterward, NHL clubs sponsored junior teams all across Canada as a way of acquiring junior talent. The introduction of the NHL Draft in 1963 was the first step in eliminating junior sponsorship, though the system would remain until 1969.

JUNIOR A & MAJOR JUNIOR

In 1933–34, junior hockey in Canada was regrouped into A and B classifications, with C and D divisions to follow later. Junior A became the job rank, with only Junior A clubs being eligible to compete for the Memorial Cup. In 1971, Junior A hockey was split into two ranks, with the leagues that would become the Ontario Hockey League, the Western Hockey League, and the Quebec Major Junior Hockey League all classified as "Major Junior."

▶ The Ontario Hockey League had to grant John Tavares "exceptional player status" to allow the Oshawa Generals to select him in the League's draft at the age of 14.

THE ONTARIO HOCKEY LEAGUE

The Ontario Hockey League can trace its roots back to the formation of the OHA in 1890. In fact, the League was still known as the OHA until 1974, when the Major Junior division was renamed the Ontario Major Junior Hockey League. It would not become the OHL until the 1980–81 season. In 2009, John Tavares ended his four-year OHL career with a record 215 goals; he had begun playing in the League at age 15.

THE CHL

The Canadian Hockey League was founded in 1975 as the Canadian Major Junior Hockey League. It is an umbrella group that oversees the OHL, the WHL, and the QMJHL. The CHL is responsible for staging the annual Memorial Cup tournament and for organizing a handful of other annual events, including the CHL Top Prospects Game. It also hands out national awards in numerous categories, including Player of the Year, Rookie of the Year, and Coach of the Year.

THE WESTERN HOCKEY LEAGUE

Through 1966, each of Canada's western provinces had its own Junior A hockey league. In 1966–67, teams from Alberta and Saskatchewan formed the Canadian Major Junior Hockey League, which became the Western Canada Hockey League a year later, and then the Western Hockey League in 1978–79. Led by goalie Grant Fuhr and top scorer Barry Pederson, the WHL's Victoria Cougars set a league record with 60 wins when they went 60-11-1 in 1980–81.

THE QUEBEC MAJOR JUNIOR HOCKEY LEAGUE

The QMJHL was formed in 1969 by a merger of the Quebec Junior Hockey League and the Metropolitan Montreal Junior Hockey League. Originally featuring two teams based in Ontario, "The Q" would begin expanding into the Maritime Provinces and the US in 1994. In 1983–84, Mario Lemieux set a league record with 133 goals in 70 games. Mike Bossy holds the career record, with 309 goals in four-plus seasons.

MIGHTY MOOSEHEADS

Nathan MacKinnon made a statement with the Halifax Mooseheads prior to being selected by Colorado with the first overall pick of the 2013 NHL draft. The Nova Scotia native helped the Mooseheads defeat Baie-Comeau Drakkar to win the President's Cup as champions of the Quebec Major Junior Hockey League in 2013. MacKinnon came up large in the Memorial Cup with a hat trick in Halifax's 6-4 triumph over the Portland Winterhawks.

THE USHL

While several American cities compete in the three leagues of the Canadian Hockey League, the United States has its own deep junior system. At the highest level is the United States Hockey League, an all-junior league since 1979. The USHL is based in the Midwest and is strictly amateur, which allows its players to go on to play NCAA (National Collegiate Athletic Association) college hockey. Each year, NHL teams have been drafting a growing number of USHL players.

CANADIAN JUNIOR A TODAY

Originally known as Tier II Junior A, the level of hockey just below Major Junior in Canada is now known simply as Junior A. As in the old days of the Memorial Cup, there are 10 provincial Junior A leagues stretching from coast to coast, organized under the Canadian Junior Hockey League. Provincial and regional playoffs lead toward the national Royal Bank Cup. From 1971 to 1995, the championship was known as the Centennial Cup.

Mario Lemieux spent three seasons with the Laval Voisins of the QMJHL from 1981 to 1984. He went from 30 to 84 to a record 133 goals in that time, and from 96 to 184 to a record 282 points.

◀ *Barry Pederson led the 1980–81 Victoria Cougars with 65 goals, 82 assists, and 147 points. A year later, he set a Boston Bruins rookie record that still stands with 44 goals.*

OTHER AMERICAN JUNIOR LEAGUES

Ranking just below the USHL is the North American Hockey League, which has teams mainly in the central and southwest United States. NAHL players are also eligible for the NCAA and though the caliber of play is lower than that of the USHL, the NHL Draft usually sees a handful of NAHL players selected each year. Below the NAHL are various regional Junior A leagues, as well as Junior B and Junior C leagues.

COLLEGE & HIGH-SCHOOL HOCKEY

McGill University in Montreal played a key role in hockey's formative years of the 1870s and 1880s, but as the sport became professionalized in the early 1900s, more and more players were drawn to the game as a means to escape the farms, factories, and mines. By 1970, Ken Dryden, a promising young NHL goaltender with the Montreal Canadiens, became newsworthy for putting his law-school education ahead of a possible NHL career. University hockey in the United States dates back to the 1890s, but it wasn't until the 1980s, after a US Olympic Team made up of collegiate players won a surprise gold medal, that the National Collegiate Athletic Association (the NCAA) truly became a viable route to the NHL.

THE EARLY YEARS IN CANADA

Though McGill formed its first hockey team in 1877, the first game played between two university hockey teams was played in Kingston, Ontario, between Queen's University and the Royal Military College in 1886. It is a rivalry that continues to this day. The Canadian Intercollegiate Hockey Union was formed on January 7, 1903, with McGill winning the first championship of the three-team league that also included Queen's and the University of Toronto, whose hockey program began in 1891.

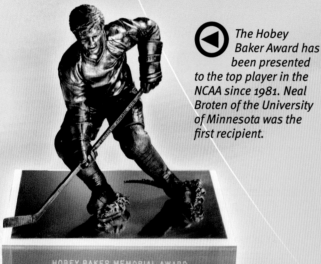

The Hobey Baker Award has been presented to the top player in the NCAA since 1981. Neal Broten of the University of Minnesota was the first recipient.

EARLY YEARS IN THE USA

The first documented hockey game between American universities was played between Yale and Johns Hopkins in Baltimore, Maryland on February 3, 1896, though reports in the *Baltimore Sun* say it drew the biggest crowd of the season, which would indicate games had been played before that date. On January 19, 1898, Brown University defeated Harvard at Boston in a rivalry that is now the oldest continuing hockey series in the United States.

THE FROZEN FOUR

The creation of a true national championship tournament in 1948 spurred the development of NCAA hockey. Dartmouth had been a powerhouse in the early 1940s but lost the first tournament championship to the University of Michigan, which has gone on to win more titles than any other NCAA school. Since 1999, the event has been known as "The Frozen Four" to distinguish it from the final round of the NCAA's annual basketball tournament, known as "The Final Four."

NCAA TO THE NHL

A handful of Canadian-born players who had won hockey scholarships to American universities were among the first NCAA players to reach the NHL. Red Berenson starred at Michigan for three years before joining the Montreal Canadiens in 1962. Lou Nanne played at the University of Minnesota in the early 1960s before joining the Minnesota North Stars at the end of the decade. Goalies Tony Esposito (Michigan Tech) and Ken Dryden (Cornell) both starred in the NCAA as well.

HOBEY BAKER

The first great hockey star from the United States was Hobey Baker. Between 1910 and 1914, he became a legend at Princeton University, leading the Tigers to two intercollegiate championships while also starring at football. He then played amateur hockey in New York City. Baker died in 1918 when he crashed his plane shortly after World War One, but the Hobey Baker Award for the top player in the NCAA is a fitting memorial and ensures his place in history.

SIMPLY PERFECT

Minnesota repeated as national champion in impressive fashion by becoming the first women's hockey team to complete a perfect season with a 6-3 victory over Boston University in 2013. Goaltender Noora Raty, who represented Finland in the 2014 Sochi Games, was named the tournament's Most Outstanding Player as the Golden Gophers finished their 41-game season without a hiccup. She joined United States Olympians Amanda Kessel and Megan Bozek as well as defenseman Milica McMillen and Hannah Brandt on the all-tournament team to boot.

NCAA FIRSTS IN THE NHL DRAFT

The first NCAA player to be selected in the NHL Draft was Michigan Tech center Al Karlander, who was taken by the Detroit Red Wings in 1967. However, 1979 was the first time for an NCAA player to be selected in the first round when the Buffalo Sabres selected University of Minnesota defenseman Mike Ramsey 11th overall. The first NCAA player to be chosen first overall was Michigan State's Joe Murphy, who was picked by the Red Wings in 1986.

◀ Mike Ramsey went from the University of Minnesota to the 1980 US Olympic hockey team before joining the Buffalo Sabres late in the 1979-80 season. He would play 18 seasons in the NHL.

MOST NHL DRAFT SELECTIONS PRODUCED BY NCAA SCHOOLS THROUGH 2013

Michigan 71
Minnesota 69
Boston University 56
Michigan State 49
Wisconsin 49
Michigan Tech 46
Denver 46
North Dakota 40
Boston College 39
Providence 37
Cornell 36

THE STATE OF HOCKEY

Minnesota high schools have been playing hockey in some form since the 1890s. St. Paul Academy iced its first hockey team in 1905 and is still active in the sport to this day. Today, more than 150 Minnesota high schools (and approximately 250 schools in total) have hockey teams, most with boys' and girls' programs. Teams are divided into either A or AA, with each of those two classes divided into eight regional sections.

THE STATE TOURNAMENT

First held in 1945, the games of the Minnesota State High School Tournament now fill the 18,000-seat Xcel Energy Center in St. Paul and attract huge television audiences. The tournament features eight winners of regional tournaments playing off for the state championship at both the A and AA levels. High-school (or prep-school) hockey is popular around New England and in other states as well, but it has become a quasi-religious experience in Minnesota.

MOST NHL DRAFT SELECTIONS PRODUCED BY US HIGH SCHOOLS THROUGH 2013

Cushing Acad. (MA)	22
Edina (MN)	
Shattuck St. Mary's (MN)	21
Northwood Prep. (NY)	19
Belmont Hill (MA)	17
Avon Old Farms (CT)	15
Hill-Murray (MN)	
Catholic Memorial (MA)	16
Deerfield (IL)	15
Hotchkiss (CT)	14
St. Sebastian's (MA)	
Minnetonka (MN)	
Mount St. Charles (RI)	13
Culver Mil. Acad. (IN)	12
Roseau (MN)	
St. John's Prep (MA)	
Culver Mil. Acad (Ind)	

▶ The Buffalo Sabres selected Phil Housley from South St. Paul High School sixth overall in the 1982 NHL Entry Draft. He began his 21-year NHL career in 1982-83.

HIGH-SCHOOL DRAFT HIGHLIGHTS

Every year since 1980, at least two American high-school players, and a high of 69 in 1987, have been selected in the NHL Draft. In 1983, the Minnesota North Stars made Brian Lawton of Mount St. Charles High School in Woonsocket, Rhode Island, the only high-school player to be selected first overall in the draft. First-round picks to go on to NHL stardom include Tom Barrasso, Phil Housley, Jeremy Roenick, and Brian Leetch.

PART VIII NHL CLUBS

From as few as three teams in the early years to the 30 clubs of today, the NHL has grown into a global sports presence, attracting players and fans around the world.

▶ *Chicago captain Jonathan Toews and Washington's Jay Beagle (83) follow the puck during the 2015 Winter Classic at Nationals Park. Troy Brouwer's goal with 12.9 seconds remaining in the third period lifted the Capitals to a 3-2 victory.*

ANAHEIM DUCKS

The city of Anaheim, California, was awarded an NHL expansion franchise (along with South Florida) at the NHL's Board of Governors meeting in December 1992 and began play in 1993–94. The expansion fee was $50 million, of which $25 million in the case of Anaheim went directly to the Los Angeles Kings because of territorial indemnification. Originally owned by the Disney Corporation, the team was named the Mighty Ducks of Anaheim after the successful Disney film. Henry and Susan Samueli purchased the team in the spring of 2005 and renamed it the Anaheim Ducks on June 22, 2006. A year later, Anaheim won the Stanley Cup.

FIRST GAME & FIRST WIN

The Ducks played their first NHL regular-season game on October 8, 1993, hosting the Detroit Red Wings, but losing 7-2. Sean Hill fired the team's first shot on goal at 7:50 of the first period and scored the first goal (on a powerplay) at 4:13 of the second. He also took the team's first penalty (for holding) at 11:31 of the first period. The team's first win came five days later with a 4-3 victory over Edmonton.

◀ *Jonas Hiller didn't let the new surroundings of Dodger Stadium affect his play, making 36 saves in a 3-0 win over Los Angeles on Jan. 25, 2014.*

HILLER HITS HOMER AT DODGER STADIUM

Jonas Hiller turned aside all 36 shots he faced as Anaheim skated to a 3-0 victory over Los Angeles in front of over 54,000 fans at Dodger Stadium on January 25, 2014. The Swiss netminder made himself at home while playing in his first-ever outdoor game on the West Coast, highlighting his performance by denying Anze Kopitar on a penalty shot in the first period. Corey Perry and Matt Beleskey provided an early cushion by scoring in the opening session before Andrew Cogliano sealed the win with an empty-net tally in the third. Hall-of-Famer Wayne Gretzky dropped the ceremonial first puck.

THE FIRST SEASON

Both the Ducks (33-46-5) and the Florida Panthers (33-34-17) posted 33 wins in 1993–94 to set an NHL record for the most victories by an expansion club. The Ducks' 19 wins on the road also established a new league record. Twenty Ducks players set personal highs for most games played and 15 reached new career highs in points. Bob Corkum led the team with 23 goals, while Terry Yake (21 goals, 31 assists) led with 52 points.

▲ *Center Terry Yake spent just one season in Anaheim, but he was the Ducks' top scorer during their inaugural 1993–94 campaign.*

OTHER FIRSTS

Goalie Ron Tugnutt got the victory in the team's first win, but it was teammate Guy Hebert who posted the first shutout, blanking the Maple Leafs 1-0 in Toronto on December 15, 1993. Tim Sweeney got the only goal and it was the first shorthand goal in team history. The first hat trick in Ducks' history came on October 19, 1993 when Terry Yake scored three goals in a 4-2 win over the Rangers.

TEEMU SELANNE: STRONG TO THE FINNISH

Originally acquired in a multi-player deal with Winnipeg on February 7, 1996, Teemu Selanne established club records with 51 goals and 109 points. A year later, he broke his own mark with 52 tallies and – over his two stints with the club – has set records for most seasons, games, goals, assists and points. The veteran Finn recorded 684 goals, putting him at 11th place in NHL history. Selanne also has 1,457 points, good enough for 15th place all-time.

PAUL KARIYA

The Ducks' first pick (fourth overall) in their inaugural Entry Draft in 1993 was Paul Kariya. He made his NHL debut during Anaheim's second season of 1994–95 and became the team's first player to score 50 goals and top 100 points (108) in 1995–96. Kariya also became the first Ducks player to be selected to the NHL's First All-Star Team that year and first to win an NHL award when he received the Lady Byng Trophy for gentlemanly conduct.

▶ *Ryan Getzlaf and Corey Perry have become big stars in Anaheim. In 2010–11, Perry joined Teemu Selanne and Paul Kariya as the only 50-goal scorers in franchise history and became the first Ducks player to win the Hart Trophy as NHL MVP.*

FIRST PLAYOFF APPEARANCE

The Ducks enjoyed their first winning season in their fourth year of 1996–97 with a record of 36-33-13 for 85 points. Paul Kariya and Teemu Selanne were both First-Team All-Stars and Anaheim went 13-3-7 in its last 23 games to make the playoffs for the first time. The Ducks became the seventh team in NHL history to win their inaugural playoff series, defeating Phoenix in seven games before losing to Detroit in the second round.

 Between them, Paul Kariya (#9) and Teemu Selanne hold down nine of the top 10 positions on the Ducks single-season goal-scoring list and eight of the top 10 for points.

FIRST STANLEY CUP FINAL

In his first year as team coach, Mike Babcock led the Ducks to a club record 40 wins and 95 points in 2002–03, a 26-point improvement over the previous season. In the playoffs, Jean-Sebastien Giguere posted three straight shutouts in a sweep of Minnesota in the Western Conference Final and would win the Conn Smythe Trophy as playoff MVP despite the Ducks losing to New Jersey in seven games in the Stanley Cup Finals.

Jean-Sebastien Giguere is the Ducks all-time leader among goaltenders with 206 career victories and 32 shutouts.

FIRST STANLEY CUP VICTORY

Coach Randy Carlyle led the Ducks to new team records with 48 wins and 110 points in 2006–07 en route to the club's first Pacific Division title. In the playoffs, the Ducks defeated Minnesota, Vancouver, and Detroit before downing Ottawa by four games to one in the Stanley Cup Finals. In his first season in Anaheim, Scott Niedermayer, who'd helped New Jersey defeat the Ducks in 2003, won the Conn Smythe Trophy.

GETZLAF: POSTSEASON POWER

Ryan Getzlaf leads by example, and the captain has no problem turning it up a notch in the postseason. The 19th overall pick of the 2003 draft, Getzlaf has recorded a franchise-best 94 points (27 goals, 67 assists) in the playoffs to outdistance even the legendary Teemu Selanne (69 points – 35 goals, 34 assists). Getzlaf continued to add to his total in 2015, notching 18 assists and 20 points – eclipsing the club record in points (18) that he had set in 2009.

COMEBACK KIDS

Anaheim set a league single-season record in 2014-15 by posting 18 victories when trailing at any point of the third period while tying a league mark with 12 wins when losing after 40 minutes. Undaunted, the Ducks routinely found a way to rally - and became the first team to overcome a third-period deficit in three consecutive contests to open their Western Conference first-round series versus Winnipeg as evidence. Anaheim skated to a 4-2 triumph in Game 1 as Corey Perry collected two goals to highlight a four-point performance, tying Joffrey Lupul (2006) and Andy McDonald (2007) for the franchise record.

ARIZONA COYOTES

The Arizona Coyotes began their existence as the Winnipeg Jets in the World Hockey Association. Led by Bobby Hull, the Jets were three-time WHA champions during the League's seven-year existence and were one of four WHA teams admitted to the NHL for the 1979–80 season. At their best during the heyday of the Edmonton Oilers, Winnipeg iced strong teams during the 1980s, but could never get out of their division in the playoffs. The Jets struggled as a small-market club in the 1990s and were sold to new owners, who officially moved the team to Phoenix on July 1, 1996. The franchise began its first season as the Arizona Coyotes in 2014–15.

Oliver Ekman-Larsson provided some scoring punch from the blue line in 2014-15.

IN THE BEGINNING: WHA

The Winnipeg Jets joined the 12-team WHA in 1971 with startup set for the 1972–73 season. Many doubted the rival league would get off the ground, but the WHA proved it meant business on June 27, 1972, when Winnipeg signed Bobby Hull to a 10-year, $2.75 million contract. In 1972–73, Hull finished the first season with 51 goals and 52 assists in 63 games. His 77 goals in 1974–75 set an unofficial pro hockey record at the time.

ROOKIE PRO

Dale Hawerchuk had 45 goals and 58 assists for 103 points as a rookie with the Jets in 1981–82. He was the first 18-year-old (and the first player who came directly to the NHL from junior hockey) to score 100 points as a rookie pro. Hawerchuk would top 100 points again for five straight seasons between 1983–84 and 1987–88, and was the first Jets player to score 50 goals in the NHL, with 53 in 1984–85.

IN THE BEGINNING: NHL

With a 4–2 loss, the Jets opened their first NHL season in Pittsburgh on October 10, 1979. Their first NHL goal came from Morris Lukowich, who would go on to lead the team in scoring in 1979–80 with 35 goals, 39 assists, and 74 points. After going 20-49-11 that first season, the Jets were a woeful 9-57-14 in 1980–81, but their last-place finish allowed them to select Dale Hawerchuk first overall in the 1981 NHL Entry Draft.

EKMAN-LARSSON EXCELS

Oliver Ekman-Larsson scored 23 goals during the 2014-15 season, tying Phil Housley for the franchise record among defensemen. The 23-year-old Swede capped off his campaign in impressive fashion, collecting two goals and an assist in Arizona's 5-3 victory over San Jose on April 4, 2015. "Don't expect me to score 23 goals every year," Ekman-Larsson joked. Housley reached the 23-goal plateau on two occasions, doing so in both 1990-91 and 1991-92 while playing for Winnipeg before the franchise moved to Arizona.

TWO GOALS, TWO RECORDS

On March 2, 1993, Teemu Selanne scored twice for the Winnipeg Jets during a 7-4 loss to the Quebec Nordiques. The two goals gave Selanne 54 for the 1992–93 season, breaking both Dale Hawerchuk's franchise record and Mike Bossy's NHL rookie record. S elanne went on to finish the season with 76 goals and 132 points, winning the Calder Trophy as rookie of the year (which Hawerchuk had also won, back in 1981–82).

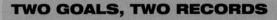

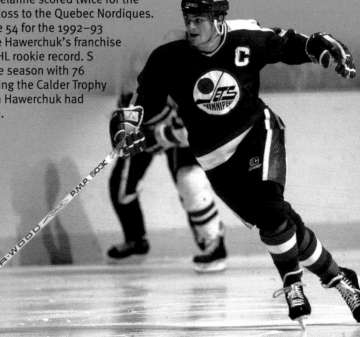

In his nine seasons with the Jets from 1981–82 through 1989–90, Dale Hawerchuk scored 40 goals or more seven times and topped 100 points on six occasions.

DOAN FINALLY DOES IT

Shane Doan accomplished a great deal during his 16-year career with the Winnipeg Jets/Phoenix Coyotes franchise. The one thing missing, however, was a hat trick – something he finally remedied on January 7, 2012. Doan scored in all three periods – with the final tally coming with one second left in the third – in the Coyotes' 5-1 rout of the New York Islanders. Doan, who was playing in his 1,161st NHL contest, would have had a league-record 39 two-goal games in his career if he was just a bit slower on the trigger.

▶ *Shane Doan has seen a great deal since he began his career with the Winnipeg Jets in 1995. On January 7, 2012, Doan finally recorded a hat trick – the first while playing his 16th season.*

IN THE BEGINNING: PHOENIX

The team played its first game as the Phoenix Coyotes in Hartford on October 5, 1996, and lost 1-0. Two nights later, the first win came in a 5-2 victory at Boston. Mike Gartner scored the first goal and finished with a hat trick. The Coyotes' first game in Phoenix was on October 10, 1996, when they beat San Jose 4-1.

BEHIND THE BENCH

Wayne Gretzky, who had a share in club ownership, was named coach of the Coyotes on August 8, 2005. He made his regular-season coaching debut on October 5, 2005 in a 3-2 loss to Vancouver and achieved his first win as head coach when Phoenix beat the Minnesota Wild 2-1 in the Coyotes' home opener on October 8. Gretzky would coach the team for four seasons through 2008–09.

◀ *Keith Tkachuk's 52 goals in 1996–97 were tops in the NHL, making him the first American-born player to lead the League in goals.*

SMITH SCORES A GOAL

Mike Smith became the 11th different goaltender to score a goal when he found the empty net in a 5-2 win against Detroit on October 19, 2013. Smith made one of his 31 saves before dropping the puck to the ice and taking aim at the opposition's goal. He had just enough mustard on his shot as it crossed the goal line with one-tenth of a second remaining. Smith's tally was the first by a goaltender since Martin Brodeur netted his third – two in the regular season and one in the playoffs – in New Jersey's 4-1 triumph over Carolina on March 21, 2013.

GAME-WINNING GOALS

Jeremy Roenick set a franchise record for game-winning goals in a single season with 12 for the Coyotes in 1999–2000. Shane Doan holds the franchise record for game-winning goals: he tied Keith Tkachuk for the team lead with his 40th career game-winning goal versus Dallas on March 5, 2008 and moved into top spot with the game winner against Pittsburgh on October 30, 2008. On January 4, 2011, he collected the 50th game-winning goal of his career versus Columbus.

FRANCHISE LEADERS

Dale Hawerchuk is the Jets/Coyotes franchise leader in goals scored (with 379) and in points (929) in the 713 games he played with the team over nine seasons in Winnipeg. Hawerchuk's 550 assists are second all-time behind Thomas Steen, who had 553. In 2010–11, Shane Doan (who played one season in Winnipeg before the team relocated) tied Teppo Numminen for the most seasons played at 15 and surpassed Numminen's record of 1,098 games played.

ONE-GAME HIGHS

The franchise record for goals in one game is five, set by Willy Lindstrom in a 7-6 Winnipeg win over Philadelphia on March 2, 1982, and matched by Alex Zhamnov in a 7-7 tie against Los Angeles on April 1, 1995. Lindstrom also added an assist in his game to become the first of four players who have had six points in one game, including Dale Hawerchuk (who did it three times), Thomas Steen, and Ed Olcyzk.

BOSTON BRUINS

When the NHL was formed in 1917, the Boston Athletic Association was the defending American Amateur Hockey League champion. Boston was already a hockey hub, and it was appropriate that the Bruins would become the NHL's first American team. Grocery store magnate Charles F. Adams was formally awarded the franchise on November 1, 1924; his family would own the team until 1975. The name Bruins was chosen from the many selections offered by fans, the news media, and club employees, and the team was originally clad in the brown and yellow colors of Adams' grocery-store chain. After a slow start, the Bruins quickly became an NHL power.

EDDIE SHORE

One of hockey's greatest defensemen, Eddie Shore personified the rough and tumble of the game in the 1920s and 1930s. A supremely talented player with a temper to match, he excelled at rushing the puck from end-to-end. Boston had yet to make the playoffs when Shore joined the team in 1926–27, but they were Stanley Cup champions by 1929 and Shore was still the NHL's best defenseman when Boston won the Cup again in 1939.

1929-30

After winning the Stanley Cup in 1929, the Bruins were even better throughout the 1929–30 season. Boston posted a record of 38-5-1 that season for a winning percentage of .875 that has never been matched and would translate to 71-9-2 and 144 points in today's 82-game schedule. The Bruins did not lose two games in a row during the regular season, but in the Stanley Cup Finals the Montreal Canadiens swept them in a best-of-three series.

NO DOUBTING THOMAS

Tim Thomas's parents always had faith in their son. So, in an attempt to fund his plans to attend goalie camp in Canada, the working-class parents sold their $1,500 wedding bands for $200. The transaction enabled Thomas to continue his dream – which spanned through numerous Finnish clubs – until he gained considerable success in the NHL. Thomas became a two-time Vezina Trophy winner as well as the Conn Smythe Trophy recipient during the Bruins' Stanley Cup run in 2011.

IGINLA'S IMPACT

Jarome Iginla scored twice while playing in his 1,300th NHL game as Boston breezed to a 4-1 triumph over Minnesota on March 17, 2014. Playing in his first season with the Bruins, the 36-year-old Iginla scored twice on March 29 to reach the 30-goal plateau for the 12th time in his career as Boston posted a 4-2 victory over Washington and clinched the Atlantic Division title. With 560 career goals, Iginla pulled into a tie with Guy Lafleur for 24th place on the NHL's all-time goals list.

▼ *Before Tim Thomas secured a Stanley Cup ring, his parents sold their wedding bands just so he could attend a goalie camp.*

ART ROSS

A star player during the 1900s and 1910s, Art Ross was hired as coach and general manager of the Bruins for their first season of 1924–25. Ross quickly built Boston into a powerhouse, winning 10 division titles and the Stanley Cup three times by 1941. On and off, he coached the team until 1945 and served as general manager until 1954. He also improved the design of the pucks and goal nets used in the NHL.

THE KRAUT LINE

Childhood friends from the Kitchener, Ontario area, where there is a strong German heritage, center Milt Schmidt and wingers Woody Dumart and Bobby Bauer were teamed in Boston for the first time on March 21, 1937. The high-scoring trio quickly became known as the Kraut Line and helped the Bruins win the Stanley Cup in 1939 and 1941 before all three joined the Royal Canadian Air Force for military service during World War Two.

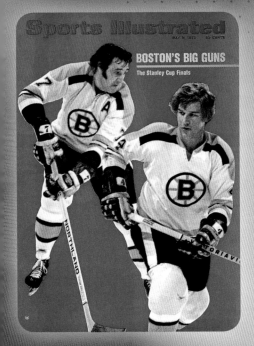

ORR & ESPO END THE HARD TIMES

The Bruins struggled in the 1960s, missing the playoffs eight years in a row from 1959–60 through to 1966–67. Bobby Orr's arrival in 1966 signaled the beginning of better times. Another key moment came on May 15, 1967 when the Bruins acquired Phil Esposito, Ken Hodge, and Fred Stanfield in a one-sided six-player swap with Chicago. After NHL expansion, Orr and Esposito combined to rewrite the record book and lead the Bruins back to greatness.

◀ *Phil Esposito and Bobby Orr led the Bruins to Stanley Cup championships in 1970 and 1972. The Bruins remained a top team for decades but did not win the Stanley Cup again until 2011.*

BRUINS WHO LED THE NHL IN SCORING

Name	Season	GP	G	A	Pts
Cooney Weiland	1929–30	44	43	30	73
Milt Schmidt	1939–40	48	22	21	43
Bill Cowley	1940–41	46	17	45	62
Herb Cain	1943–44	48	36	46	82
Phil Esposito	1968–69	74	49	77	126
Bobby Orr	1969–70	76	33	87	120
Phil Esposito	1970–71	78	76	76	152
Phil Esposito	1971–72	76	66	67	133
Phil Esposito	1972–73	78	55	75	130
Phil Esposito	1973–74	78	68	77	145
Bobby Orr	1974–75	80	46	89	135

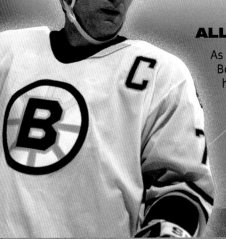

◀ *With Raymond Bourque following after Eddie Shore and Bobby Orr, the Bruins boast three of the greatest defensemen in NHL history.*

ALL-AROUND EXCELLENCE

As a rookie in 1979–80, defenseman Raymond Bourque became the first non-goaltender in NHL history to win the Calder Trophy as Rookie of the Year and be named to the First All-Star Team in the same season. Bourque went on to play 21 years with the Bruins; he won the Norris Trophy as the NHL's best defenseman five times and led Boston in scoring five times. He is the Bruins' all-time leader in games played (1,518), assists (1,111), and points (1,506).

1970–71

After winning the Stanley Cup in 1970, the Bruins followed up with a record-breaking season in 1970–71. Phil Esposito, Bobby Orr, and John Bucyk all established individual records while the club set 37 team records, including NHL highs for most wins (57), most points (121), and most goals (399). In the playoffs, however, red-hot rookie goaltender Ken Dryden and the Montreal Canadiens upset Boston in the first round. A year later, the Bruins bounced back to win the Stanley Cup again.

CHEEVERS' MASK

During the 1970s, Gerry Cheevers was a great clutch goaltender in the NHL, helping Boston win the Stanley Cup in 1970 and 1972, and reach the Finals again in 1977 and 1978. He also wore one of the most distinctive masks in hockey history with its pattern of stitches. Around 1966, Boston trainer John "Frosty" Forristall began painting stitch marks on the mask to indicate stitches that might have been after a shot hit Cheevers' mask in practice.

▲ *Other goalies had gaudier statistics, but Gerry Cheevers could be counted on to make the big save when it mattered most.*

RASK UP TO THE TASK

Tuukka Rask admitted that he could've played in more games after winning the Vezina Trophy at the conclusion of the 2013–14 season. The Finn got his wish the following campaign, as he appeared in 12 more contests – 70 in all – to tie the franchise record. Rask posted a 34-21-13 mark with a 2.30 goals-against average during his 70 appearances, which matched Jack Gelineau (1950–51), Jim Henry (1951–52, 1952–53, 1953–54) and Eddie Johnston (1963–64) for the most in team history.

BUFFALO SABRES

After missing out on an expansion team in 1967, Buffalo was awarded a club (along with the Vancouver Canucks) when the NHL added two more teams in 1970. The name "Sabres" was selected in a contest and a lucky spin of the wheel gave the team first choice in the 1970 NHL Draft. Buffalo selected Gilbert Perreault, a top prospect who immediately became the team's best player. He won the Calder Trophy in 1970–71 and would spend his entire 17-year career with the Sabres. The offense was later led by Pat LaFontaine and Alexander Mogilny, while Dominik Hasek would give the Sabres one of the greatest goalies in NHL history.

FAST STARTERS

After missing the playoffs in their first two seasons, the Sabres reached the postseason for the first time in 1972–73. They missed again in the following year but Buffalo had a breakout season in 1974–75, topping its division with a record of 49-16-15 for 113 points to tie Montreal and Philadelphia for the most points in the NHL's overall standings. The Sabres eliminated the Canadiens in the semifinals but lost to the Flyers in the Stanley Cup Final.

THE FRENCH CONNECTION

The Sabres top line of Gilbert Perreault centering Rick Martin and Rene Robert starred from 1972 to 1979. Dubbed "The French Connection" after their Quebec backgrounds and the hit movie of the same name, they were the greatest line in Sabres' history. Perreault remains the franchise leader in most major offensive categories, while Martin was the first Sabre to score 50 goals in a season in 1973–74 and Robert was first to record 100 points in 1974–75.

The trio of Gil Perreault (left), Rick Martin, and Rene Robert (#14) gave Buffalo one of the NHL's most exciting lines of the 1970s.

ALL-TIME OFFENSIVE LEADERS

Games:	Gilbert Perreault, 1,191
Goals:	Gilbert Perreault, 512
Assists:	Gilbert Perreault, 814
Points:	Gilbert Perreault, 1,326
Penalty Minutes:	Rob Ray, 3,189
Game-Winning Goals:	Gilbert Perreault, 81
Powerplay Goals:	Dave Andreychuk, 161
Shorthand Goals:	Craig Ramsay, 27
Hat Tricks:	Rick Martin, 21

Pat LaFontaine had 53 goals for the Sabres in 1992–93 and helped Alexander Mogilny score 76 that season.

A FLURRY OF 50S

Rick Martin had 49 goals heading into the last game of the season in 1973–74. He scored three against St. Louis to reach 52 for the year and then scored 52 again in 1974–75. Heading into the last game of the season in 1975–76, Martin once again had 49 goals but was held scoreless by the Toronto Maple Leafs. However, Danny Gare, who had 47 goals, scored three that night against Gord McRae to reach 50.

SINGLE-SEASON OFFENSIVE LEADERS

Goals:	76, Alexander Mogilny in 1992–93
Assists:	95, Pat LaFontaine in 1992–93
Points:	148, Pat LaFontaine in 1992–93
Penalty Minutes:	354, Rob Ray in 1991–92
Game-Winning Goals:	11, Danny Gare in 1979–80
	11, Alexander Mogilny in 1992–93
Powerplay Goals:	28, Dave Andreychuk in 1991–92
Shorthand Goals:	8, Don Luce in 1974–75
Plus-Minus:	+61, Don Luce in 1974–75
Hat Tricks:	7, Rick Martin in 1975–76
	7, Alexander Mogilny in 1992–93

STARRY NIGHT

Buffalo hosted the NHL All-Star Game for the only time on January 24, 1978 when stars from the Wales Conference faced the stars from the Campbell Conference at the Memorial Auditorium. With 1:39 remaining, the Sabres' Rick Martin scored for the Wales to tie the contest at 2-2 and send the game into overtime for the first time in All-Star history. At 3:55 of the extra session, Gilbert Perreault scored to give the Wales a 3-2 victory.

MAY DAY!

The Sabres had not won a postseason series since 1983 when they opened the 1993 playoffs against a strong Boston Bruins club that had finished 23 points ahead of them (109-86) in the standings. But Buffalo won the first three games, including two in overtime, and took Boston to overtime again in game four. Brad May evaded Raymond Bourque and then beat goalie Andy Moog at 4:48 of overtime to give the Sabres a surprising sweep.

 Brad May only scored four goals in 84 career playoff games, but no one who has ever heard the play-by-play call will forget his series winner for the Sabres in 1993.

DOMINATING PERFORMANCE

Dominik Hasek, who had been named top player in Czechoslovakia in 1987, 1989, and 1990, played parts of two seasons in Chicago before joining the Sabres in 1992. He became Buffalo's number-one goaltender in 1993–94. "The Dominator" responded by recording a 1.95 goal-against average, the lowest mark seen in the NHL since Bernie Parent's 1.89 in 1973–74.

WINNING BY LOSING?

A sizable contingent of fans at First Niagara Center cheered when Sam Gagner scored 56 seconds into overtime, sending visiting Arizona to a 4-3 victory over Buffalo on March 27, 2015. With the Sabres going nowhere fast, the fans were very vocal about turning their attention to next season.

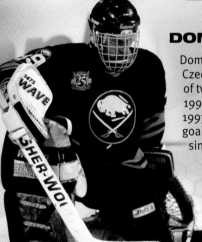

DOMINATING THE HARDWARE

Dominik Hasek won the Vezina Trophy as the NHL's best goalie six times in eight seasons between 1993–94 and 2000–01. His Hart Trophy wins of 1996–97 and 1997–98 make him the only goalie in NHL history with back-to-back MVP awards. Hasek set team records with 13 shutouts in 1997–98 and with a 1.87 goals-against average and .937 save percentage in 1998–99. He also led the Sabres to their second appearance in the Stanley Cup Finals in 1999.

 Dominik Hasek was said to have "a slinky for a spine." His style was unorthodox, but there was no arguing with the results.

 Ryan Miller has provided quite the presence in net for both the Buffalo Sabres and the United States Olympic team.

GOOD COMPANY

A former Sabres captain who spent nine-plus years of his 12-year playing career in Buffalo, Lindy Ruff was named coach of the Sabres on July 21, 1997 and has become far and away the most successful coach in franchise history. On January 6, 2011, Ruff became the 16th coach in NHL history to win 500 games and joined Toe Blake as the only two coaches to win all their games with one team.

RYAN'S GOODBYE

Ryan Miller made a career out of fighting off every shot that came his way. On February 28, 2014, the goaltender was tasked with another assignment – trying to fend off the tears after learning he was traded from the team that drafted him nearly 15 years ago. "I kind of figured this is what would happen," Miller said shortly after learning he was traded as part of a five-player deal from cellar-dwelling Buffalo to Stanley Cup contender St. Louis. Miller exited the Sabres as the franchise's leader with 284 victories and 540 games played.

CALGARY FLAMES

Originally entering the NHL (along with the New York Islanders) as the Atlanta Flames in 1972–73, the team officially moved to Calgary on June 24, 1980. Though generally coming out on the losing end in the "Battle of Alberta" in the 1980s, the Flames upset the Edmonton Oilers in the 1986 Smythe Division Final and went on to play for the Stanley Cup for the first time. In 1989, the Flames became the first team ever to beat the Montreal Canadiens on Forum ice to win the Stanley Cup. Another trip to the Finals in 2004 thrilled fans all across Canada, but the Flames lost to the Tampa Bay Lightning in seven games.

MAGIC MAN

Sweden's Kent Nilsson played two seasons with the Winnipeg Jets in the World Hockey Association and spent the 1979–80 season with the Atlanta Flames before moving to Calgary. In 1980–81, the slick center with the magic moves scored 49 goals; he also finished second in the NHL behind Wayne Gretzky with 82 assists and third behind Gretzky and Marcel Dionne with 131 points. Nilsson's 82 assists and 131 points both remain Flames single-season highs.

MOUSTACHE MAN

Early on in their second season of 1981–82, the Flames acquired Lanny McDonald from the Colorado Rockies. In his first full season in Calgary (1982–83), McDonald scored 66 goals to set a franchise record. He spent the rest of his career in Calgary, retiring in 1989 with 500 goals and 506 assists for 1,006 points in 1,111 games. McDonald also scored the go-ahead goal for the Flames in the decisive game of the 1989 Stanley Cup Finals.

▲ *Instantly recognizable by his bushy red moustache, Lanny McDonald was a big star who remains one of the most popular players in Flames history.*

▼ *With 314 goals for Calgary, Joe Nieuwendyk is one of only three Flames (along with Jarome Iginla and Theo Fleury) to top 300 goals with the team.*

'JOHNNY HOCKEY'

Standing 5-foot-9 and 150 pounds, Johnny Gaudreau does not exactly cut an imposing figure. The 21-year-old Gaudreau had little difficulty cutting opponents down to size on the ice, however, collecting 24 goals and 40 assists to tie Ottawa's Mark Stone for the most points among rookies during the 2014-15 season. A former Hobey Baker Award winner at Boston College, Gaudreau scored three goals and set up three others in the final five games of the season to send the Flames back to the playoffs for the first time since the 2008-09 campaign.

▲ *Kent Nilsson topped the 100-point mark twice during his five seasons in Calgary and just missed in 1985–86 when he had 99 points.*

SINGLE-GAME STANDARDS

On January 11, 1989, Joe Nieuwendyk set a club record with five goals in an 8-3 win over the Winnipeg Jets. The Flames' single-game record for points is seven, set by Sergei Makarov with two goals and five assists in a 10-4 win over Edmonton on February 25, 1990. The team record for assists in one game is six: it was set by Guy Chouinard on February 25, 1981 and matched by Gary Suter on April 4, 1986.

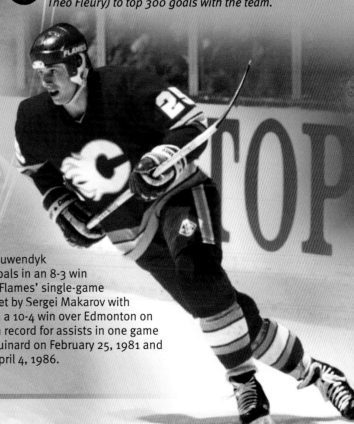

SINGLE-GAME TEAM RECORDS

The Flames' team record for goals in a game is 13 in a 13-1 victory over San Jose on February 19, 1993. Also a record is the 12-goal margin of victory, though this is closely followed by an 11-0 victory over the Colorado Rockies on April 1, 1982, which is the team's biggest win by shutout. The largest loss by shutout was an 11-0 defeat by Vancouver on March 1, 1992.

50 & 100

Eight different Flames (including Joe Nieuwendyk and Jarome Iginla twice) have scored 50 goals, and eight (including Kent Nilsson and Theo Fleury twice) have produced 100 points, but only two players in team history have reached both milestones in the same season. The first was Joe Mullen, who had 51 goals and 59 assists for 110 points in 1988–89. Second was Fleury, who had 51 goals and 53 assists for 104 points in 1990–91.

The Flames' all-time scoring leader, Jarome Iginla reached the 1,000-point plateau with his second goal, and third point of the night, in a 3-2 win over St. Louis on April 1, 2011.

THE PRESIDENTS' TROPHY

The Flames have twice-posted the NHL's best record in the regular season: the first time was in 1987–88 when Calgary went 48-23-9 for 105 points and edged Montreal by two points in the overall standings. One of the highest totals in NHL history, the Flames' 397 goals that season is also a club record. In 1988–89 Calgary set club records with 54 wins (54-17-9) and 117 points, once again edging out Montreal by two points.

AL-AROUND EXCELLENCE

Calgary's first-round draft choice (15th overall) in 1981, Al MacInnis was allowed to develop slowly: he didn't spend a full season in the NHL until 1984–85, but his booming slapshot quickly made him one of the League's best offensive defensemen. MacInnis was a key contributor to Calgary's Stanley Cup win in 1989 and he topped 100 points in 1990–91 with 28 goals and 75 assists. His 609 assists in 13 years with the Flames remains a franchise record.

JAROME NETS 500TH

Aesthetically pleasing it was not, but Jarome Iginla wasn't making any apologies after scoring his 500th career goal on January 7, 2012. The Flames captain became the 42nd player in NHL history to reach the milestone after his intended centering feed caromed off the skates of a pair of Minnesota Wild defenders and past goaltender Niklas Backstrom midway during the third period. Iginla became the 15th player to accomplish the feat with one team.

Quiet by nature, Miikka Kiprusoff has made quite the statement for Calgary. The talented Finn secured his 300th career win in February 2012.

QUITE THE GOAL-KIPPER

Miikka Kiprusoff was a virtual unknown when Calgary acquired him from San Jose in 2003. His 1.69 goals-against average in 2003–04 was the NHL's lowest since 1939–40 and he led the team on a surprising run to the Stanley Cup Finals. After moving past Mike Vernon for the franchise's all-time lead in wins to start the 2011–12 season, the Finn became the 27th goaltender in NHL history to record 300 wins on February 8, 2012. He denied Joe Pavelski and Logan Couture late in the third period to preserve a 4-3 win over the Sharks.

FOUR TIMES 40

Joe Nieuwendyk became the second rookie in NHL history to score 50 goals with 51 for the Flames in 1987–88. Hakan Loob also scored 50 for Calgary that year, while Mike Bullard came close with 48 and Joe Mullen scored 40. The only other team in NHL history to produce four 40-goal scorers in the same season are the Edmonton Oilers, where four teammates topped 40 four times during the 1980s.

RUSSELL LAYS IT ON THE LINE

Defenseman Kris Russell wasn't shy about putting his body in harm's way, blocking an NHL-record 283 shots during the 2014-15 season. The 5-foot-10, 173-pounder eclipsed the mark of 273 by then-Ottawa blue-liner Anton Volchenkov (2006-07) by denying two attempts in a 4-1 loss to St. Louis on April 2. Russell set a league record by blocking a staggering 15 shots in the Flames' 4-3 shootout win over Boston on March 5. "I would rather block a shot than have a bull chase me," Russell later told CBC.

CAROLINA HURRICANES

The Carolina Hurricanes began as the New England Whalers, one of the most successful franchises in the World Hockey Association. They were one of four WHA teams to enter the NHL in 1979–80, when they became known as the Hartford Whalers. The team transferred from Hartford to North Carolina on June 25, 1997, playing first in Greensboro before finally opening a brand-new arena in Raleigh on October 29, 1999. In 2002, the Hurricanes reached the Stanley Cup Final for the first time in franchise history, but were beaten by the Detroit Red Wings. Carolina won the Cup in 2006, when it defeated the Edmonton Oilers in a seven-game series.

ALL-TIME GREATS

During their WHA existence, the Whalers boasted several luminaries, including Dave Keon and Gordie Howe. Howe returned to the NHL at the age of 51 in 1979–80 as a member of the Whalers. He finished his 32nd season and 26th in the NHL with 15 goals, including his 800th career regular-season tally. That same year, the Whalers traded for another Hall of Famer, Bobby Hull, and he and Howe played on the same line for nine games.

IN THE BEGINNING: WHA

Former Montreal Canadiens center Larry Pleau was the first Whaler signed in the WHA, followed by Brad Selwood, Rick Ley, and Jim Dorey of the Toronto Maple Leafs. On July 27, 1972, the Whalers signed former Boston Bruins defenseman Ted Green as captain. On October 12, 1972, the Whalers played their first home game at Boston Garden before a crowd of 14,442, defeating the Philadelphia Blazers 4-3. The Whalers went on to win the WHA's Avco World Trophy.

▶ *Ron Francis starred in the NHL from the age of 18 until he reached 41. He spent 14 full seasons, and parts of two others, with the Hurricanes/ Whalers franchise.*

IN THE BEGINNING: NHL

The Whalers played their first NHL regular-season game at Minnesota on October 11, 1979. The North Stars won 4-1 with Gordie Roberts (who was named after Gordie Howe) scoring the first Whalers NHL goal at 14:15 of the third period. Hartford's record of 27-34-19 for 73 points in 80 games was enough to qualify for the playoffs as the 14th of 16 teams, but the Whalers were swept in three straight by Montreal in a best-of-five series.

STOUGHTON SETS THE STANDARD

Blaine Stoughton had seen limited success in three NHL seasons before a breakout year in the WHA in 1976–77. Returning to the NHL with Hartford in 1979–80, Stoughton tied the Sabres' Danny Gare and the Kings' Charlie Simmer for the NHL lead with 56 goals that season, which remains a Whalers/ Hurricanes single-season high. Stoughton is the only player in the team's NHL history to score 50 goals, which he did again when he scored 52 times in 1981–82.

100-POINT SCORERS

Mike Rogers led the team in scoring with 105 points (44 goals, 61 assists) in 1979–80 and in 1980–81 had 105 again (40, 65). No one else in franchise history has bettered that mark, with only Ron Francis (101 points in 1989–90) and Eric Staal (100 in 2005–06) reaching the century mark. John Cullen had 110 points in 1990–91, but he collected 94 of them with the Penguins that season before being traded to Hartford.

RON FRANCIS

Hartford selected Ron Francis fourth overall in the 1981 NHL Entry Draft and he joined the team as an 18-year-old in 1981–82. After 10 seasons with the Whalers, he spent seven full years in Pittsburgh before rejoining his original franchise in 1998 when he signed with Carolina as a free agent. Overall in his 23-year career, Francis ranks second to Wayne Gretzky in NHL history with 1,249 assists and fourth in points with 1,798.

ALL-TIME OFFENSIVE LEADERS

Seasons:	Ron Francis, 16
Games:	Ron Francis, 1,186
Goals:	Ron Francis, 382
Assists:	Ron Francis, 793
Points:	Ron Francis, 1,175
Penalty Minutes:	Kevin Dineen, 1,439

SINGLE-GAME GOALS

The franchise record of four goals in a single game has been achieved three times: twice in Hartford and once in Carolina. Jordy Douglas scored four for Hartford in a 5-3 win over the New York Islanders on February 3, 1980, while Ron Francis scored four in an 11-0 Whalers romp over the Oilers on February 12, 1984. Eric Staal scored four for the Hurricanes in a 9-3 win over Tampa Bay on March 7, 2009.

STANLEY CUP SCORERS

Eric Staal was Carolina's playoff scoring leader in the Stanley Cup-winning spring of 2006, collecting points in 20 of 25 postseason games and leading the NHL with 19 assists and 28 points. Rod Brind'Amour led the team with 12 goals in the postseason. In game seven of the Finals against Edmonton, Aaron Ward and Frantisek Kaberle gave Carolina a 2-0 lead before Justin Williams clinched a 3-1 victory with an empty-net goal with 1:01 remaining.

Jared Staal, top, began his NHL career by joining brothers Jordan (11) and Eric to start the game against the New York Rangers on April 26, 2013.

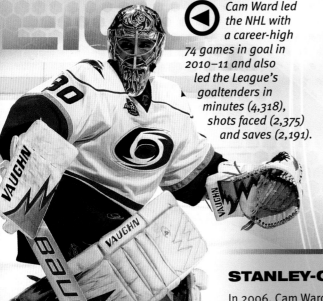

Cam Ward led the NHL with a career-high 74 games in goal in 2010–11 and also led the League's goaltenders in minutes (4,318), shots faced (2,375) and saves (2,191).

SINGLE-SEASON OFFENSIVE LEADERS

Goals:	56, Blaine Stoughton in 1979–80 (Hartford)
	45, Eric Staal in 2005–06 (Carolina)
Assists:	69, Ron Francis in 1989–90 (Hartford)
	56, Rod Brind'Amour in 2006–07 (Carolina)
Points:	105, Mike Rogers in 1979–80, 1980–81 (Hartford)
	100, Eric Staal in 2005–06 (Carolina)
Penalty Minutes:	358, Torrie Robertson in 1985–86 (Hartford)
	204, Stu Grimson in 2003–04 (Carolina)

STAAL IN THE FAMILY

Carolina enjoyed a family affair as 22-year-old Jared Staal made his NHL debut while starting on the same line with brothers Eric and Jordan on April 26, 2013. "That's something they're going to remember the rest of their lives," Hurricanes coach Kirk Muller said after the contest. Ironically, Carolina's opponent was the New York Rangers, but brother Marc Staal was unable to play for them due to an eye injury.

CAM COMES THROUGH IN 500TH GAME

Cam Ward has seen a lot during his career with Carolina, from winning the Conn Smythe Trophy in 2006 to even being credited with scoring a goal against New Jersey in 2011. Ward provided another highlight by emerging victorious in his 500th career appearance with a 4-1 victory over Philadelphia on February 24, 2015. The veteran netminder made 23 saves in the win to become the fourth active goaltender to reach the 500-game milestone, joining Henrik Lundqvist of the New York Rangers, Marc-Andre Fleury of Pittsburgh and Ryan Miller of Vancouver.

STANLEY-CUP STOPPER

In 2006, Cam Ward became the first rookie goalie since Patrick Roy 20 years earlier to lead his team to a Stanley Cup victory. He also joined Roy (1986), Ron Hextall (1987), and Ken Dryden (1971) as rookie goalies to win the Conn Smythe Trophy as playoff MVP. Since his rookie season, Ward has gone on to break most of the franchise's all-time goaltending records and set a single-season mark of 39 wins in 2008–09.

CHICAGO BLACKHAWKS

Two ownership groups were looking to land an NHL franchise for Chicago when coffee baron Major Frederic McLaughlin's group was officially awarded the team on September 25, 1926. As the story goes, the Major had belonged to the 86th Blackhawk Division of the American army during World War One and named his team in its honor (though it was usually spelled as two words – Black Hawks – until 1985–86). In its first 12 years, the team won the Stanley Cup twice, but there would be hard times ahead until the 1960s when Bobby Hull and Stan Mikita led them to success ... much as Jonathan Toews and Patrick Kane did more than 40 years later, with three titles in six seasons.

▶ *Jonathan Toews battles both Pittsburgh defenseman Rob Scuderi and the snow in their game at Soldier Field.*

HOW THEY STARTED

Many of the players who made up Chicago's original lineup of 1926–27 had been acquired from the Portland Rosebuds of Western Hockey League, including coach Pete Muldoon and the team's first big star, Dick Irvin. Although the Blackhawks made the playoffs in their first season, owner Frederic McLaughlin fired Pete Muldoon after the season and would continue to burn through coaches at an alarming rate during his 18 years of ownership.

GARDING THE GOAL

Though the early era Blackhawks were very poor on offense, goalie Charlie Gardiner kept them competitive. Gardiner joined the team in its second season of 1927–28. He led the NHL with 12 shutouts in 1930–31 and helped Chicago reach the Stanley Cup Final for the first time. In 1931–32, Gardiner won the Vezina Trophy and repeated his success in 1933–34 when his 1.63 goals-against average set a team record that has never been beaten.

MULDOON'S CURSE

Though just a myth (sportswriter Jim Coleman who wrote all about it in 1943 would later admit to making it up), Pete Muldoon was said to have cursed the Blackhawks, preventing the club from ever finishing in first place after he was fired in 1927. Chicago would win the Stanley Cup in 1934, 1938, and 1961, but despite several close calls, they would not finish first in the regular-season standings until 1966–67.

CRAWFORD IN CONTROL

Corey Crawford received his second William M. Jennings Trophy in three seasons when he joined Montreal's Carey Price in winning the award in 2015. Crawford, who also shared the honor in 2013 with then-teammate Ray Emery, put forth one of his best seasons to date – posting a 32-20-5 record with a 2.27 goals-against average and .924 save percentage. He joined Price by playing in at least 25 games for their respective teams, which tied for an NHL low in allowing 189 goals.

DARLING DEBUT

Scott Darling didn't miss a step in relief of Corey Crawford, turning aside all 42 shots he faced in his playoff debut to lead Chicago to a 4-3 win over Nashville in double overtime of Game 1 of their 2015 Western Conference first-round series. The 26-year-old Darling logged 67:44 of ice time in the longest relief appearance in a playoff game without yielding a goal, according to the Elias Sports Bureau. Darling made the most of his first postseason start by finishing with 35 saves in a 4-2 win over the Predators in Game 3 before turning aside 50 shots in Chicago's 3-2 victory in triple overtime in Game 4.

OTHER GOALTENDING RECORDS

Ed Belfour set a franchise high with 43 wins for Chicago as a rookie in 1990–91. Tony Esposito's 15 shutouts as a rookie in 1969–70 are also a franchise record, as are his career totals of 413 wins and 74 shutouts. Starting with two seasons in Detroit and then five-plus years in Chicago, Glenn Hall played 502 consecutive complete games in goal from 1955 through November 7, 1962, setting one of hockey's most incredible records.

THE MADHOUSE ON MADISON

For their first three seasons, the Blackhawks played at the 6,000-seat Chicago Coliseum. The Chicago Stadium was completed in March of 1929 and the Blackhawks played their first game there on December 15, 1929. It was their home until the United Center opened on January 25, 1995. The Stadium held approximately 18,000 people but was sometimes filled with over 20,000. Noise from the crowd and the huge pipe organ made the Chicago Stadium the NHL's loudest rink.

TOEWS SOLDIERS ON

Jonathan Toews is used to a winter wonderland – after all, he is from Winnipeg, Manitoba. With continual snow flurries wreaking havoc on the ice, the captain collected two goals and an assist to lead the Blackhawks to a 5-1 victory over Pittsburgh in front of nearly 63,000 fans at an outdoor game at Soldier Field on March 1, 2014. After setting up Patrick Sharp for the game's first goal, Toews doubled the advantage with a backhander between the pads of Marc-Andre Fleury midway through the second before capping the scoring with 2:08 to play. The contest represented the first on NHL ice between Toews and superstar Sidney Crosby.

SINGLE-SEASON POINTS LEADERS

Points	Player
131	Denis Savard, 1987–88 (44G-87A in 80 GP)
121	Denis Savard, 1982–83 (35G-86A in 78 GP)
119	Denis Savard, 1981–82 (32G-87A in 80 GP)
116	Denis Savard, 1985–86 (47G-69A in 80 GP)
107	Bobby Hull, 1968–69 (58G-49A in 74 GP)
	Jeremy Roenick, 1992–93 (50G-57A in 84 GP)
	Jeremy Roenick, 1993–94 (46G-61A in 84 GP)
105	Denis Savard, 1984–85 (38G-67A in 79 GP)
103	Jeremy Roenick, 1991–92 (53G-50A in 80 GP)
101	Steve Larmer, 1990–91 (44G-57A in 80 GP)

SINGLE-SEASON GOAL-SCORING LEADERS

Goals	Player
58	Bobby Hull, 1968–69 (74 GP)
54	Bobby Hull, 1965–66 (65 GP)
	Al Secord, 1982–83 (80 GP)
53	Jeremy Roenick, 1991–92 (80 GP)
52	Bobby Hull, 1966–67 (66 GP)
50	Bobby Hull, 1961–62 (70 GP)
	Bobby Hull, 1971–72 (78 GP)
	Jeremy Roenick, 1992–93 (84 GP)

Bobby Hull scored his 200th career goal and Stan Mikita got his 100th in a 6-2 win over the New York Rangers on December 11, 1963.

COACH Q: 700 CLUB

Joel Quenneville continued his ascent up the coaching ranks by becoming the third person in NHL history to win 700 games as the Blackhawks breezed to a 4-0 triumph over St. Louis on March 19, 2014. Quenneville trails only Chicago senior adviser of hockey operations Scotty Bowman (1,244) and Al Arbour (782). The victory over the Blues was a special one for Quenneville, who guided that team from 1996 to 2004 – and won the Jack Adams Trophy as the coach of the year in 2000.

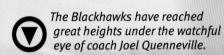

The Blackhawks have reached great heights under the watchful eye of coach Joel Quenneville.

HULL, MIKITA ... & MULVEY

Bobby Hull scored a franchise record 604 goals during his 15 seasons in Chicago. Stan Mikita established club highs in seasons (22), games (1,394), assists (926), and points (1,467). Hull is also the franchise leader in hat tricks with 28, which includes 24 three-goal games and four four-goal games. The only player in Chicago history to score five goals in a game is Grant Mulvey in a 9-5 win over St. Louis on February 3, 1982.

Denis Savard was a slick stickhandler who piled up points during his 10 seasons in Chicago.

Duncan Keith, Jonathan Toews, and Patrick Kane (88) celebrate a Chicago goal. All three players were key reasons why the Blackhawks won their first Stanley Cup since 1961 in 2010.

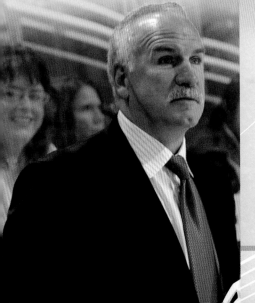

KANE, KEITH, & TOEWS

Duncan Keith and right-winger Patrick Kane became the first Chicago players since Chris Chelios in 1996 to be named to the NHL's First All-Star Team in 2010. For leading Chicago to the Stanley Cup for the first time in 49 years, Jonathan Toews became the first Blackhawks player to win the Conn Smythe Trophy as playoff MVP and tied Denis Savard for the club record of 29 postseason points with seven goals and 22 assists.

COLORADO AVALANCHE

Before relocating to Denver on June 21, 1995, the Colorado Avalanche had been the Quebec Nordiques for 23 seasons – seven in the World Hockey Association and 16 after entering the NHL in 1979–80. The Nordiques enjoyed rapid improvement in the 1980s with stars like Peter Stastny and Michel Goulet, before falling on hard times in the 1990s but were able to rebuild with draft picks. In their very first season in Colorado, Joe Sakic and Peter Forsberg led the team to the Stanley Cup. Beginning with their final season in Quebec and stretching through 2002–03, the Nordiques/Avalanche won a record nine consecutive division titles and were Stanley Cup champions again in 2001.

▲ Paul Stastny, left, and the Avalanche were quick to welcome Nathan MacKinnon, who was the top overall pick of the 2013 draft. Colorado won the Central Division title the following season.

BATTLE OF QUEBEC

The arrival of the Quebec Nordiques in the NHL in 1979 gave the Montreal Canadiens their first local rival since the Montreal Maroons folded in 1938. "The Battle of Quebec" was fierce – on the ice, in the newspapers, and in family living rooms. A 1982 playoff upset by the Nordiques took the battle to a new level and led to the infamous "Good Friday Brawl" on April 20, 1984. Eleven players were tossed from that game.

PETER THE GREAT

After joining the Nordiques in 1980–81 along with his brother Anton (Marian would arrive the following season), Peter Stastny went on to become one of the most dominant offensive players in hockey. In fact, only Wayne Gretzky had more points in the 1980s (1980–81 through 1989–90) than the 1,059 collected by Stastny. He topped 100 points seven times in the decade, including a franchise record 139 points (46 goals, 93 assists) in 1981–82.

LANDESKOG MAKES HIS MARK

Gabriel Landeskog became the first Colorado player since Chris Drury to win the Calder Trophy after collecting 22 goals and 30 assists during his rookie season in 2011–12. Landeskog also inadvertently established a craze called "Landeskoging." The 19-year-old, who scored the overtime winner against Anaheim on March 12, had been drained by a bout with the flu. As a result, he fell face-first to the ice with his fists clenched near his head after the goal – causing many to mimic his actions.

GOAL-SCORING LEADERS

Though Michel Goulet holds the franchise's top three positions among the single-season leaders in goals with 57 (1982–83), 56 (1983–84), and 55 (1984–85), Milan Hejduk is the only player in franchise history to lead the NHL in goals. Hejduk won the Maurice "Rocket" Richard Trophy with 50 goals in 2002–03. Other 50-goal scorers in franchise history are: Goulet (53 in 1985–86), Joe Sakic (54 in 2000–01; 51 in 1995–96), and Jacques Richard (52 in 1980–81).

▶ Joe Sakic spent his entire 20-year career with the Nordiques/Avalanche franchise. He finished among the NHL's top-10 scorers ten times and his 1,641 career points rank him eighth in League history.

TOP POINTS PRODUCERS

Six different players in franchise history have combined to produce 21 100-point seasons for the Nordiques and/or Avalanche: Peter Stastny (seven times), Joe Sakic (six times), Michel Goulet (four times), Peter Forsberg (twice), Jacques Richard, and Mats Sundin. Forsberg is the only player in team history to lead the NHL in scoring, passing Markus Naslund who, like Forsberg, is a native of Örnsköldsvik, Sweden, in the final game of the 2002–03 season to win the Art Ross Trophy with 106 points.

IGINLA STILL GOING STRONG

Playing in his first season with Colorado, Jarome Iginla became the oldest player in franchise history to lead the team in goals when he netted 29 during the 2014–15 campaign. The 37-year-old Iginla recorded his fourth multi-goal performance in impressive fashion, netting a power-play tally with 33 seconds remaining in the third period to send the Avalanche to a 3-2 victory over Chicago in the regular-season finale. Iginla, who scored 589 times and has 1,226 points in his NHL career, fell just one tally shy of notching his 13th career 30-goal season.

HEJDUK: THE NATURAL CHOICE

When Adam Foote announced his retirement after the 2010–11 season, the team didn't have to look too far to find its next captain. Veteran Milan Hejduk readily accepted the honor of becoming the third captain since the team relocated from Quebec City, joining Joe Sakic (1992–2009) and Foote (2009–11). The Czech native spent his entire career with the Avalanche/Nordiques and ranks fourth all-time in franchise history in points.

▼ *Peter Forsberg's best statistical season came in the Avalanche's first season in Colorado when he had 30 goals and 86 assists for 116 points in 1995–96.*

YOU'VE GOTTA HAVE HART

In addition to becoming the first Swedish player to lead the NHL in scoring (2002–03), Peter Forsberg also became the first Swede to win the Hart Trophy as NHL MVP. Two years earlier, Joe Sakic was the first Avalanche to win the Hart Trophy. Sakic joined Bobby Clarke, Wayne Gretzky, and Mark Messier as the only players in history to captain their team to the Stanley Cup and win the Hart Trophy in the same season.

SINGLE-GAME HIGHS

The franchise record of five goals in a single game was accomplished twice while the team was based in Quebec. Mats Sundin scored five goals in a 10-4 win over Hartford on March 5, 1992 and Mike Ricci scored five in an 8-2 win over San Jose on February 17, 1994. Ricci is also one of six players in franchise history to have recorded five assists in a single game. Peter Forsberg had five assists on three different occasions.

ST. PATRICK (PLAYER)

Acquired from Montreal on December 5, 1995, Patrick Roy would set most of the goaltending records in franchise history, both for a single season and all-time. Roy is the franchise leader among goalies in games played (478), minutes (28,317), wins (262), goals-against average (2.27), save percentage (.918), and shutouts (37). He also holds the single-season records for shutouts (nine in 2001–02), goals-against average (1.94 in 2001–02), and save percentage (.925 in 2001–02).

ST. PATRICK (COACH)

After a successful playing career, Patrick Roy traded in the goalie mask and pads for a suit and tie, when he was hired by the Avalanche as the coach and vice president of hockey operations on May 23, 2013. In his first game, on October 2, he made quite an impression: he was embroiled in a shouting match with Ducks coach Bruce Boudreau and nearly broke the partition separating the benches. Roy went on to win the 2014 Jack Adams Award as coach of the year.

◄ *Patrick Roy was a big reason why Colorado won the Stanley Cup in 1996 and 2001. The Avalanche reached at least the third round of the playoffs five times in his eight seasons with the club.*

COLUMBUS BLUE JACKETS

The addition of the Columbus Blue Jackets, along with the Minnesota Wild, to the NHL for the 2000–01 season saw the League become a 30-club circuit and completed a wave of expansion that began on June 25, 1997, when those two cities were formally admitted into the NHL, along with Nashville and Atlanta. The name "Blue Jackets" was announced by principal owner John H. McConnell on November 11, 1997 and pays homage to Ohio's contributions to American history and the great pride and patriotism exhibited by its citizens, especially during the Civil War when citizens of both the state of Ohio and the city of Columbus wore the blue uniform of the Union Army.

BIRTH OF THE BLUE JACKETS

The history of the franchise began on November 1, 1996, when Columbus Hockey Limited, a partnership formed by five investors interested in attracting an expansion team, submitted an application and a $100,000 fee to the NHL office. A formal presentation to the League was made on January 13, 1997 and plans for an arena announced on May 31. Doug MacLean was hired as general manager on February 11, 1998, and soon became the club president as well.

WHAT ABOUT BOB?

Sergei Bobrovsky made quite the impression in his first season with Columbus, winning the 2013 Vezina Trophy to become the team's third recognized NHL award recipient. Acquired from Philadelphia for second- and fourth-round draft picks, the Russian posted a 21-11-6 record and a stingy 2.00 goals-against average. Bobrovsky dominated down the stretch with a 9-2-3 mark and 1.49 GAA in March while collecting three of his four shutouts.

EXPANSION DRAFT

The Expansion Draft to stock the Blue Jackets and Wild was held in Calgary on June 23, 2000, a day before that year's Entry Draft. Of the 26 players Columbus selected, many would never suit up for the team but among those chosen was Lyle Odelein, who would become the first captain, and Geoff Sanderson, who went on to score 30 goals in just 68 games during the team's first season and also led the club with 56 points.

ENTRY DRAFT

The first player chosen by the Blue Jackets in their initial Entry Draft was Rostislav Klesla, who was selected fourth overall in 2000. A native of the Czech Republic who played his junior hockey in the United States and Canada, Klesla played briefly in Columbus in 2000–01 and made the NHL All-Rookie Team of 2001–02. Entering 2010–11, Klesla was the only Columbus player who had taken part in every season the team has played.

 Lyle Odelein was a rugged defenseman who helped the Blue Jackets ice a competitive team during their inaugural season.

Sergei Bobrovsky skated away with the Vezina Trophy following his first season in Columbus.

FIRST GAME & FIRST WIN

The Blue Jackets played their first NHL regular-season game on October 7, 2000, hosting the Chicago Blackhawks but losing 5-3. Bruce Gardiner scored the first goal at 7:34 of the first period. The team's first win was a 3-2 victory in their third game, which was played in Calgary on October 12. It was the first of 22 wins that season for Ron Tugnutt, setting a new record for a goalie on an expansion team.

OTHER FIRSTS

Robert Kron won the opening face-off from Alexei Zhamnov in the team's first game, while Kevyn Adams was the first Columbus player with a shot on goal at 1:41 of the first period. Serge Aubin drew the team's first penalty at 10:59. Ron Tugnutt posted the Blue Jackets' first shutout in a 2-0 win at Montreal on December 18, 2000 and Geoff Sanderson scored the first hat trick in a 3-2 win over Nashville on February 10, 2001.

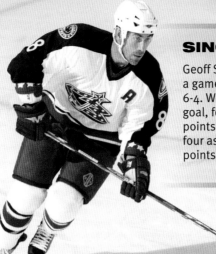

SINGLE-GAME STANDARDS

Geoff Sanderson set a Blue Jackets record with four goals in a game on March 29, 2003, leading Columbus over Calgary 6-4. With an assist in that game, he and Andrew Cassels (one goal, four assists) both tied Espen Knutsen's club mark of five points, which was later tied again by David Vyborny (one goal, four assists) on February 28, 2004. Knutsen achieved his five points with a club-record five assists on March 24, 2001.

LEAGUE LEADER

Rick Nash finished third in voting for the Calder Trophy as Rookie of the Year in 2003 behind winner Barret Jackman of St. Louis and Henrik Zetterberg of Detroit. In 2003–04, Nash set a franchise record with 41 goals and tied for the Maurice "Rocket" Richard Trophy as the league leader with Calgary's Jarome Iginla and Atlanta's Ilya Kovalchuk. At age 19, Nash was the youngest player in history to lead the NHL in goals.

FAST START

Slated to pick second in the 2002 Entry Draft, Columbus traded with Florida to land first choice and selected Rick Nash. The youngest player in the NHL in 2002–03, Nash became just the eighth number-one draft choice to score a goal in his first NHL game (versus Chicago's Jocelyn Thibault on October 10, 2002) and the first since Mario Lemieux in 1984 to do so in the same year in which he was drafted.

▶ Steve Mason's club-record 10 shutouts in 2008–09 were the most by an NHL rookie since Tony Esposito had 15 for Chicago in 1968–69.

▲ Geoff Sanderson reached the 30-goal plateau twice in his three full seasons with Columbus. He and Rick Nash are the only players in franchise history to score 30 goals in a season.

ROOKIE SENSATION

Goalie Steve Mason posted a record of 33-20-7 with a 2.29 goals-against average in 2008–09 and led the League with 10 shutouts. He received 121 of a possible 132 first-place votes, easily capturing the Calder Trophy as Rookie of the Year. Mason also finished runner-up to Boston's Tim Thomas for the Vezina Trophy and was fourth in voting for the Hart Trophy as NHL MVP. He was named to the Second All-Star Team.

 ▲ Rick Nash led the Blue Jackets in goals for the seventh straight season with 32 in 2010–11. He also led the team in points for the fifth time in seven years.

CALVERT TO THE RESCUE

After recording a franchise-best 43 wins and 93 points during the 2013–14 season, Columbus notched its first postseason victory in dramatic fashion. Matt Calvert scored his second goal of the game at 1:10 of double overtime as the Blue Jackets skated to a 4-3 triumph over Pittsburgh on April 19, 2014. Calvert converted his second attempt to clean up a rebound of Cam Atkinson's initial shot to even the Eastern Conference first-round series at one game apiece. Four nights later, Nick Foligno scored 2:49 into overtime as Columbus overcame an early three-goal deficit to post a 4-3 win over the Penguins and record its first-ever home postseason victory.

LUCKY 13 FOR JOHANSEN, JACKETS

Ryan Johansen recorded a goal and an assist to extend his franchise-best point streak to 13 games in Columbus' 3-1 victory over Boston on January 17, 2015. Johansen scored eight goals and set up as many others during the streak, while torching the Bruins with two tallies and four assists in three meetings. The fourth overall pick of the 2010 draft, Johansen began the season with a 10-game point streak while adding a nine-game stretch as part of the Blue Jackets' season-ending 13-game point streak (12-0-1). The latter surge eclipsed Columbus' previous mark of 12, set with an 8-0-4 surge from February 26–March 22, 2013.

DALLAS STARS

As a true hotbed of American hockey, it was not surprising that the NHL added a team in Minnesota when the League expanded from 6 to 12 teams in 1967. However, on June 9, 1993, Minnesota lost its first NHL franchise after 26 seasons when the North Stars transferred south to Texas. The word "North" was dropped from the team name and the Dallas Stars were born. By their fourth season the Stars had developed into a real powerhouse: they won five straight division titles from 1996–97 through 2000–01, won the Stanley Cup in 1999, and remained one of the NHL's top clubs well into the 2000s.

NORTH STARS' FIRST STAR

Like so many players of that era, the addition of six NHL Expansion teams breathed new life into Wayne Connelly's career. Connelly had scored just 25 goals in parts of five seasons with the Montreal Canadiens and Boston Bruins, but exploded for 35 with the North Stars in 1967–68. Only Bobby Hull (44), Stan Mikita (40), and Gordie Howe (39) scored more goals that season, but Connelly would never again approach that total in the NHL.

100-POINT SEASONS

Dino Ciccarelli's 106 points in 1981–82 rank as the second-highest single-season total in franchise history behind Bobby Smith, who had 43 goals and 71 assists for 114 points that same season. Neal Broten, with 105 points (29 goals, 76 assists) in 1985–86, and Ciccarelli again, when he had 103 points (52 goals, 51 assists) in 1986–87, are the only other players in franchise history to top the 100-point plateau. Signed as a free agent in 1979, Ciccarelli made his debut in 1980–81 and set a rookie playoff scoring record with 14 goals as the North Stars reached the Stanley Cup Finals for the first time.

THE GOLDY SHUFFLE

Bill Goldsworthy led all NHL players with 15 points in the 1968 playoffs and had his first big breakout season with a team-leading 36 goals in 1969–70. He was Minnesota's top goal scorer six times in seven years from that season through 1975–76, including a 48-goal effort in 1973–74 that stood as a team record for eight years. Goldsworthy celebrated his goals with a high-stepping fist pump known as "the Goldy Shuffle."

Jordie Benn (28) was joir. by younger brother Jamie (1. in the former's NHL debut on January 3, 2012. The two quickly came together t assist on a first-period goal.

Mike Modano began his NHL career in 1989–90 when the franchise was based in Minnesota. After four seasons as a North Star, Modano made the trek to Dallas and set team records for seasons (21), games (1,459), goals (557), assists (802) and points (1,359).

BENN BROTHERS UNITE

When Jordie Benn was recalled from Texas of the American Hockey League on January 3, 2012, it reunited him with his younger brother, Jamie. The two Benns then combined to assist on Loui Eriksson's first-period goal in a 5-4 loss to the Detroit Red Wings. Jamie Benn, who made the All-Star team later in the season, finished with a goal and two assists in the loss. Jordie Benn was held off the scoresheet in his next game before being assigned back to the AHL.

BIG BENN CHIMES IN

Captain Jamie Benn finished the 2014–15 season with a flourish, collecting 16 points (eight goals, eight assists) in seven games to edge New York Islanders star John Tavares for the Art Ross Trophy as the NHL's scoring leader. Benn capped the surge in scintillating fashion, recording his second career hat trick before adding an assist with nine seconds remaining in the final contest of the season – a 4-1 victory over Nashville on April 11. The 25-year-old Benn, who finished with a career high in goals (35), assists (52) and points (87), became the first player in franchise history to win the award.

THE PRESIDENTS' TROPHY

In 1996–97, the Dallas Stars posted the first 100-point season in franchise history when they finished second in the NHL's overall standings behind the Colorado Avalanche with 104 points. A year later, Dallas won the Presidents' Trophy for the first time with a league-leading 109 points. The Stars set a franchise record with 114 points and won the Presidents' Trophy again in 1998–99; they also went on to win the Stanley Cup that year.

BELFOUR AT HIS BEST

Goalie Ed Belfour joined the Dallas Stars in 1997–98 and was a key in the team's jump to elite status. In the playoffs of 1999, Belfour, who had combined with Roman Turek to win the Jennings Trophy, outdueled Patrick Roy as the Stars defeated Colorado in seven games to win the Western Conference championship. Belfour got the better of Dominik Hasek in the Stanley Cup Final as Dallas captured the franchise's first NHL title in six games.

TWO-WAY TALENT

Jere Lehtinen has won the Selke Trophy as the NHL's Best Defensive Forward three times in his career (1998, 1999, and 2003), tying him with former Stars teammate Guy Carbonneau, who won the award three times with Montreal, for the second-most Selke Trophy wins behind longtime Stars GM Bob Gainey (who won it four times with the Canadiens). Offensively, Lehtinen's seven 20-goal seasons are the third most in Stars' history behind Brian Bellows (10) and Mike Modano (16).

TURCO'S TURN

Marty Turco played 26 games for Dallas in 2000–01 and his 1.90 goals-against average was the second-best by a rookie netminder in the "modern" era since 1943–44, trailing only Al Rollins' 1.77 in 1950–51. Turco tied Ed Belfour's club records with 37 wins and nine shutouts in 2002–03 and set a new mark with a 1.72 average. He established a new franchise high with 41 wins in 2005–06 when Dallas won a club-record 53 games.

STANLEY CUP SUCCESS

After 10 stellar seasons in St. Louis, Brett Hull signed with the Dallas Stars in 1998–99. Battling injuries and playing under the Stars' tight defensive system, Hull's 58 points (32 goals, 26 assists) was his lowest total in any full NHL season, but he scored the Stanley Cup winner for Dallas over Buffalo in triple overtime. Joe Nieuwendyk led all postseason performers with 11 goals and was rewarded with the Conn Smythe Trophy.

◄ Dave Reid of Dallas celebrates Joe Nieuwendyk's third period goal that gave the Stars a 2-1 win over Buffalo in game three of the 1999 Stanley Cup Final. Dallas went on to win the series in six games.

▼ In his nine seasons with the team between 2000 and 2010, Marty Turco became the franchise's all-time leader in games played by a goaltender (502), wins (262), and shutouts (40).

DETROIT RED WINGS

In 1936, its tenth season in the NHL, Detroit won the Stanley Cup for the first time. Though Detroit was the last of the four American franchises that would become part of the so-called "Original Six" to win the Stanley Cup, the Red Wings have since gone on to win more Cup titles than any other US-based club. Detroit originally entered the NHL in 1926–27 with a roster stocked mainly through the purchase of the Victoria Cougars of the Western Hockey League. Until 1930, Detroit was known as the Cougars and then as the Falcons for two seasons before being renamed the Red Wings in 1932.

 General manager Jack Adams smiles as captain Ted Lindsay kisses the Stanley Cup after defeating Montreal in 1954.

HOME SWEET HOME?

Detroit spent its first season in the NHL playing home games across the border in Windsor, Ontario. Their first game was a 2-0 loss to Boston on November 18, 1926. The Detroit Olympia hosted its first game on November 22, 1927 (a 2-1 loss to Ottawa) and was home to the Red Wings until December 15, 1979. On December 27, 1979, the team played its first game at the Joe Louis Arena, losing 3-2 to St. Louis.

SINGLE-SEASON GOAL-SCORING LEADERS

65	Steve Yzerman	1988–89 (80 GP)
62	Steve Yzerman	1989–90 (79 GP)
58	Steve Yzerman	1992–93 (84 GP)
56	Sergei Fedorov	1993–94 (82 GP)
55	John Ogrodnick	1984–85 (79 GP)
52	Mickey Redmond	1972–73 (76 GP)
	Ray Sheppard	1993–94 (82 GP)
51	Mickey Redmond	1973–74 (76 GP)
	Steve Yzerman	1990–91 (80 GP)
50	Danny Grant	1974–75 (80 GP)
	Steve Yzerman	1987–88 (64 GP)
49	Gordie Howe	1952–53 (70 GP)
	Frank Mahovlich	1968–69 (76 GP)
47	Gordie Howe	1951–52 (70 GP)
	Marcel Dionne	1974–75 (80 GP)
46*	Brendan Shanahan	1996–97 (79 GP)
45	Steve Yzerman	1991–92 (79 GP)

* Also scored one goal in two games with Hartford that season

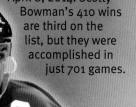

▶ *Steve Yzerman is the longest-serving team captain in NHL history, first donning the "C" at age 21 in 1986–87 and wearing it through his final season of 2005–06.*

BENCH BOSSES

Jack Adams took over as coach and general manager of Detroit in 1927–28. He held both positions for 20 seasons through 1946–47 and remained on as general manager through 1961–62. Adams' mark of 413-390-161 stood as the franchise record for wins before Mike Babcock notched his 414th career regular-season victory with a 4-2 triumph over Buffalo on April 8, 2014. Scotty Bowman's 410 wins are third on the list, but they were accomplished in just 701 games.

NHL'S GOAL-SCORING LEADERS

The first Detroit player to lead the NHL in goals was Larry Aurie, who tied Nels Stewart for the NHL lead with 23 goals in 1936–37. The only other Red Wings to lead the NHL in goals were Ted Lindsay (tops with 33 goals in 1947–48), Sid Abel (who led with 28 the following season), and Gordie Howe (who led the NHL in goals five times between 1950–51 and 1962–63).

ART ROSS TROPHY WINNERS

Ted Lindsay was the first Red Wing to lead the NHL in scoring with 78 points (23 goals, 55 assists) in 1949–50. Linemates Sid Abel (34-35-69) and Gordie Howe (35-33-68) finished second and third in scoring that year. Howe led the NHL in scoring for each of the next four seasons and won the Art Ross Trophy again in 1956–57 and 1962–63. No other Detroit player has ever led the NHL in scoring.

GOALIES BY THE NUMBERS

Terry Sawchuk's 44 wins as a rookie in 1950–51 and again in 1951–52 continue to stand as the Red Wings' single-season record. Sawchuk's 12 shutouts in 1951–52, 1953–54, and 1954–55, and Glenn Hall's dozen (1955–56) are also a franchise high. Chris Osgood set a team record with 13 straight wins between January 30 and March 20, 1996, while the 72 games in goal played by Tim Cheveldae in 1991–92 established a single-season Red Wings record.

ALL-TIME CAREER LEADERS

Most Seasons	25	Gordie Howe
Most Games	1,687	Gordie Howe
Most Goals	786	Gordie Howe
Most Assists	1,063	Steve Yzerman
Most Points	1,809	Gordie Howe
		(786 G, 1,023 A)
Most Wins	351	Terry Sawchuk
Most Shutouts	85	Terry Sawchuk
Most Penalty Minutes	2,090	Bob Probert

NO RELATION...

On January 23, 1944, Syd Howe scored a hat trick in Detroit's 15-0 win over the New York Rangers. His three goals that night gave him 149 as a Red Wing, breaking Herbie Lewis's club record of 148. Eleven days later, on February 3, 1944, the Red Wings crushed the Rangers again: Howe had six goals in the 12-2 victory, making him the first player in 23 years to score that many goals in a single game.

PETR THE GREAT

Petr Mrazek stole the show while making his postseason debut, stopping a career-high 44 shots to lift Detroit to a 3-2 victory over Tampa Bay in Game 1 of their Eastern Conference first-round series on April 16, 2015. The rookie wasn't done turning heads, making 22 saves in a 3-0 triumph over the Lightning five days later before stopping all 28 shots he faced in a 4-0 victory on April 25. Mrazek's two shutouts in his playoff debut series matched the accomplishment of Earl Robertson, who turned the trick in 1937 for Detroit.

 Detroit's Gordie Howe beats Toronto's Johnny Bower for a goal in a game at Maple Leaf Gardens in the early 1960s.

NYQUIST STEPS UP

Gustav Nyquist began the 2013–14 season with Calder Cup champion Grand Rapids of the American Hockey League. With the Red Wings encountering injuries to captain Henrik Zetterberg and dynamo Pavel Datsyuk, Detroit recalled Nyquist on Nov. 20, 2013 and saw him make an immediate impact. Scoring twice in his debut versus Carolina, he eventually earned a spot on Sweden's Olympic team when teammate Johan Franzen pulled out with a concussion. The 24-year-old highlighted a sensational first season by recording a six-game goal streak and tallied 23 times in a 28-game stretch.

IRON MAN

Nicklas Lidstrom's resume is decorated to say the least. The seven-time Norris Trophy winner bolstered his career accomplishments on Feb. 12, 2012 when he set an NHL record for most games played while competing for just one franchise (1,550), breaking former Red Wing great Alex Delvecchio's mark. Lidstrom played 14 more games and retired after his 20th season. Two years later, the Swede returned to see his No. 5 jersey raised to the rafters at Joe Louis Arena – joining Gordie Howe (No. 9), Steve Yzerman (No. 19), Ted Lindsay (No. 7), Terry Sawchuk (No. 1), Delvecchio (No. 10) and Sid Abel (No. 12).

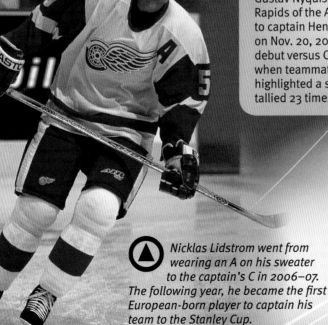 *Nicklas Lidstrom went from wearing an A on his sweater to the captain's C in 2006–07. The following year, he became the first European-born player to captain his team to the Stanley Cup.*

EDMONTON OILERS

Originally formed as the Alberta Oilers for the inaugural season of the World Hockey Association in 1972–73, the team was renamed the Edmonton Oilers before the 1973–74 season and was one of four WHA teams admitted to the NHL in 1979–80. Wayne Gretzky joined the Oilers as a 17-year-old in 1978–79 and was retained when the team joined the NHL. With Gretzky and other young stars such as Mark Messier, Jari Kurri, Paul Coffey, and Grant Fuhr, the Oilers improved rapidly. They won the Stanley Cup for the first time in their fifth season of 1983–84 and over the next six years, went on to secure it four more times.

Wayne Gretzky is surrounded by Mark Messier (left), Kevin Lowe (right), and the rest of his Oilers teammates after winning the Stanley Cup for the fourth time in 1988.

SEVEN ASSISTS IN ONE GAME

On February 15, 1980, just 57 games into his NHL career, Wayne Gretzky tied Billy Taylor's NHL record with seven assists in one game and led the Oilers to an 8-2 win over Washington. Gretzky achieved seven assists in a game again on December 11, 1985 in a 12-9 win over Chicago. Later that season, he went on to do so a third time, on February 14, 1986, when the Oilers beat Quebec 8-2.

Defenseman Kevin Lowe was the first player selected by the Oilers (21st overall) in their first NHL Entry Draft in 1979. He became coach of the team in 1999.

ALL-TIME CAREER LEADERS

Most Seasons	15	Kevin Lowe
Most Games	1,037	Kevin Lowe
Most Goals	583	Wayne Gretzky
Most Assists	1,086	Wayne Gretzky
Most Points	1,669	Wayne Gretzky
Most Wins	226	Grant Fuhr
Most Shutouts	23	Tommy Salo
Most Penalty Minutes	1,747	Kelly Buchberger

SINGLE-SEASON LEADERS

Most Goals	*92	Wayne Gretzky (1981–82)
Most Assists	*163	Wayne Gretzky (1985–86)
Most Points	*215	Wayne Gretzky (1985–86; 52G, 163A)
Most Points, Right Wing	135	Jari Kurri (1984–85; 71G, 64A)
Most Points, Left Wing	106	Mark Messier (1982–83; 48G, 58A)
Most Points, Defenseman	138	Paul Coffey (1985–86; 48G, 90A)
Most Points, Rookie	75	Jari Kurri (1980–81; 32G, 43A)
Most Wins	40	Grant Fuhr (1987–88)
Most Shutouts	8	Curtis Joseph (1997–98)
		Tommy Salo (2000–01)
Most Penalty Minutes	286	Steve Smith (1987–88)

*NHL record

POWER SUPPLY

Ryan Smyth tied Glenn Anderson for the most power-play goals in franchise history when he netted his 126th tally on March 6, 2014. "Captain Canada' accomplished the feat midway through the third period as he capped a rush by shovelling Jordan Eberle's feed past New York Islanders netminder Evgeni Nabokov. The goal also put him one ahead of franchise icon Wayne Gretzky.

FIVE GOALS IN ONE GAME

Wayne Gretzky scored five goals in a game in a 9-2 win over St. Louis on February 18, 1981, a 7-5 win over Philadelphia on December 30, 1981, an 8-2 win over St. Louis on December 15, 1984, and a 10-4 win over Minnesota on December 15, 1984. Jari Kurri scored five in a 13-4 win over New Jersey on November 19, 1983, while Pat Hughes did so in a 10-5 win over Calgary on February 3, 1984.

JORDAN RULES

Jordan Eberle enjoyed a career year in 2014-15, scoring 24 goals to share top honors with Ryan Nugent-Hopkins while posting team-bests in assists (39), points (63) and power-play points (21). Eberle recorded the first of his three multi-goal performances of the season on October 24, 2014, scoring midway into the second period and again early in the third before adding an assist on an insurance tally by Nugent-Hopkins to lift the Oilers to a 6-3 win over Carolina. "It's funny how it works, you get one (goal) and the net turns into a soccer net," Eberle said.

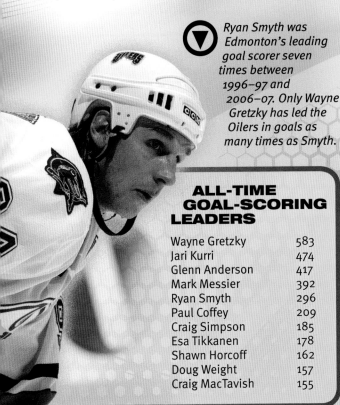

▼ *Ryan Smyth was Edmonton's leading goal scorer seven times between 1996–97 and 2006–07. Only Wayne Gretzky has led the Oilers in goals as many times as Smyth.*

100-POINT SEASONS

A total of seven players in Oilers' history have combined to produce 28 100-point seasons. Wayne Gretzky topped the century mark in each of his nine seasons in Edmonton, while Jari Kurri produced six 100-point seasons and Mark Messier had five. Glenn Anderson and Paul Coffey both topped 100 points on three occasions, while Jimmy Carson and Doug Weight did so once each.

50-GOAL SCORERS

Wayne Gretzky, Jari Kurri, Glenn Anderson, and Mark Messier are the only players in Oilers' history to score 50 goals or more in a season. Combined, they did so 15 times. Gretzky had eight seasons with 50 goals or more, including seasons with 92, 87, 73, 71, and 62 goals. Kurri topped 50 goals four times, including seasons with 71 and 68. Anderson had two 50-goal seasons, while Messier had one.

ALL-TIME GOAL-SCORING LEADERS

Wayne Gretzky	583
Jari Kurri	474
Glenn Anderson	417
Mark Messier	392
Ryan Smyth	296
Paul Coffey	209
Craig Simpson	185
Esa Tikkanen	178
Shawn Horcoff	162
Doug Weight	157
Craig MacTavish	155

CRAZY EIGHT

By all accounts, Edmonton center Sam Gagner had himself quite a night on February 2, 2012. Gagner collected four goals and four assists to become the 13th NHL player to accomplish an eight-point performance in one game. The sizzling performance tied the club record, held by Hall of Famers Wayne Gretzky and Paul Coffey – and fell two points shy of tying the NHL record of 10, set by Toronto's Darryl Sittler. What made the 22-year-old Gagner's night startling was that he entered the contest with five goals and nine assists all season.

GOALTENDING RECORDS

Bill Ranford has played more games in goal for Edmonton (449) than anyone else, but had a losing record of 167-193-54. Grant Fuhr is second with 423 games. His record of 226-117-54 for a .637 winning percentage ranks second in team history behind Andy Moog, who had a mark of .707 by going 143-53-21 in his 235 games. Tommy Salo's goals-against average of 2.22 in 2000–01 is the lowest single-season total in club history.

▶ *Sam Gagner recorded the NHL's first eight-point game since 1988 when he had four goals and four assists in the Oilers' 8-4 victory over the Chicago Blackhawks on February 2, 2012. The 22-year-old Gagner finished the season with 18 goals and 29 assists.*

FLORIDA PANTHERS

On December 10, 1992, NHL owners approved the addition of new expansion teams in Anaheim and Miami that would see the NHL grow to 26 franchises for the 1993–94 season. Then, on April 19, 1993, the Miami-area team was officially named the Florida Panthers in part because the Florida panther had been designated the official state animal – even though fewer than 100 were left in the wild. The team's first president was Bill Torrey, who had previously built the expansion New York Islanders. Bob Clarke, the former Philadelphia Flyers star, was the team's first general manager and Roger Neilson was the first head coach.

FIRST PLAYERS

On June 23, 1993, the Panthers selected former New York Rangers' goalie John Vanbiesbrouck with the first pick in the NHL Expansion Draft. Two days later, Florida made center Rob Niedermayer, young brother of New Jersey Devils' defenseman Scott Niedermayer, the club's first selection (fifth overall) in the 1993 Entry Draft. In the team's first trade, Dave Tomlinson (who had been obtained from Toronto) was sent to Winnipeg for Jason Cirone on August 3, 1993. Both the Panthers and the Mighty Ducks of Anaheim posted 33 wins in 1993-94 to set an NHL record for the most victories by an expansion club. The Panthers (33-34-17) set another record with 83 points and were in playoff contention until the final week of the regular season.

THE FIRST GAME

On October 6, 1993, the Florida Panthers played their first NHL regular-season game against the Blackhawks in Chicago. Coverage in Miami included the NHL's first Spanish-language broadcast on radio station WCMQ. Team captain Brian Skrudland fired the team's first shot on goal at 1:07 of the first period, but Chicago's Ed Belfour made the save. Right-winger Scott Mellanby scored the Panthers' first goal on a powerplay at 12:31. The game ended in a 4-4 tie.

◄ *Roberto Luongo played with Florida from 2000 to 2006 before returning to the club at the trade deadline in 2014.*

TEAM FIRSTS (GAME, WIN)

On October 6, 1993, Florida played its first NHL regular-season game against the Blackhawks in Chicago. Coverage in Miami included the league's first Spanish-language broadcast on radio station WCMQ. Scott Mellanby scored the first power-play goal for the Panthers, who settled for a 4-4 tie. Florida fell to St. Louis the following night before John Vanbiesbrouck recorded a shutout and Scott Levins and Tom Fitzgerald each scored in a 2-0 win over Tampa Bay on October 9.

JAGR'S MILESTONES

Jaromir Jagr passed Phil Esposito for fifth place on the NHL all-time goals list by scoring for the 718th time in his career in a 3-1 win versus Detroit on March 19, 2015. Jagr accomplished the feat midway into the second period, opening the scoring with a wrist shot from the left faceoff circle that handcuffed Petr Mrazek. Acquired from New Jersey on February 26, Jagr also moved past Ron Francis for fourth place when he eclipsed 1,800 points in his career with two assists against Boston on April 9 and set up another goal two days later to move past Adam Oates for sixth place on the career assists list with 1,080.

A BIG BREAKTHROUGH

Under new head coach Doug MacLean in 1995–96, the Panthers enjoyed a big year in their third season. After 50 games, the club boasted a 31-14-5 mark and ranked among the NHL elite. Although a slump followed, Florida finished the season 41-31-10 for 92 points and made the playoffs. Not expected to go very far, the Panthers knocked off Boston, Philadelphia, and Pittsburgh to reach the Stanley Cup Final, but were swept in four games by the Colorado Avalanche.

TWENTY-ROUND SHOOTOUT

Although unable to convert on his first attempt in the shootout, Nick Bjugstad made good on his second – in the NHL-record 20th round, no less – as Florida skated to a 2-1 victory over Washington on December 17, 2014. Bjugstad's game-winning tally put an end to the longest shootout in league history, eclipsing the previous mark by five full rounds – when the New York Rangers defeated the Capitals on November 26, 2005. Florida scored in the shootout on five different occasions to extend the contest before Bjugstad deked goaltender Braden Holtby to the ice and fired the puck into the open net.

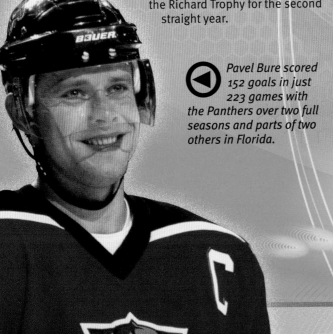

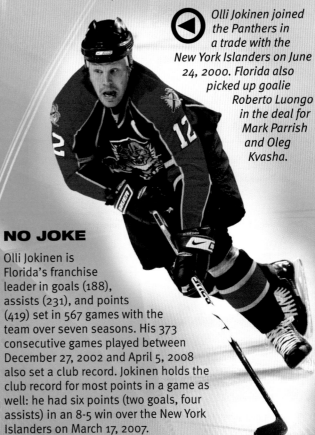

GOALS IN ONE GAME

On January 23, 1996, Johan Garpenlov became the first player in Panthers' history to score a hat trick with three goals in a 5-4 win over Washington. On October 30, 1998, Mark Parrish set a club record with four goals in a 7-3 win over Chicago. Pavel Bure equaled the record twice: in a 7-5 win over Tampa Bay on January 1, 2000 and a 7-3 win over Atlanta on February 10, 2001.

Olli Jokinen joined the Panthers in a trade with the New York Islanders on June 24, 2000. Florida also picked up goalie Roberto Luongo in the deal for Mark Parrish and Oleg Kvasha.

Miami Arena workers remove rubber rats from the ice. The rats became a strange symbol of the Panthers success during the 1995–96 season.

RAT TRICK

Scott Mellanby used his stick to kill a rat in the Panthers' dressing room before the second game of the 1995–96 season, then scored two goals in a 4-3 win over Calgary. John Vanbiesbrouck dubbed it "a rat trick." Newspapers reported the story and club fans soon picked up on it, throwing plastic and rubber rats on the ice to celebrate every goal. The craze gained international attention during the Panthers' surprise run to the Stanley Cup Final.

NO JOKE

Olli Jokinen is Florida's franchise leader in goals (188), assists (231), and points (419) set in 567 games with the team over seven seasons. His 373 consecutive games played between December 27, 2002 and April 5, 2008 also set a club record. Jokinen holds the club record for most points in a game as well: he had six points (two goals, four assists) in an 8-5 win over the New York Islanders on March 17, 2007.

RUSSIAN ROCKET

On January 17, 1999, the Panthers acquired Pavel Bure from the Vancouver Canucks in a multiplayer deal. In his first full season with Florida in 1999–2000, Bure set club records with 58 goals and 94 points. He won the Maurice "Rocket" Richard Trophy and finished two points behind Jaromir Jagr for the Art Ross Trophy. In 2000–01, Bure set a new club record with 59 goals and won the Richard Trophy for the second straight year.

Pavel Bure scored 152 goals in just 223 games with the Panthers over two full seasons and parts of two others in Florida.

LUONGO'S RETURN

Roberto Luongo's second tour of duty in South Florida couldn't have started any better. Acquired at the NHL's trade deadline from Vancouver, he turned aside all 25 shots he faced to lead the Panthers to a 2-0 victory over Buffalo on March 7, 2014. The Montreal native, who had played with Florida from 2000 to 2006 before heading to the Canucks, registered his 27th shutout with the Panthers and 66th career. The blanking tied him with Hall-of-Famer Patrick Roy for 14th place on the NHL all-time list.

END OF A DROUGHT

The Panthers snapped a nine-game postseason losing streak which stretched nearly 15 years on April 15, 2012, when they posted a 4-2 triumph over the New Jersey Devils in Game 2 of the Eastern Conference quarterfinals. The home victory was the team's first since April 17, 1997 – a span of 5,478 days. Veteran Stephen Weiss set a franchise record for the quickest goal when he scored 23 seconds into the game. Weiss tallied again in the win, but the Devils went on to claim the series in seven games.

LOS ANGELES KINGS

Minor pro hockey in California dates back to the 1920s and thrived during the 1940s and '50s. When the NHL finally announced formal plans to expand on February 9, 1966, Los Angeles was included among the six new teams that would begin play in 1967–68. Canadian-born entrepreneur Jack Kent Cooke paid the $2 million expansion fee and called his team the Kings. He also built a state-of-the-art suburban arena dubbed "the Fabulous Forum." Although the team has boasted some of the greatest players in hockey history – including Wayne Gretzky and Marcel Dionne – it wasn't until 2012 that the Kings finally raised the Stanley Cup. They repeated the feat in 2014.

MARCEL DIONNE

In 1975–76, Marcel Dionne joined the Kings from Detroit and set new club records that season with 40 goals and 94 points. A year later, he became the first Los Angeles player to top both the 50-goal and 100-point plateaus, scoring 53 times and adding 69 assists for 122 points. In 1979–80, Dionne became the first King to win the Art Ross Trophy with a career-high 137 points on 53 goals and 84 assists.

ROGIE VACHON

On November 4, 1971, Los Angeles acquired Rogie Vachon from Montreal. He went on to star with the Kings through 1977–78. Vachon was named a Second-Team All-Star in 1974–75 and *The Hockey News* awarded him NHL Player of the Year that season after leading the Kings to a franchise-record 105 points; his 2.24 goals-against average was a career best. Vachon was a Second-Team All-Star again in 1976–77 when he established a franchise record with eight shutouts.

Rogie Vachon and his smiling mask were the face of the franchise in the 1970s. He held the franchise record in wins (171) until Jonathan Quick broke the mark on March 22, 2014.

FRANCHISE LEADER

Luc Robitaille was considered too poor a skater to make it in the NHL; he wasn't selected until the ninth round of the 1984 Entry Draft when the Kings picked him 171st overall. When Robitaille reached the NHL in 1986–87, he scored 45 goals and won the Calder Trophy as Rookie of the Year. He went on to play 14 of his 19 NHL seasons with the Kings and is franchise leader with 557 goals.

Justin Williams' penchant for coming up large in do-or-die Game 7 matchups allowed him to win both the Conn Smythe Trophy and the Stanley Cup in 2014.

TRIPLE CROWN LINE

The Los Angeles Kings' Triple Crown Line became the first line in NHL history where all three players topped 100 points during the 1980–81 season. Center Marcel Dionne led the way with 135 points (58 goals, 77 assists) while right-winger Dave Taylor had 112 (47-65) and left-winger Charlie Simmer had 105 (56-69). Before teaming up with Dionne in 1978–79, Simmer had been a decent minor league scorer while second-year player Taylor was virtually unknown.

WILLIAMS: MR. GAME 7

Justin Williams has a knack for stepping up with everything on the line. The forward improved to 7-0 in Game 7s after collecting a goal and an assist in the final contest of the Western Conference series versus defending Stanley Cup champion Chicago on June 1, 2014. Williams, who went on to win the Conn Smythe Trophy, tied Hall of Famer Glenn Anderson by scoring his seventh goal in a Game 7 matchup and notched his seventh assist on defenseman Alec Martinez's overtime-winning goal.

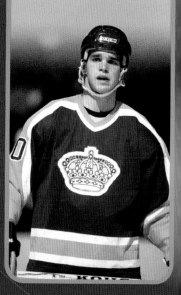

KING JONATHAN

Jonathan Quick became the king of the Kings goaltenders by recording his franchise-best 172nd victory in style. The 2012 Conn Smythe Trophy winner turned aside all 24 shots he faced to register his 30th career shutout in a 4-0 triumph over Florida on March 22, 2014. The win allowed Quick to surpass Rogie Vachon for the top mark in team history and he would eclipse his shutout record on October 23, 2014. Vachon was on hand to congratulate Quick after the game.

 While rarely given much offensive support, Jonathan Quick stood tall to carry the Kings into the postseason. For his efforts, the Connecticut native secured a spot in the 2012 All-Star Game.

SINGLE-SEASON SCORING LEADERS

168	Wayne Gretzky (54G, 114A) in 1988–89
163*	Wayne Gretzky (41G, 122A) in 1990–91
150	Bernie Nicholls (70G, 80A) in 1988–89
142*	Wayne Gretzky (40G, 102A) in 1989–90
137*	Marcel Dionne 137 (53G, 84A) in 1979–80
135	Marcel Dionne (58G, 77A) in 1980–81
130	Marcel Dionne (59G, 71A) in 1978–79
130*	Wayne Gretzky (38G, 92A) in 1993–94
126	Marcel Dionne (46G, 80A) in 1984–85
125	Luc Robitaille (63G, 62A) in 1992–93

*NHL leader

THAT 70'S LINE

Veteran Jeff Carter and younger stars Tyler Toffoli and Tanner Pearson comprised "That 70's Line", a term based on the players' jersey numbers with a nod to the television show as well. The trio became a hit in guiding the Kings to their second Stanley Cup title in 2014, with Carter and Toffoi continuing to pay dividends the following season. Carter led the team with 28 goals and Toffoli added 23 tallies and 49 points, but Pearson's absence due to a broken left leg proved to be too much to overcome as the Kings missed the playoffs.

ROB BLAKE

During his 20-year NHL career, Rob Blake played 13-plus seasons in two stints with the Kings. In 1997–98, he won the Norris Trophy as the NHL's Best Defenseman and is franchise leader among defensemen in games played (805), goals (161), assists (333), points (494), and powerplay goals (92). His 23 goals in 1997–98 were a career high, but rank second behind Steve Duchesne's 25 in 1988–89 as the best single-season mark for a Kings defenseman.

Rob Blake took over the Kings captaincy from Wayne Gretzky in 1995–96. He was captain until being traded in 2001, and then again in 2007–08.

BERNIE'S BIG NIGHT

On December 1, 1988, Bernie Nicholls had two goals and six assists to lead the Kings past Toronto 9-3. His six assists and eight points surpassed the club records of five assists and six points shared by several players, including teammate Wayne Gretzky, who had a goal and five assists versus Detroit eight days before. Nicholls' six assists were later matched by Tomas Sandstrom in a 10-3 win over Detroit on October 9, 1993.

Luc Robitaille led or shared the Kings lead in goals scored eight times in his career, a mark matched only by Marcel Dionne whose total of 550 goals was a Kings record broken by Robitaille.

Only Wayne Gretzky, Mario Lemieux, Steve Yzerman, and Phil Esposito have had more points in a season than the 150 Bernie Nicholls had in 1988-89.

TEAM RECORDS

The Kings' record for most wins in a season is 46, established in 1990–91 (46-24-10, 102 points) and again in 2009–10 (46-27-9, 101 points). Most points are 105 (42-17-21) in 1974–75 and the most losses are 52 (14-52-10) in 1969–70. The team record for most goals in a season is 376 (1988–89), while the record for most goals in one game came in a 12-1 victory over Vancouver on November 29, 1984.

MINNESOTA WILD

The NHL announced its return to Minneapolis-St. Paul on June 25, 1997, when the League also welcomed Nashville, Atlanta, and Columbus as new expansion cities. This hotbed of American high school and college hockey had lost its original NHL franchise when the Minnesota North Stars moved to Dallas in 1993. On January 22, 1998, the team name Wild for the new Minnesota franchise was announced. In its first season of 2000–01, the club drew record numbers for an expansion team, selling out for every home game at the Xcel Energy Center. The sellout streak lasted through 409 preseason, regular-season, and playoff games until September 22, 2010.

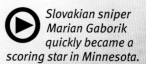

▶ Slovakian sniper Marian Gaborik quickly became a scoring star in Minnesota.

THE FIRST DRAFT PICK

Minnesota won a coin flip with Columbus and chose to take the higher pick (third overall) in the 2000 NHL Entry Draft, leaving Columbus to select first in the Expansion Draft held on June 23, 2000. A day later, the Wild took Marian Gaborik as the team's first pick in the NHL Entry Draft. Gaborik entered the NHL as an 18-year-old in 2000–01 and quickly established himself as the team's offensive leader.

FIRST GAME

On October 6, 2000, the Minnesota Wild played their first NHL regular-season game on the road in Anaheim. The Ducks won 3-1. Marian Gaborik scored the team's first goal at 18:59 of the second period. After a 4-1 loss in Phoenix the next night, the Wild returned home for the first game at the Xcel Energy Center on October 11, 2000 and collected their first point in a 3-3 tie with Philadelphia.

WILD'S FIRST (WIN, SEASON)

The Wild's first win came in their sixth game on October 18, 2000. Marian Gaborik scored twice in the final 2:28 to give Minnesota a 6-5 victory over Tampa Bay. The rookie's first goal snapped a tie at 17:32 of the third period, then the first empty-net goal in team history came with 57.6 seconds remaining for an all-important insurance tally. The high-scoring game was a contrast to the rest of the season for Minnesota, which surrendered just 210 goals (12th best in the NHL). Manny Fernandez set an expansion team record with a 2.24 goals-against average.

WELCOME MATT

Veteran center Matt Cullen did his best to ensure victory on January 10, 2012. Playing in his 1,000th NHL contest, Cullen netted what appeared to be the game winner in the third period against the San Jose Sharks. No longer a consistent goal-scorer, the tally was Cullen's third in 24 matches. After the Sharks answered, Cullen scored in the first round of the shootout after his shot caromed off the stick of Antti Niemi and into the net as the Wild posted a 5-4 victory.

FIRST PLAYOFF APPEARANCE

Jacques Lemaire earned the Jack Adams Award as Coach of the Year for guiding the Wild to their first playoff appearance in their third season of 2002–03. In the opening round, the Wild trailed Colorado by three games to one, but rallied to win the series in seven. No team in NHL history had ever staged two such rallies in one playoff year, but after falling behind Vancouver three games to one in round two, the Wild won again.

WES WALZ

Of the 18 goals scored by Wes Walz in the Wild's first season, seven of them came shorthanded, which set a record for an NHL expansion team and remains the top total in franchise history. Walz was a talented two-way performer who fitted the team's defensive approach and he became the first Wild player to be a finalist for an individual award in 2003 when he was up for the Selke Trophy as Best Defensive Forward.

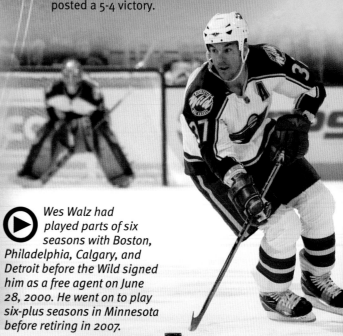

▶ Wes Walz had played parts of six seasons with Boston, Philadelphia, Calgary, and Detroit before the Wild signed him as a free agent on June 28, 2000. He went on to play six-plus seasons in Minnesota before retiring in 2007.

PARISE'S HOMECOMING

Minnesota native Zach Parise opted to leave the New Jersey Devils and sign a 13-year, $98 million deal in July 2012 to become the new face of the Wild. Parise paid immediate dividends with his new team, highlighted by his goal 27 seconds into overtime as Minnesota skated to a 2-1 home triumph over Calgary on Feb. 26, 2013. The United States Olympian kept his foot on the gas and led the Wild with 18 goals and 38 points in the 48-game lockout-shortened season. Parise's production was certainly welcome by Minnesota, which snapped a four-year playoff drought.

DUBNYK SAVES SEASON

Minnesota was spiraling out of control with six straight losses and 12 in 14 contests when it acquired Devan Dubnyk from Arizona for a third-round draft pick on Jan. 14, 2015. The goaltender paid immediate dividends by turning aside all 18 shots he faced in blanking Buffalo the following night, marking the first of four shutouts in a nine-game span. Dubnyk became a fixture in net, posting a 27-9-2 mark with five blankings, a 1.78 goals-against average and .936 save percentage – earning a Vezina Trophy nomination in the process.

MARIAN GABORIK

After an impressive debut as an 18-year-old in 2000–01, Marian Gaborik scored 30 goals during the Wild's second season. He went on to score 30-or-more five times in his eight seasons in Minnesota, including 2007–08 when he set franchise records with 42 goals and 83 points. Gaborik scored five goals in a 6-3 win over the Rangers on December 20, 2007, becoming the first NHL player in 11 years to score five in one game.

Minnesota acquired goaltender Devan Dubnyk for a third-round pick on January 14, 2015, and its fortunes promptly changed.

GOALTENDING RECORDS

Niklas Backstrom has become the Wild's career leader in wins and shutouts; he also holds the single-season marks in those categories. His 33 wins in 2007–08 broke Manny Fernandez' club record of 30 from 2005–06 before Backstrom broke his own record with 37 wins in a club-high 71 games played in goal in 2008–09. His eight shutouts that season broke the club record of five previously shared with Dwayne Roloson.

Mikko Koivu was the Wild's first pick (sixth overall) in the 2001 NHL Entry Draft. After four more years in his native Finland and one year in the minors, Koivu made his NHL debut in 2005–06.

DEVAN DAZZLES IN PLAYOFFS

After a remarkable regular-season run in 2014–15, Devan Dubnyk continued his sterling play by making 19 saves in a 4-2 triumph over St. Louis in Game 1 of their first-round series on April 16. Dubnyk became the first netminder in franchise history to earn a victory in his playoff debut and followed that up two contests later by turning aside all 17 shots he faced in a 3-0 win over the Blues. The blanking linked Dubnyk with Ilya Bryzgalov and Darcy Kuemper as the only goaltenders in franchise history to secure a postseason shutout.

CAPTAIN KOIVU

For most of the Wild's history, the team had a system of rotating captains with as many as five players wearing the "C" in some seasons. Mikko Koivu, who had been one of three captains in 2008–09, was named the franchise's first full-time captain on October 20, 2009. His older brother Saku Koivu wore the "C" for the Montreal Canadiens from 1999 to 2009, tying Jean Beliveau for the team's longest tenure as captain.

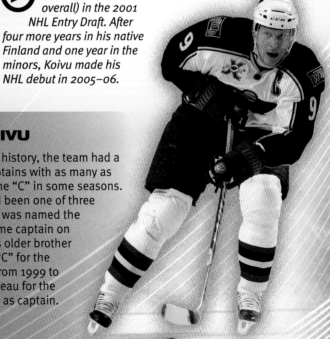

MONTREAL CANADIENS

The Montreal Canadiens were formed on December 4, 1909 for the inaugural season of the National Hockey Association (forerunner of the NHL). They are not only the oldest team in professional hockey, but also the most successful – with a record 24 Stanley Cup victories. From Georges Vezina to Howie Morenz, Maurice Richard to Guy Lafleur and Patrick Roy, the Canadiens' legacy of greatness is passed on from generation to generation. In fact, these words from the World War One poem *In Flanders Fields* are inscribed on the wall of their locker room: "To you from failing hands we throw the torch, be yours to hold it high."

PRICE IS RIGHT

Carey Price put forth a season for the ages in 2014–15, claiming the Hart and Vezina trophies after setting a franchise record in wins by going 44-16-6 – surpassing the previous mark of 42 by Jacques Plante (1955–56, 1961–62) and Ken Dryden (1975–76). Price led the league in goals-against average (1.96) and save percentage (.933) and his nine shutouts were second only to Pittsburgh's Marc-Andre Fleury (10). The Canadiens netminder made it look so easy that he even skated over to a young fan and posed for a picture during a stoppage in the third period of a 3-1 win against the New York Islanders on March 14.

Canadiens legend Georges Vezina recorded the first shutout in NHL history on February 18, 1918 when Montreal blanked Toronto 9-0.

THE CHICOUTIMI CUCUMBER

Georges Vezina joined the Canadiens for the 1910–11 season and did not miss a game, regular season or playoffs, until tuberculosis cut short his career (and shortly afterward his life) in 1925. Known as "The Chicoutimi Cucumber" for his ability to remain cool under pressure, Vezina helped the Canadiens win Stanley Cup titles in 1916 and 1924. After his death in 1926, Canadiens' management donated the Vezina Trophy to the NHL to honor his memory.

TRAGIC HERO

Howie Morenz joined the Canadiens in 1923–24 and immediately helped his team win the Stanley Cup. With blazing speed, he went on to earn two scoring titles, three Hart Trophy selections as League MVP, and helped the Canadiens win the Stanley Cup again in 1930 and 1931. Morenz died tragically on March 8, 1937, a few weeks after breaking his leg in a game. Over 10,000 fans attended a service at the Montreal Forum, where he lay in state.

Patrick Roy celebrates with the Stanley Cup after the Canadiens' victory in 1993. It was fitting for the game's most celebrated team to win the Cup in its centennial year.

LATE BLOOMER

Arriving in 1971 as the heir apparent to his childhood hero Jean Beliveau, Guy Lafleur finally blossomed with 53 goals and 119 points in 1974–75. He won his first of three straight scoring titles in 1975–76 and led the Canadiens to the first of four straight Stanley Cup titles. Lafleur's combination of speed, style, and scoring skill made him the most exciting player in the NHL and the biggest star of a great Canadiens dynasty.

ALL-TIME CAREER LEADERS

Most Seasons	20	Henri Richard, Jean Beliveau
Most Games	1,256	Henri Richard
Most Goals	544	Maurice Richard
Most Assists	728	Guy Lafleur
Most Points	1,246	Guy Lafleur (518G, 728A)
Most Wins	314	Jacques Plante
Most Shutouts	75	George Hainsworth
Most Penalty Minutes	2,248	Chris Nilan

Montreal Canadiens captain Brian Gionta is credited with scoring the team's 20,000th NHL goal.

LEGENDARY SCORER

The most beloved player in Canadiens' history, Maurice Richard overcame injuries early in his career to become the first player in NHL history to score 50 goals in a season (in just 50 games in 1944–45) and first to score 500 in a career. At his best when it mattered most, "The Rocket" had a burning desire that helped the Canadiens to secure the Stanley Cup eight times in his 18-year career.

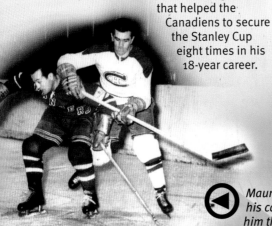

TWO TIMES FOR 20,000

Captain Brian Gionta etched his name into the record books on March 5, 2013 when he scored on the power play to mark the Canadiens' 20,000th NHL goal. Gionta's deflection eluded New York Islanders netminder Evgeni Nabokov to cap his team's scoring in a 6-3 loss in Long Island. The Montreal franchise, of course, predates the league and it amassed an additional 610 goals during the previous eight years. With that math in mind, Michael Cammalleri netted the franchise's 20,000th overall goal versus Ottawa on December 28, 2009.

MAX'S MEMORABLE NIGHT

Max Pacioretty became the first NHL player to receive two penalty shots in one period in Montreal's 5-2 victory over Vancouver on February 6, 2014. Pacioretty was thwarted by Montreal native Roberto Luongo's right pad on his first attempt before losing control of the puck on the second just over two minutes later. While Luongo also stopped Pacioretty on a penalty shot in the teams' previous meeting earlier in the season, the latter wasn't going to be denied. Pacioretty capped his third career hat trick with an empty-net goal to seal the win.

◀ *Maurice Richard was closely checked throughout his career. His ability to play through it earned him the admiration of Canadiens fans, though his temper sometimes got the better of him.*

HAINSWORTH SHUTOUTS

George Hainsworth set an NHL record, unlikely to be broken, with 22 shutouts in 1928–29. He also did so during a 44-game season! Though scoring was at an all-time low that year, Hainsworth still posted nine more shutouts than anyone else in the NHL. He played every minute in goal for the Canadiens, allowing just 43 goals for a 0.92 goals-against average. Forward passing rules were changed the following season to open up the game.

FIFTIES DYNASTY

Stars such as Maurice Richard, Doug Harvey, Jean Beliveau, and Bernie Geoffrion not only rank among the greatest of their day but the greatest of all time. From 1951 to 1960, they helped the Canadiens reach the Stanley Cup Final 10 years in a row. In each of the last five years of that streak, the Canadiens were Stanley Cup champions and capped their streak in 1960 with eight straight wins to sweep through the playoffs.

SEVENTIES STARS

From 1976 to 1979, the Canadiens won four straight Stanley Cup titles and enjoyed some of the greatest seasons in NHL history, including 1976–77 when they went 60-8-12 for an NHL-record 132 points. Boasting stars such as Guy Lafleur, Steve Shutt, Larry Robinson, and Ken Dryden, the Canadiens dominated on offense and defense, combining to earn 19 individual trophies and 16 all-star selections during this stretch. Altogether, 15 players played on each of the four championship teams.

PATRICK ROY

As a rookie with the Canadiens in 1985–86, Patrick Roy led his team to a surprising Stanley Cup victory and became the youngest winner of the Conn Smythe Trophy as playoff MVP. Over the next six seasons, Roy established himself as one of the top goalies in the NHL. In 1993, he posted a playoff record of 16-4, including 10 wins in overtime, to earn the Conn Smythe Trophy again after another Stanley Cup victory.

▶ *Jacques Plante was a great goaltender and a great innovator who literally changed the face of the game.*

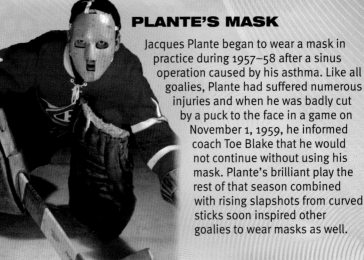

PLANTE'S MASK

Jacques Plante began to wear a mask in practice during 1957–58 after a sinus operation caused by his asthma. Like all goalies, Plante had suffered numerous injuries and when he was badly cut by a puck to the face in a game on November 1, 1959, he informed coach Toe Blake that he would not continue without using his mask. Plante's brilliant play the rest of that season combined with rising slapshots from curved sticks soon inspired other goalies to wear masks as well.

NASHVILLE PREDATORS

Nashville was welcomed into the NHL with Atlanta, Minnesota, and Columbus as expansion clubs on June 25, 1997 and was the first of this group to begin play when the team faced off in 1998–99. David Poile was hired as general manager on July 9, 1997 and Barry Trotz became coach on August 6. Both continue to serve with the club in those roles. The fans of Nashville's team chose the name Predators on November 13, 1997. "The image of a predator is one who succeeds and wins," said club president Jack Diller, "something we hope our team will do often."

FIRST ENTRY DRAFT

A trade with the San Jose Sharks landed Nashville the second pick in the 1998 NHL Entry Draft. The Predators chose highly regarded junior prospect David Legwand. He spent most of the 1998–99 season with the Ontario Hockey League's Plymouth Whalers, but made his NHL debut against New Jersey on April 17, 1999. Legwand is the only player in Predators' history to see action in every season and he is also the franchise leader in games, goals, assists, and points.

FIRST GAME & FIRST WIN

The Predators hosted the Florida Panthers in their first NHL regular-season game on October 10, 1998. Florida's Ray Whitney scored the only goal of a 1-0 game and the Panthers' Kirk McLean earned the shutout. Three nights later, the Predators defeated the Carolina Hurricanes 3-2 to net the first victory in franchise history in their second game. Andrew Brunette notched the first goal in franchise history at 5:12 of the first period; Mike Dunham earned the victory.

FIRST PLAYERS

On June 1, 1998 the Predators acquired their first player when they obtained Marian Cisar from the Los Angeles Kings for future considerations. Free agents Jayson More, Rob Valicevic, and Mark Mowers were signed later in the same month. Roster building began in earnest on June 26, 1998 at the Expansion Draft in Buffalo. Greg Johnson and Andrew Brunette, as well as goaltenders Mike Dunham and Tomas Vokoun, were key members of the inaugural club chosen in the Expansion Draft.

◀ *David Legwand had his best offensive season in 2006–07, setting career highs with 27 goals, 36 assists, and 63 points. His plus/minus rating of +23 established a franchise record.*

THE FIRST SEASON

The Predators finished their first season with a record of 28-47-7 for 63 points. Cliff Ronning, acquired from Phoenix on October 31, 1998, led the team with 35 assists and 53 points. Sergei Krivokrasov's 25 goals were also tops on the team. Among the highlights of the Predators' first season was the one and only visit by Wayne Gretzky to Nashville. "The Great One" had five assists as the Rangers beat the Predators 7-4.

FIRST PLAYOFF APPEARANCE

In 2003–04, Tomas Vokoun established himself as one of the best goalies in the game. Vokoun was second among NHL goaltenders with 73 games played and third in wins with 34 as he led the Predators to the playoffs for the first time that season. After losing their first two playoff games in Detroit, Vokoun stopped 82 of 83 Red Wings shots in 3-1 and 3-0 victories at home before the Predators were eliminated in six games.

▶ *Before going on to stardom in Nashville, Tomas Vokoun was originally chosen by Montreal with the 226th selection in the 1994 NHL Entry Draft.*

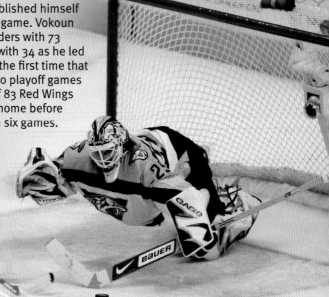

RECORD-SETTING PERFORMANCES

The 2005–06 season was a big one for several Predators players. Tomas Vokoun broke his own club record with 36 wins and the team went 49-25-8 to top 100 points for the first time with 106. Paul Kariya had signed with Nashville as a free agent and he and Steve Sullivan became the first players in franchise history to reach the 30-goal plateau with 31 apiece. Kariya also set club records with 54 assists and 85 points.

Paul Kariya spent only two seasons in Nashville (2005–06 and 2006–07), but his 85- and 76-point performances are the two highest totals in franchise history.

WEBER & SUTER – THE 1-2 PUNCH

The Predators certainly liked what they saw in defensemen Shea Weber and Ryan Suter, so much so that they selected them both in the 2003 draft. Weber would later be named as the team's fifth captain in franchise history while Suter serves as an alternate. The pair participated in the 2012 NHL All-Star Game, although on opposing sides – much like in their gold-medal game in the 2010 Vancouver Olympics. This time, the American-born Suter got the better of the Canadian Weber.

RECORD-SETTING SEASON

For much of the 2006–07 season it appeared Nashville was to finish first in the Central Division. Though they set franchise records with 51 wins and 110 points, injuries and a late-season slump saw the Predators finish three points behind the Red Wings. Shortly before the trade deadline, Nashville acquired Peter Forsberg from Philadelphia. Though it was hoped his playoff experience would help, Nashville was eliminated in the first round by San Jose for the second season in a row.

MOST POINTS, ONE GAME

Marek Zidlicky set a franchise record with five assists in a 7-3 win over San Jose on February 18, 2004. Only two other players in Predators' history have had five points in a single game: Dan Hamhuis had a goal and four assists in a 9-4 win at Pittsburgh eight games after Zidlicky on March 4, 2004, while J.P. Dumont had a goal and four assists in a 6-5 overtime win at Ottawa on October 22, 2009.

NEW PEKK-ING ORDER

In his first full NHL season in 2008–09, rookie Pekka Rinne posted a record of 29-15-4 and set a new club high with seven shutouts, which ranked him fourth in the League. His 2.38 goals-against average was sixth in the NHL and his .917 save percentage placed him tenth. Rinne was 32-16-5 in 2009–10 and tied his own club record with another seven shutouts, this time ranking third in the NHL.

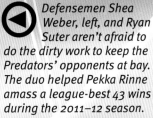

Defensemen Shea Weber, left, and Ryan Suter aren't afraid to do the dirty work to keep the Predators' opponents at bay. The duo helped Pekka Rinne amass a league-best 43 wins during the 2011–12 season.

Pekka Rinne's goals-against average of 2.12 in 2010–11 ranked him third in the NHL and established a new franchise best.

SMITH'S TERRIFIC NIGHT

Craig Smith collected two goals and an assist as Nashville recorded a franchise playoff-best total in a 6-2 rout of Chicago in Game 2 of the Western Conference first-round series on April 17, 2015. The six tallies eclipsed the club's previous high, which was set in a 5-2 victory over San Jose in 2007 and a 5-3 win versus Detroit the following year. Smith's second goal of the contest was sandwiched during a three-tally flurry in a 2:19 span in the third period, also marking a franchise record.

NEW JERSEY DEVILS

The New Jersey Devils began their existence in Missouri as the Kansas City Scouts in 1974. Two seasons later, the team relocated to Denver in 1976 and played six seasons as the Colorado Rockies before officially transferring to New Jersey on June 30, 1982. Over its first 13 seasons in three different cities through 1986–87, the franchise had only once made the playoffs and was famously mocked as a "Mickey Mouse operation" by Wayne Gretzky after a 13-4 Oilers romp in 1983. The Devils were finally able to erase their image as the League's laughing stock during the 1990s and became Stanley Cup champions in 1995, 2000, and 2003.

EARLY DAYS AS THE DEVILS

The Devils made their debut in the New Jersey Meadowlands in a preseason game on September 21, 1982, dropping a 3-2 decision to the New York Rangers. The first regular-season game was played against Pittsburgh on October 5 and ended in a 3-3 tie. Don Lever scored the Devils' first goal. The first victory at the Meadowlands came in a 3-2 win over the Rangers in front of a capacity crowd of 19,023 on October 8, 1982.

PLAYOFF PUSH

Coach Jim Schoenfeld and goalie Sean Burke joined the Devils midway through the 1987–88 season and sparked the transformation into a strong playoff team. Burke's brilliance upon joining New Jersey after the 1988 Calgary Olympics began to put the Devils into contention and they clinched a playoff spot for the first time since moving to New Jersey when John MacLean scored in overtime for a 4-3 victory over Chicago on the last night of the season.

LOU TO THE RESCUE

The fortunes of the New Jersey Devils began to take a turn for the better when Lou Lamoriello was named club president on April 30, 1987. He added the role of general manager to his duties prior to training camp for the 1987–88 season then saw the Devils reach the playoffs for just the second time in franchise history. Previously, Lamoriello had been the guiding force behind Providence College's successful hockey program for more than 20 years.

ELIAS' MILESTONES

Nearly three weeks after passing John MacLean for the franchise record in goals, Patrik Elias tallied and set up two others in his 1,000th career game to lead the Devils to a 5-2 victory over Florida on January 6, 2012. The veteran celebrated three more significant milestones three years later, including notching both his 600th career assist and 1,000th point in a 4-1 triumph over Buffalo on January 6, 2015. Elias, who had a goal and two assists versus the Sabres, added his 400th career tally in a 4-1 win over Toronto on February 6.

SINGLE-SEASON GOAL-SCORING LEADERS

48	Brian Gionta	2005–06 (82 GP)
46	Pat Verbeek	1987–88 (73 GP)
45	John MacLean	1990–91 (78 GP)
	Zach Parise	2008–09 (82 GP)
43	Alexander Mogilny	2000–01 (75 GP)
42	John MacLean	1988–89 (74 GP)
41	Wilf Paiement	1976–77 (78 GP)
	John MacLean	1973–74 (80 GP)
	Claude Lemieux	1991–92 (74 GP)
40	Patrik Elias	2000–01 (82 GP)

Adam Henrique stepped up his offense to help the New Jersey Devils in 2013–14.

TORRID STREAK FOR HENRIQUE

Adam Henrique found his scoring touch after the NHL resumed following a break for the 2014 Winter Olympics. He scored nine times during his franchise-tying six-game goal-scoring streak, which ended in New Jersey's 2-1 victory over rival Philadelphia on March 11, 2014. The 24-year-old tied six others for the franchise record and is the first player to score nine goals over a six-game span since John MacLean in December 1988.

Kirk Muller was selected second overall at the 1984 NHL Entry Draft after a successful junior career and a stint with Canada's national team at the Sarajevo Olympics.

DEVILS DEFENSEMAN

Scott Stevens spent 13 seasons with the Devils, from 1991–92 to 2003–04. He captained the team to its Stanley Cup victories in 1995, 2000, and 2003. In 2006, he became the first player in franchise history to have his number retired. Though best remembered for his physical play, Stevens' 60 assists in 1993–94 remain a franchise record and his 18 goals and 78 points that year are the most ever achieved by a Devils defenseman.

CAPTAIN KIRK

The Devils selected Kirk Muller second overall behind Mario Lemieux in the 1984 NHL Entry Draft. He entered the NHL as an 18-year-old in 1984–85 and quickly became an offensive force. His six points (three goals, three assists) in one game in an 8-6 win over Pittsburgh on October 29, 1986 are a franchise record. Named team captain in 1987–88, Muller's 94 points (37 goals, 57 assists) for the Devils that year remain a franchise high for centers.

Scott Stevens got to hoist the Stanley Cup three times as captain of the New Jersey Devils.

HOME SWEET HOME

Just a few weeks after Scott Stevens had his number 4 retired on February 3, 2006, the Devils retired Ken Daneyko's number 3 on March 24, 2006. Daneyko spent his entire 20-year NHL career with the Devils from 1983–84 through 2002–03, setting club records for seasons played and for games played with 1,283. A solid stay-at-home defenseman, Daneyko won the Masterton Trophy for perseverance, sportsmanship, and dedication to hockey in 2000.

Martin Brodeur has led all NHL goalies in wins a record nine times in his career. He's led all goalies in games played on six occasions and in shutouts five times.

SHOT DOWN AGAIN

For all of its success, New Jersey has struggled with the shootout. The Devils lost all 13 games that spanned into the bonus format during the 2013–14 season to run their streak of ineptitude to an NHL-record 17 consecutive contests. The lost points came back to haunt New Jersey, as it fell just five points shy of qualifying for the playoffs. The latter portion of the campaign was particularly brutal for the Devils, who lost five shootouts in a nine-game stretch.

LONG-TIME TEAM LEADER

Martin Brodeur has more wins than any goalie in NHL history. He set the Devils' club record for wins on February 15, 1997 when a 4-1 win at Montreal gave him his 107th victory, one more than Chris Terreri had at the time. The NHL's all-time shutout leader passed Terreri for top spot in Devils' history, with just the seventh shutout of his career in a 4-0 win over Florida on October 7, 1995.

NEW YORK ISLANDERS

NHL president Clarence Campbell had said that the League was unlikely to expand before 1973, but on November 8, 1971, it was announced teams in Long Island and Atlanta would be added for the 1972–73 season. Despite a dismal 12-60-6 record in their first season, the New York Islanders quickly improved. By their third season, they made the playoffs, topped 100 points by their fourth, and won the first of four straight Stanley Cup championships in 1980. General manager Bill Torrey built his team for success through the NHL Draft, landing future stars such as Denis Potvin, Clark Gillies, Bryan Trottier, and Mike Bossy between 1973 and 1977.

IN THE BEGINNING

The Islanders and Atlanta Flames selected 21 players apiece in the Expansion Draft on June 7, 1972. Among the key players acquired by the Islanders were goalie Billy Smith, defenseman Gerry Hart, and forward Ed Westfall. A day later, the Islanders made Billy Harris the first overall selection in the NHL Amateur Draft. The Islanders hosted the Flames in their first NHL regular-season game on October 7, 1972, but were beaten 3-2. Westfall got the team's first goal.

NEW COACH & A FUTURE CAPTAIN

On June 10, 1973, Al Arbour was hired to take over as coach for the Islanders' second season. He brought a sense of toughness and discipline that quickly improved the team's fortunes. A week after hiring Arbour the Islanders selected Denis Potvin first overall in the Amateur Draft. Potvin had broken Bobby Orr's junior scoring records in the Ontario Hockey Association. He made an immediate impact in the NHL and became captain of the Islanders in 1979.

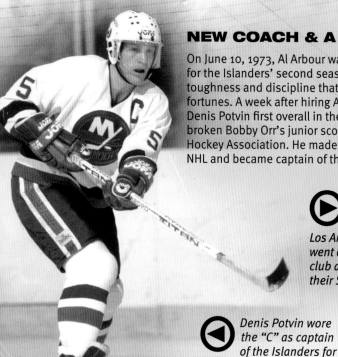

Billy Smith joined the Islanders after playing five games with the Los Angeles Kings in 1971–72. He went on to spend 17 years with the club and was a key component in their Stanley Cup dynasty.

Denis Potvin wore the "C" as captain of the Islanders for nine seasons from 1979–80 through to his retirement at the end of the 1987–88 campaign.

FIRST PLAYOFF APPEARANCE

After making the playoffs in 1974–75, the Islanders upset their highly favored rival, the New York Rangers, in their first postseason series, winning on a goal by J.P. Parise just 11 seconds into overtime in the final game. In the second round against Pittsburgh, the Islanders became the first team since the 1942 Toronto Maple Leafs to win after trailing 3-0. Facing Philadelphia in the semifinals, the Islanders staged a similar rally only to lose the seventh game.

ROOKIES OF THE YEAR

Islanders who have won the Calder Trophy are: Denis Potvin (1974), Bryan Trottier (1976), Mike Bossy (1978), and Bryan Berard (1997). Denis Potvin would later claim the Norris Trophy as the NHL's best defenseman in 1976, 1978, and 1979. Bryan Trottier won both the Art Ross (scoring leader) and Hart (MVP) trophies in 1979, while Bossy won the Conn Smythe Trophy (playoff MVP) in 1982 and the Lady Byng Trophy (sportsmanship) in 1983, 1984, and 1986.

ALL-TIME CAREER LEADERS

Most Seasons	17	Billy Smith
Most Games	1,123	Bryan Trottier
Most Goals	573	Mike Bossy
Most Assists	853	Bryan Trottier
Most Points	1,353	Bryan Trottier (500G, 853A)
Most Wins	304	Billy Smith
Most Shutouts	25	Glenn Resch
Most Penalty Minutes	1,879	Mick Vukota

SINGLE-SEASON LEADERS

Most Goals	69	Mike Bossy (1978–79)
Most Assists	87	Bryan Trottier (1978–79)
Most Points	147	Mike Bossy (1981–82; 64G, 83A)
Most Points, Center	134	Bryan Trottier (1978–79; 47G, 87A)
Most Points, Left Wing	100	John Tonelli (1984–85; 42G, 58A)
Most Points, Defenseman	101	Denis Potvin (1978–79; 31G, 70A)
Most Points, Rookie	95	Bryan Trottier (1975–76; 32G, 63A)
Most Wins	38	Jaroslav Halak (2014-15)
Most Shutouts	7	Glenn Resch (1975–76)
Most Penalty Minutes	356	Brian Curran (1986–87)

HALAK OF A SEASON

Jaroslav Halak certainly made the most of his first season with the Islanders, setting the franchise record by recording a career-high 38 victories – highlighted by yielding just 14 goals en route to winning 11 straight from November 5 to December 4, 2014. Halak made 20 saves in New York's 2-1 triumph over Ottawa on December 4 to break Hall-of-Famer Billy Smith's club-record of wins in a row, which was set during the 1981-82 season. Halak wasn't done, however, as he stopped Michael Ferland on a penalty shot in the first period and finished with 26 saves in the Islanders' 2-1 victory over Calgary on February 27. The win was the 33rd for Halak, snapping a tie with Smith (1981–82), Chris Osgood (2001–02) and Rick DiPietro (2006–07).

Bryan Trottier centered a line with sniper Mike Bossy on the right and the tough but talented Clark Gillies at left. The trio helped take the Islanders to the top.

BIG GAMES

Bryan Trottier set a team record with eight points (five goals, three assists) in a 9-4 win over the Rangers on December 23, 1978. He also scored five goals in an 8-2 win over Philadelphia on February 13, 1982. The only other Islanders player to score five goals in a game was John Tonelli on January 6, 1981 in a 6-3 win over Toronto. Mike Bossy set a club record with six assists that night.

Mike Bossy scored 573 goals in just 752 games in his career for a goals-per-game average of .762, which is tops all time among players who have scored more than 200 goals.

50-GOAL SEASONS

In his 10 seasons with the Islanders, Mike Bossy topped the 50-goal plateau nine times, missing only in his final season of 1986–87, when a back injury that would force his retirement limited him to 38 goals in 63 games. Only two other players in Islanders' history have topped the 50-goal plateau: Pat LaFontaine scored 54 goals in 1989–90 and in 1992–93, Pierre Turgeon (acquired from Buffalo in a trade for LaFontaine in 1991) had 58.

TAVARES: STAR IN MAKING

Expectations were high when New York selected John Tavares with the top overall pick of the 2009 draft – and he did not disappoint. Tavares collected a goal and an assist in his first NHL game versus Pittsburgh on October 3, 2009, recorded a pair of hat tricks in the 2010–11 season before erupting during the lockout-shortened campaign in 2012–13. The Ontario native scored 28 goals and ignited the Islanders to their first postseason appearance since 2007. Tavares was named a finalist for the Hart Trophy, ultimately falling to Washington superstar Alex Ovechkin.

BY THE NUMBERS

Denis Potvin (5), Clark Gillies (9), Bryan Trottier (19), Mike Bossy (22), Bob Nystrom (23), and Billy Smith (31) have all had their numbers retired by the Islanders. Al Arbour had a banner displaying the number 739 (his coaching victories) "retired" in 1997. The Islanders later received the NHL's permission to have Arbour step behind the bench for a final time on November 3, 2007 so that he could reach the 1,500 game milestone as team coach. He picked up one final victory in this contest.

THE LONGEST GAME

On April 18–19, 1987, the longest game in Islanders' history was played at the Capital Centre in Landover, Maryland against the Washington Capitals. It was the seventh game of their opening-round series and tied 2-2 until 8:47 of the fourth overtime period. Pat LaFontaine beat goalie Bob Mason just seconds before 2 a.m. for an Islanders victory. At the time, it was the fifth-longest game in NHL history. No seventh game has ever gone on longer.

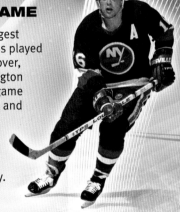

After his overtime goal in 1987, Pat LaFontaine led the Islanders in scoring the next four years in a row.

NEW YORK RANGERS

Following on quickly from the box-office success of the New York Americans at Madison Square Garden in 1925, Tex Rickard and the Madison Square Garden Corporation officially applied for an NHL franchise on April 17, 1926. They were granted a team on May 15. Conn Smythe was hired to assemble the original roster, but it was Lester Patrick who would guide the New York Rangers to success as coach and general manager. After Stanley Cup wins in 1928, 1933, and 1940, the Rangers fell on hard times until NHL expansion in 1967 and endured a record 54-year drought before once again winning the Stanley Cup in 1994.

QUITE THE SEASON: 2014–15

The Rangers enjoyed their best statistical regular season to date in 2014–15, recording franchise bests in wins (53) and points (113) en route to winning the Presidents' Trophy. Both totals eclipsed the records previously held by the 1993–94 club (52 wins, 112 points), which did the 2014–15 team one better by skating away with the Stanley Cup. Rick Nash scored a career-high 42 goals in 2014–15.

EARLY HEROES

With a star forward line featuring Frank Boucher, centering brothers Bill Cook and Bun Cook, and top defensemen in Ching Johnson and Taffy Abel, the Rangers finished their first season of 1926–27 with the third-best overall record in the newly expanded 10-team NHL, while sitting in first place in the League's American Division. Bill Cook was the NHL's scoring leader with 33 goals and four assists during the 44-game season. Cook won a second scoring title in 1932–33.

THE FIRST STANLEY CUP

The Rangers won the Stanley Cup in their second season of 1927–28. After losing game one of the Final to the Montreal Maroons, the Rangers lost goalie Lorne Chabot to an eye injury midway through game two. Rangers coach Lester Patrick took over in net and inspired his team to a 2-1 overtime victory. The following day, the Rangers signed New York Americans netminder Joe Miller, who led them to a 3-2 victory in the best-of-five series.

BEYOND 33

Bill Cook's 33 goals in 1926–27 (which he subsequently matched in 1931–32) remained a Rangers club record until the 1958–59 season. That year, Andy Bathgate became the first player in the club's history to score 40 goals. Bathgate's 40 stood as the club record until the 1971–72 season when Vic Hadfield became the first Rangers player to score 50 goals. The Rangers' only other 50-goal scorers are Adam Graves (52 in 1993–94) and Jaromir Jagr (54 in 2005–06).

▲ Derek Stepan (21) and Chris Kreider gave the fans a thrill at Yankee Stadium by leading the Rangers to victory.

DOUBLE OVERTIME

Bill Cook became the first player in NHL history to score the Stanley Cup-winning goal in overtime when the Rangers beat the Leafs 1-0 on April 13, 1933. The Leafs were two men short at the time and Cook remains the only player to score an overtime Cup-winning goal on the powerplay. In 1940, the Rangers beat the Leafs in overtime to win the Stanley Cup again. This time it was Bryan Hextall who scored the winner.

ALL-TIME CAREER LEADERS

Most Seasons	18	Rod Gilbert
Most Games	1,160	Harry Howell
Most Goals	406	Rod Gilbert
Most Assists	741	Brian Leetch
Most Points	1,021	Rod Gilbert (406G, 615A)
Most Wins	339	Henrik Lundqvist
Most Shutouts	55	Henrik Lundqvist
Most Penalty Minutes	1,226	Ron Greschner

KING HENRIK: WINS

After becoming the first goaltender in NHL history to record 30 victories in each of his first seven seasons in the league, Henrik Lundqvist etched his name into the franchise's record books in impressive fashion. The Swede secured his 300th win after turning aside all 30 shots in a 3-0 triumph against Detroit on March 9, 2014. Five days later, Lundqvist also made 30 saves in a 4-2 win over Winnipeg to equal Mike Richter for the franchise mark in victories, only to secure the mark for himself on March 18 as New York erupted for a season high in goals in an 8-4 triumph over Ottawa.

HOME RUN AT YANKEE STADIUM

Playing outdoors at Yankee Stadium, the Rangers scored six unanswered goals to leave New Jersey out in the cold in a 7-3 triumph on January 26, 2014. Mats Zuccarello scored twice and Rick Nash also tallied for the fifth consecutive game as New York erased an early two-goal deficit. Devils goaltender Martin Brodeur certainly struck out with his performance after yielding six goals before being pulled to start the third. The Rangers improved to 2-0-0 at Yankee Stadium with a 2-1 victory over the New York Islanders three days later.

MESSIER DELIVERS

In his first season with the Rangers in 1991–92, Mark Messier had 107 points (35 goals, 72 assists), led the team to first place in the NHL's overall standings, and won the Hart Trophy as MVP. Messier famously scored a hat trick after "guaranteeing" a victory over New Jersey in game six of the 1994 Eastern Conference Final. After eliminating the Devils, the Rangers beat Vancouver to win the Stanley Cup for the first time since 1940.

KING HENRIK: SHUTOUTS

Registering a shutout was nothing new for Henrik Lundqvist, who recorded 10 in 2007-08 to become the first Rangers goaltender to lead the league in that category since Ed Giacomin (eight) in 1970–71. Lundqvist stood atop the NHL once again in 2010-11, securing a career-high 11 shutouts to remain in hot pursuit of Giacomin for the franchise record. The 2012 Vezina Trophy winner finally surpassed Giacomin on March 22, 2014, turning aside all 21 shots he faced for his 50th career blanking in a 2-0 victory over NHL shutout king Martin Brodeur and New Jersey. "My parents flew in to be here and share this moment with me – to break the shutout record, and that means a lot to me," Lundqvist said. "I'm really happy right now."

▶ *Henrik Lundqvist led the NHL in shutouts for a second time with a career-high 11 in 2010–11.*

◀ *Mark Messier was already a star when he arrived in New York, but he became a legend in 1994 when he led the Rangers to their first Stanley Cup victory in 54 years.*

100-POINT PAIR

Center Jean Ratelle was the first player in Rangers' history to collect 100 points in a season when he reached the milestone on February 18, 1972. He finished the 1971–72 campaign with 46 goals and 63 assists for 109 points in just 63 games. Vic Hadfield (50 goals, 56 assists) also topped 100 points that season. Ratelle and Hadfield played with Rod Gilbert on the Rangers' top line, known as the G-A-G Line for "Goal-A-Game."

FIVE IN ONE GAME

Don Murdoch set a Rangers record with five goals in a game in a 10-4 win over the Minnesota North Stars on October 12, 1976. He and Toronto's Howie Meeker from 1947 are the only modern-era rookies to score five goals in an NHL game. Mark Pavelich is the only other Rangers player to score five goals in one game when he led New York to an 11-3 win over the Hartford Whalers on February 23, 1983.

A CASE FOR THE DEFENSE

The first Rangers player to win the Norris Trophy as the NHL's Best Defenseman was Doug Harvey. He won the award in 1961–62, after having already won it six times in the previous seven seasons with the Montreal Canadiens. Harry Howell won the Norris for the Rangers in 1966–67 just before Bobby Orr won in each of the next eight seasons. Brian Leetch won the Norris twice for the Rangers, first in 1991–92 and then in 1996–97.

OTTAWA SENATORS

The rebirth of NHL hockey in Ottawa formally began on June 12, 1989, when a Letter of Intent for an expansion team was filed with the League. On December 6, 1990, it was announced that Ottawa and Tampa Bay had been awarded franchises to begin play in 1992–93. The Senators' 10-70-4 record that season was one of the worst in history and improvement was slow until the fifth season of 1996–97, when the team made its first playoff appearance. Soon the Senators were among the best teams in the NHL, topping 100 points six times in eight seasons from 1998–99 through 2006–07, winning four division titles, and reaching the Stanley Cup Final in 2007.

FIRST PLAYERS

Goalie Peter Sidorkiewicz was the first player selected by the Senators in the NHL Expansion Draft on June 18, 1992. Two days later, Ottawa selected Alexei Yashin with its first choice (second overall) at the 1992 NHL Entry Draft, but Yashin would not join the Senators for another year. Norm MacIver was obtained from Edmonton in the NHL Waiver Draft on October 4, 1992 and led the team with 63 points (17 goals, 46 assists) the first season.

ALEXEI & ALEXANDRE

Alexei Yashin joined the Senators in 1993–94 and led the team with 30 goals, 49 assists, and 79 points. He was selected to play in the NHL All-Star Game that season and finished fourth in voting for the Calder Trophy as Rookie of the Year. Alexandre Daigle, whom the team chose first overall in the 1993 Entry Draft, had 20 goals and 31 assists, but never developed into the star he was expected to become.

YASHIN'S BIG YEAR

From 1993–94 through 2000–01, Alexei Yashin spent seven seasons in Ottawa and led the team in goals and points in every season except 1995–96. His best season came in 1998–99 with 44 goals, 50 assists, and 94 points. Yashin was sixth in points in the NHL and his 44 goals tied him with Jaromir Jagr and Tony Amonte for second behind Teemu Selanne's 47. He finished second to Jagr in voting for the Hart Trophy as NHL MVP.

Defenseman Cody Ceci only scored three times during his rookie season, but two were game-winning goals.

HOSSA & A HOST OF RECORDS

Marian Hossa was a rookie with the Senators in 1998–99 and finished runner-up behind Colorado's Chris Drury for the Calder Trophy that season. He topped 30 goals for the first time in 2000–01 and broke Alexei Yashin's club record by scoring 45 times in 2002–03 to rank fourth in the NHL. As a team, the Senators set club records in 2002–03 with 52 wins and 113 points. They went on to match those marks in 2005–06.

FIRST GAME

The Senators hosted the Montreal Canadiens in their first regular-season NHL game on October 8, 1992. With a national television audience watching on *Hockey Night in Canada*, Ottawa defeated Montreal 5-3. The first Senators goal was scored on a powerplay when Neil Brady beat Patrick Roy 26 seconds into the second period. Sylvain Turgeon was credited with the game-winning goal and Doug Smail iced the victory with an empty-net goal at 19:46 of the third period.

50 & 100

On August 23, 2005, Marian Hossa was traded to Atlanta for Dany Heatley. In his first season with the Senators in 2005–06, Heatley scored 50 goals to become the first player in franchise history to reach the milestone. Both he and Daniel Alfredsson (43 goals, 60 assists) had 103 points, becoming the first Ottawa players to top the century mark. Heatley had 50 goals and 55 assists for a club-record 105 points in 2006–07.

COLOSSAL KARLSSON

Erik Karlsson set a franchise record for assists by a defenseman when he notched his 47th helper in a 5-2 win over Washington on February 22, 2012. The Norris Trophy winner, who finished with 59 assists to shatter Norm MacIver's mark, notched 25 more points than any other defenseman in the league. Karlsson also tied Steve Duchesne's record for most goals by a blue-liner with 19.

OTTAWA'S ALL-TIME LEADER

Daniel Alfredsson won the Calder Trophy as Rookie of the Year in 1995–96, collecting 26 goals and 35 assists for 61 points in his first NHL season. He has spent his entire career in Ottawa and became the Senators' all-time leader in games played, goals, assists, and points. On April 6, 2010, he played his 1,000th game for the team and scored a hat trick against the Buffalo Sabres on October 22, 2010 to reach the 1,000-point plateau.

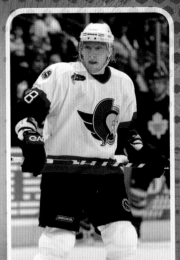

◀ Captain Daniel Alfredsson continues to lead by example. During the 2011–12 season, the veteran Swede registered his most goals (27) since he recorded 40 in 2007–08.

▶ Marian Hossa scored 188 goals in the six full seasons he spent in Ottawa. Only Daniel Alfredsson, Alexei Yashin, and Jason Spezza have scored more for the Senators.

400 FOR ALFIE

After missing a fair portion of 2010 due to a balky back, Daniel Alfredsson returned with the vigor of a man half his age. The 39-year-old Swede netted his 400th goal at the 3:31 mark of overtime to lift the Senators to a 4-3 win over the Calgary Flames on December 30, 2011. The NHL's longest serving active captain, Alfredsson's blast from the left point sailed past Leland Irving to send Scotiabank Place into a frenzy. The tally was Alfredsson's 1,050th point, also a team record.

CECI CLUTCH IN HERITAGE CLASSIC

Codi Ceci isn't known for his offense, although his goals have proven timely. The defenseman recorded his second tally of the season as Ottawa netted four unanswered goals en route to a 4-2 victory over Vancouver in the Heritage Classic on March 2, 2014. With more than 50,000 people in attendance at BC Place Stadium, Ceci converted an odd-man rush and solved fellow rookie Eddie Lack from the right circle to snap a tie midway through the second period. The tally was Ceci's first since December 16, which also served as a game-winner.

▲ Jason Spezza topped the 30-goal plateau for three straight seasons from 2006-07 through 2008-09. He had a career-high 92 points (34 goals, 58 assists) in 2007-08.

BIG GAMES

The Senators' record for most points in one game is seven and was set by Daniel Alfredsson on January 24, 2008, when he had three goals and four assists in an 8-4 win over Tampa Bay. Marian Hossa had a club-record five assists in an 8-3 win over the Lighting on January 4, 2001. Hossa was also the first player in franchise history to score four goals in one game in an 8-1 win over Atlanta on January 2, 2003.

SPEZZA'S SINGLE-SEASON RECORD

Jason Spezza became only the second player in Senators' history to collect 500 points with the team on February 15, 2011. Spezza set up a goal by Bobby Butler to reach the 500-point plateau (181 goals, 319 assists) during a 4-3 loss to the New York Islanders in his 501st career game. Back in 2005–06, he set a Senators single-season record with 71 assists.

HAMBURGLAR TO THE RESCUE

Ottawa looked like anything but a contender on February 10, 2015, as it resided 14 points out of a playoff berth with two months remaining in the regular season. Enter Andrew Hammond (20-1-2, 1.79 GAA, .941 save percentage), who made his first NHL start with a 4-2 victory over Montreal on February 18 as the Senators ignited a sizzling 23-4-4 mark to secure the top wild-card position in the Eastern Conference.

STONE COLD SENATOR

Mark Stone put his best foot forward in his initial season in 2014–15, collecting 26 goals and 38 assists to match Calgary's Johnny Gaudreau for the most points (64) by a rookie. Stone finished with a flourish, recording eight goals and five assists on his nine-game point streak to end the season – the longest such run by any rookie in franchise history. The 22-year-old tallied twice – including the overtime winner – to secure his first career multi-goal performance in a 4-3 victory over Pittsburgh on April 7, before scoring twice in a playoff-clinching 3-1 triumph over Philadelphia four days later.

PHILADELPHIA FLYERS

The NHL was initially skeptical of Philadelphia as an expansion site due to the city's historically poor support of various minor-league teams over the years. Many were surprised on February 9, 1966 when Philadelphia was included among the six cities to join the NHL for the 1967–68 season, yet fans soon flocked to see the Flyers. The team quickly became known as "The Broad Street Bullies" for its intimidating style of play and in 1974, would become the first of the NHL's new expansion teams to win the Stanley Cup. They won it again in 1975 and have remained among the NHL's elite for most of their history.

BOBBY CLARKE: BY THE NUMBERS

From 1970–71 through 1975–76, Bobby Clarke was the Flyers' top scorer for six straight seasons and eight times overall. He was the first Flyers player to win a major award when he received the Masterton Trophy in 1972 and won the Hart Trophy as NHL MVP in 1973, 1975, and 1976. Clarke's 89 assists in 1974–75 and 1975–76 set an NHL record for centers at the time and remain the single-season high in Flyers' history.

FLYERS FIRSTS

On October 11, 1967, the Flyers played their first NHL regular-season game in Oakland when they lost 5-1 to the Seals. Their first win was a 2-1 victory in St. Louis on October 18. The following night, they played their first home game and beat Pittsburgh 1-0. Bill Sutherland scored and goalie Doug Favell earned the team's first shutout. Leon Rochefort scored the first hat trick in a 4-1 win at Montreal on November 4, 1967.

VORACEK'S CAREER YEAR

Forward Jakub Voracek recorded his best season to date in 2014–15, posting a career-best 59 assists to go along with his club-leading 81 points. Voracek finished one assist behind Washington's Nicklas Backstrom for the league lead, while his overall total was 20 more than his previous career best – set in 2013–14. Voracek also remained in the scoring race throughout the season, before falling behind eventual champion Jamie Benn of Dallas during the final week.

BOBBY CLARKE: BEGINNINGS

Though a junior sensation, 10 out of 12 NHL teams passed on selecting Bobby Clarke in the 1969 Amateur Draft (and some more than once) because he'd been diagnosed with diabetes. Philadelphia took a chance on him with their second pick, 17th overall, midway through the second round. By his second season of 1970–71, Clarke had emerged as the Flyers' top scorer. He was named captain during the 1972–73 season and was the team's undisputed leader.

ALL-TIME CAREER LEADERS

Most Seasons	15	Bobby Clarke
Most Games	1,144	Bobby Clarke
Most Goals	420	Bill Barber
Most Assists	852	Bobby Clarke
Most Points	1,210	Bobby Clarke (358G, 852A)
Most Wins	240	Ron Hextall
Most Shutouts	50	Bernie Parent
Most Penalty Minutes	1,817	Rick Tocchet

 With captain Claude Giroux at the helm, the resilient Flyers always had a chance during the 2013–14 season.

FIRST TO 50 & 100

On March 29, 1973, Bobby Clarke became the first Flyer (and ninth player in NHL history) to record 100 points in a season with a third-period goal in a 4-2 win over the Atlanta Flames. Three days later, Rick MacLeish became the first Flyer (and eighth player in NHL history) to record 50 goals in one season during a 5-4 loss at Pittsburgh. The goal was also MacLeish's 100th point of the 1972–73 season.

SINGLE-SEASON GOAL-SCORING LEADERS

61	Reggie Leach	1975–76 (80 GP)
58	Tim Kerr	1985–86 (76 GP)
	Tim Kerr	1986–87 (75 GP)
54	Tim Kerr	1983–84 (79 GP)
	Tim Kerr	1984–85 (74 GP)
53	Mark Recchi	1992–93 (84 GP)
51	John LeClair	1995–96 (82 GP)
	John LeClair	1997–98 (82 GP)
50	Reggie Leach	1979–80 (76 GP)
	Bill Barber	1975–76 (80 GP)
	John LeClair	1996–97 (82 GP)
	Rick MacLeish	1972–73 (78 GP)

▶ *Tim Kerr scored 363 goals in 601 games over 11 seasons in Philadelphia. He ranks third all-time on the Flyers' career goal-scoring list.*

STANLEY CUP SUCCESS

The Flyers became the first 1967 expansion team to win a game in the Stanley Cup Final, when Bobby Clarke scored in overtime to beat Boston 3-2 in game two of the 1974 series. They went on to take the series in six games, defeating the Bruins 1-0 on a goal by Rick MacLeish in Game Six. A year later, Philadelphia faced Buffalo in the first all-expansion Final and took the Stanley Cup again with another six-game victory.

RALLYING CRY

The Flyers didn't fret during the 2013–14 season when they found themselves trailing in the third period – and with good reason. Philadelphia set a franchise record by overcoming such a deficit for the 10th time on February 3, 2014 when it scored four goals in the final session en route to a 5-2 victory over San Jose. Captain Claude Giroux keyed this comeback with a goal and two assists as the Flyers posted their first victory over the Sharks since 2000. The Flyers added to their record by rallying from a two-goal deficit for a 5-4 triumph over Washington on March 2.

▶ *Eric Lindros had 290 goals and 369 assists for 659 points in just 468 games over his eight seasons in Philadelphia. His average of 1.36 points per game is by far the best in club history.*

BERNIE BY THE NUMBERS

Ron Hextall has surpassed his total of 232 career victories for the Flyers, but Bernie Parent still holds numerous Philadelphia goaltending records. His 47 wins of 1973–74 were an NHL record for many years and are still a Flyers' high, though his 29 losses in 1969–70 (tied by Antero Niittymaki in 2006–07) are still on the team's books. Parent set a team record with 12 shutouts in 1973–74 and went on to match this in 1974–75.

◀ *Bernie Parent was brilliant during the Flyers' Stanley Cup-winning seasons of 1973–74 and 1974–75, winning the Vezina Trophy and the Conn Smythe Trophy in both years.*

THE BIG E

Eric Lindros is the only player in Flyers' history to lead the NHL in scoring, although he did not win the Art Ross Trophy. During the 1994–95 season (shortened to 48 games due to a lockout), Lindros tied Pittsburgh's Jaromir Jagr for the League lead with 70 points but since Jagr had 32 goals to Lindros's 29, he received the Art Ross Trophy. However, Lindros earned the Hart Trophy as NHL MVP that year.

SINGLE-GAME STANDARDS

A total of nine different Flyers have combined to score four goals in a game 16 times, led by Tim Kerr, who scored four goals on four occasions. Tom Bladon scored four goals in an 11-1 win over the Cleveland Barons on December 11, 1977 and also added four assists for a club-record eight-point game. The Flyers' single-game record for assists is six and was set by Eric Lindros in an 8-5 win over Ottawa on February 26, 1997.

PITTSBURGH PENGUINS

The history of pro hockey in Pittsburgh dates back to the early 1900s, but the city's original NHL franchise lasted only from 1925 to 1929. Pittsburgh re-entered the NHL as one of six new expansion teams for the 1967–68 season, but success came slowly for the Penguins until they selected Mario Lemieux with the first choice in the 1984 Entry Draft. Lemieux led the Penguins to back-to-back Stanley Cup titles in 1991 and 1992, and became part owner of the club in 1999. With the team struggling on the ice again, the Penguins landed Sidney Crosby with the top draft pick in 2005 and in 2009, became Stanley Cup champions.

50 X 2 = 100

Jean Pronovost became the first Penguin to score 50 goals on March 24, 1976 in a 5-5 tie with Boston. Pierre Larouche became the first Pittsburgh player to reach 100 points in the same game. In a 5-4 loss to Washington on April 3, 1976, Pronovost reached the 100-point plateau, while Larouche scored his 50th goal. Pronovost ended the season with 50 goals and 52 assists, while Larouche set club records with 53 goals and 111 points.

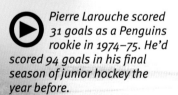

▶ *Pierre Larouche scored 31 goals as a Penguins rookie in 1974–75. He'd scored 94 goals in his final season of junior hockey the year before.*

A BUSY NIGHT

Mario Lemieux scored five goals in a regular-season game for the Penguins three times in his career. The first was on December 31, 1988 in an 8-6 win over New Jersey, when Lemieux scored once on the powerplay, once shorthanded, once at even strength, once on a penalty shot, and once into an open net. He also had three assists in that game, tying his own club record with eight points.

THE CENTURY LINE

Syl Apps Jr. centered right-winger Jean Pronovost and left-winger Lowell McDonald for four seasons from 1972–73 through 1975–76. The trio combined to collect over 200 points in all four seasons, topped 100 goals twice, and was dubbed "The Century Line." Apps led the Penguins in assists five times during his six full seasons in Pittsburgh, including 1975–76, when he achieved what was then a club record with 67 assists and a career-high 99 points.

LEMIEUX MEANS THE BEST

As a rookie in 1984–85, Mario Lemieux had 43 goals and 57 assists for 100 points. A year later, he had 48 goals and set new club records with 93 assists and 141 points. Rick Kehoe had broken Pierre Larouche's record of 53 goals when he scored 55 in 1980–81, but Lemieux shattered that mark with 70 goals in 1987–88 as he continued to push Penguins' single-season records to new heights.

SINGLE-SEASON LEADERS

Most Goals	85	Mario Lemieux (1988–89)
Most Assists	114	Mario Lemieux (1988–89)
Most Points	199	Mario Lemieux (1988–89)
Most Points, Right Wing	*149	Jaromir Jagr (1995–96; 62G, 87A)
Most Points, Left Wing	123	Kevin Stevens (1991–92; 54G, 69A)
Most Points, Defenseman	113	Paul Coffey (1988–89; 30G, 83A)
Most Points, Rookie	102	Sidney Crosby (2005–06; 39G, 63A)
Most Wins	43	Tom Barrasso (1992–93)
Most Shutouts	10	Marc-Andre Fleury 2014–15
Most Penalty Minutes	409	Paul Baxter (1981–82)

*NHL record

ALL-TIME CAREER LEADERS

Most Seasons	17	Mario Lemieux
Most Games	915	Mario Lemieux
Most Goals	690	Mario Lemieux
Most Assists	1,033	Mario Lemieux
Most Points	1,723	Mario Lemieux
Most Wins	322	Marc-Andre Fleury
Most Shutouts	38	Marc-Andre Fleury
Most Penalty Minutes	1,048	Kevin Stevens

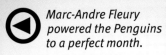

Marc-Andre Fleury powered the Penguins to a perfect month.

SIX ASSISTS

Ron Stackhouse was the first Penguin with six assists in one game in an 8-2 win over the Flyers on March 8, 1975. Greg Malone tied the record on November 28, 1979, in a 7-2 win over the Quebec Nordiques. In addition to Mario Lemieux's six-assist game against St. Louis in 1988, he also had six in a 9-4 win over San Jose on December 5, 1992, and in a 10-0 win over Tampa Bay on November 1, 1995.

JAGR & LEMIEUX

Between them, Mario Lemieux and Jaromir Jagr won the Art Ross Trophy as the NHL's leading scorer 11 times in 14 seasons between 1987–88 and 2000–01. Jagr won his first scoring title in 1994–95 and later won four in a row, from 1997–98 to 2000–01. He joined the Penguins in 1990–91 and spent 11 seasons with the team. Jagr ranks second to Lemieux in franchise history in games (806), goals (439), assists (640), and points (1,079).

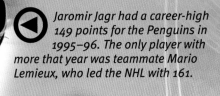

Jaromir Jagr had a career-high 149 points for the Penguins in 1995–96. The only player with more that year was teammate Mario Lemieux, who led the NHL with 161.

MARCH OF THE PENGUINS

Pittsburgh set an NHL record by winning all 15 contests to complete a perfect month of March during the 2012–13 season. This set a franchise record for a month for the Penguins, who capped the streak with shutouts against Montreal, Winnipeg and the New York Islanders. Chris Kunitz scored 11 goals and nine assists while Pascal Dupuis finished the stretch with a plus-19 rating. Marc-Andre Fleury and backup Tomas Vokoun split the netminding responsibilities, winning eight and seven games, respectively.

OTHER SCORING FEATS

On December 23, 1991, Joe Mullen scored four goals in a 6-3 win over the Islanders. In the team's next game, on December 26, Mullen scored four goals again in a 12-1 rout of Toronto. No other player in Penguins' history has ever had back-to-back four-goal games. The 12 goals the Penguins scored against the Maple Leafs tied a team record set on March 15, 1975, when they beat the Washington Capitals 12-1.

Joe Mullen won Stanley Cup championships in Pittsburgh in 1991 and 1992. He'd previously won the Stanley Cup with Calgary in 1989.

CROSBY LEADS THE WAY

In his second NHL season of 2006–07, Sidney Crosby joined Mario Lemieux and Jaromir Jagr as Art Ross Trophy winners when he led the NHL with 120 points (36 goals, 84 assists). In the playoffs of 2008, Crosby led the NHL with 21 assists and 27 points as Pittsburgh reached the Stanley Cup Final. When they beat Detroit in a Stanley Cup rematch in 2009, Crosby was the playoff leader with 15 goals.

FLEURY FINISHES STRONG

Marc-Andre Fleury made certain that Pittsburgh made the playoffs during the 2014–15 season, registering his career-high 10th shutout in a 2-0 victory over Buffalo on April 11. The 30-year-old Fleury turned aside all 28 shots he faced for his 38th career blanking, allowing Pittsburgh to secure a postseason berth for the ninth straight season. Fleury highlighted the stretch by establishing a career-best 165:06 shutout run spanning over four games from February 1–11, 2015.

Sidney Crosby led the Penguins from non-playoff team to Stanley Cup champions in four seasons.

Few players in NHL history have possessed the offensive skills that Mario Lemieux had. He played 17 seasons and put up huge numbers despite battling injuries and illness.

SAN JOSE SHARKS

On May 9, 1990, the NHL granted approval for brothers George and Gordon Gund to sell the Minnesota North Stars in return for the rights to an expansion franchise in the San Francisco Bay Area. The San Jose Sharks would begin play in the 1991–92 season and spent two years at the Cow Palace in Daly City, located just outside the San Francisco city limits, before moving to a new arena in downtown San Jose in 1993. They made the playoffs for the first time in 1993–94 and would emerge as a Western Conference power after winning their first Pacific Division title in 2001–02.

RECORD IMPROVEMENT

The Sharks were 17-58-5 (39 points) in their first season and even worse in 1992–93, when they went 11-71-2 for just 24 points and set an NHL record for losses. In 1993–94, they improved their record to 33-35-16. Led by goalie Arturs Irbe, defenseman Sandis Ozolinsh, and newly acquired former Soviet stars Igor Larionov and Sergei Makarov, the Sharks' 58-point increase from 24 to 82 marked the greatest single-season turnaround in NHL history.

Drafted first overall by the Quebec Nordiques in 1990, Owen Nolan played in San Jose from 1995 to 2003 and was captain of the team for five seasons.

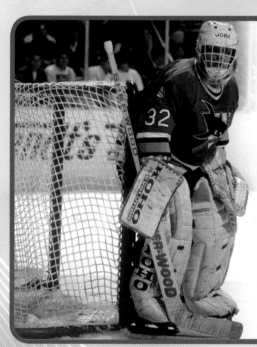

OTHER 1993-94 HIGHLIGHTS

Sergei Makarov became the first player in franchise history to score 30 goals in 1993–94, while Sandis Ozolinsh set club records for defensemen still in existence, with 26 goals and 64 points. Artus Irbe led all goaltenders with 74 games played and set what was then an NHL record for most minutes played: 4,412 minutes. The Sharks made the playoffs for the first time and stunned the top-seeded Red Wings in the opening round.

Arturs Irbe was a member of the Sharks during their first five seasons in the NHL, coming to the team in 1991 in the Dispersal Draft of Minnesota North Stars players.

THE GREAT PAVELSKI

Joe Pavelski reached the 30-goal, 30-assist plateau for the third time in his career, collecting a team-leading 37 and 32, respectively, during the 2014–15 season. Pavelski eclipsed the 30-tally mark as part of recording his fourth career hat trick in a 4-2 triumph over Arizona on February 13, tying Patrick Marleau for the second-most three-goal performances in franchise history. The win over the Coyotes gave coach Todd McLellan his 300th career victory.

40, THEN 50

Owen Nolan was the first player in Sharks' history to score 40 goals when he had 44 in 1999–2000. His 84 points and 18 powerplay goals that season also established club records at the time. In 2005–06, Jonathan Cheechoo became the Sharks' first 50-goal scorer when he won the Maurice "Rocket" Richard Trophy with a league-leading 56 goals. Cheechoo also set a new club record with 24 powerplay goals.

SCORING TITLE

On November 30, 2005, the Sharks acquired Joe Thornton from the Boston Bruins. At the time of the trade, Thornton had 33 points (nine goals, 24 assists) in 23 games for Boston. He collected 92 points (20 goals, 72 assists) in 58 games in San Jose and won the Art Ross Trophy as the NHL scoring leader with a total of 125 points on 29 goals and 96 assists. Thornton also won the Hart Trophy as MVP.

THORNTON LEADS THE WAY

Joe Thornton's 1,000th career NHL game was certainly a memorable one. On October 21, 2011, the captain helped San Jose rally from a two-goal deficit by scoring late in the second period and then set up Joe Pavelski's tying tally with 33 seconds left in regulation. Aided by Thornton's heroics, the Sharks rallied for a 4-3 shootout win over the New Jersey Devils.

▶ *The San Jose Sharks picked Patrick Marleau second overall in the 1997 NHL Entry Draft. The Boston Bruins had selected Joe Thornton with the first pick that year.*

◀ *There's no stopping Joe Thornton! The veteran played in all 82 games during the 2011–12 season for the fourth time in his career.*

29 SHOTS IN ONE PERIOD

San Jose unleashed a franchise-record 29 of its 54 total shots in the third period on March 18, 2014 – to no avail. Goaltender Roberto Luongo made 52 saves as Florida posted a 3-2 victory. What made his performance even more impressive is that he exited unscathed as the Sharks were awarded 7:09 of power-play time in the session against the league's worst penalty-killing team.

TEAM RECORDS

The Sharks established team records with 53 wins (53-18-11) and 117 points in 2009–10 and won the Presidents' Trophy for best overall record in the NHL for the first time. In 2005–06, the team scored a record 266 goals. The club record for goals in one game is 10, first set in a 10-8 win in Pittsburgh on January 13, 1996, and matched at home in a 10-2 win over Columbus on March 30, 2002.

500, THE HARD WAY!

Jeremy Roenick scored the 500th goal of his NHL career as a Sharks player against the Phoenix Coyotes on November 10, 2007. It was a major milestone but it wasn't pretty. Roenick dumped the puck into the Phoenix end from outside the blue line, the puck hit the glass behind the net, bounced off the goal, deflected off goalie Alex Auld's skate, twirled toward the goal line, and then skittered in off Auld's stick.

▼ *Evgeni Nabokov finished among the top 10 in the NHL in goals-against average four times in his nine full seasons with the Sharks.*

ROOKIE OF THE YEAR

Defenseman Brad Stuart was the first Sharks player to be a finalist for the Calder Trophy in 2000, but finished second to New Jersey's Scott Gomez in the final voting. A year later, Sharks goalie Evgeni Nabokov won the Calder Trophy. Nabokov set new franchise records for wins (32), goals-against average (2.19), and shutouts (six) in 2000–01. He was also named Sharks Player of the Year that season, and finished fourth in voting for the Vezina Trophy.

GOALIE RECORDS

In his 10 seasons in San Jose through 2009–10, Evgeni Nabokov shattered all previous career records with 293 wins and 50 shutouts. He holds the top six positions for single-season victories, including a high of 46 in 2007–08, and set a team record for shutouts with nine in 2003–04. Vesa Toskala holds the team records for goals-against average with a single-season best of 2.06 in 2003–04 and a career mark of 2.34.

ST. LOUIS BLUES

Since entering the NHL in 1967, the St. Louis Blues have employed some of the greatest players in history. Such old-time hockey heroes as Dickie Moore, Doug Harvey, Glenn Hall, and Jacques Plante helped give the team its start. Later, stars like Brett Hull, Wayne Gretzky, Dale Hawerchuk, Al MacInnis, and Chris Pronger would also spend time in St. Louis. Though they have never won the Stanley Cup, the Blues reached the Final in each of their first three seasons in the NHL and the team's run of 25 straight playoff appearances from 1980 through 2004 is the third-longest in NHL history behind Boston (29 years, 1968–96) and Chicago (28 years, 1970–97).

THE FIRST THREE YEARS

When the NHL doubled to 12 teams for the 1967–68 season, the six new expansion teams were all put together in one division and the playoffs arranged so that for the next three years an expansion team would meet an "Original Six" team for the Stanley Cup. The Blues made it to the Final three years in a row but were swept by Montreal (1968, 1969) and Boston (1970).

BIG GAMES

On November 3, 1968, Camille Henry became the first Blues player to score a hat trick in a 4-4 tie with Detroit. Just four nights later, Red Berenson set club records with six goals and seven points in an 8-0 win over Philadelphia. The only other St. Louis player to collect seven points in one game was Garry Unger, with three goals and four assists in a 9-0 win over Buffalo on March 13, 1971.

 Garry Unger never scored fewer than 30 goals during his eight full seasons in St. Louis. His 41 goals in 1972–73 tied him for sixth in the NHL that year.

FIRST TO 50 & 100

The 1980–81 season marked the first time in Blues' history that the team had a 50-goal scorer and a player topped 100 points. Wayne Babych reached the 50-goal plateau on March 12, 1981 and finished the season with 54 goals. Bernie Federko notched his 100th point of the 1980–81 season with an assist on March 28, 1981. He finished the year with 104 points on 31 goals and 73 assists.

Brett Hull was the Blues' top goal scorer for nine straight seasons from 1988–89 through 1996–97.

OTHER 50-GOAL SCORERS

Wayne Babych's 54 goals in 1980–81 remained a Blues club record until the 1989–90 season when Brett Hull shattered it with 72 goals. A year later, Hull had the third-highest goal-scoring season in NHL history when he scored 86 times. He followed that with a 70-goal effort in 1991–92, and then scored 54 and 57 in the next two years. Brendan Shanahan is the Blues' only other 50-goal scorer, with 51 in 1992–93 and 52 in 1993–94.

OSHIE TAKES OVER SOCHI, SHOOTOUT

T.J. Oshie converted four times in the shootout to lift the United States Olympic team to a 3-2 triumph over Russia in the 2014 Sochi Games. He was selected by American coach Dan Bylsma based on his success rate in the NHL's bonus format. The Blues' forward led the league in 2013–14 with nine shootout goals on 12 attempts – including five that served as the game-deciding tally.

EXCELLENT ELLIOTT

Brian Elliott became the Blues' all-time franchise leader in shutouts by notching his 21st with the club and 30th overall on March 17, 2015. Elliott edged past Jaroslav Halak for the honor by turning aside all 25 shots he faced in a 4-0 victory over Calgary. The blanking was the second in three games and fifth of the season for Elliott, who was competing in just his fourth year with the club.

ALL-TIME CAREER LEADERS

Most Seasons	13	Bernie Federko
Most Games	927	Bernie Federko
Most Goals	527	Brett Hull
Most Assists	721	Bernie Federko
Most Points	1,073	Bernie Federko (352G, 721A)
Most Wins	151	Mike Liut
Most Shutouts	21	Brian Elliott
Most Penalty Minutes	1,786	Brian Sutter

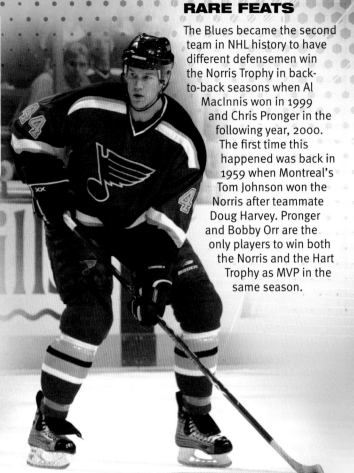

RARE FEATS

The Blues became the second team in NHL history to have different defensemen win the Norris Trophy in back-to-back seasons when Al MacInnis won in 1999 and Chris Pronger in the following year, 2000. The first time this happened was back in 1959 when Montreal's Tom Johnson won the Norris after teammate Doug Harvey. Pronger and Bobby Orr are the only players to win both the Norris and the Hart Trophy as MVP in the same season.

IMMEDIATE IMPACT

Goaltender Ryan Miller vaulted from cellar-dwelling Buffalo to the penthouse in St. Louis when he was acquired in a five-player trade from Buffalo on February 28, 2014. The United States Olympian and 2010 Vezina Trophy winner paid immediate dividends for his new team, posting a sparkling 7-0-1 mark with a rail-thin 1.61 goals-against average. Miller was viewed as the final piece to the puzzle for a team still searching for its first Stanley Cup.

THE IRONMAN

Garry Unger led the Blues six times in goals and five times in points during a seven-season stretch, from 1971–72 to 1977–78. From 1972–73 through 1975–76, he also led the team in assists for four straight seasons. Unger was the first player in team history to score 40 goals with 41 in 1972–73. His ironman streak of 914 games is the second longest in NHL history and includes a club-record 662 consecutive games with St. Louis.

Bernie Federko served as captain of the Blues during his final season in St. Louis in 1988–89.

Chris Pronger led the NHL with a plus/minus rating of +52 during his MVP season of 1999–2000.

TEAM RECORDS

The Blues established team records with 51 wins and 114 points in 1999–2000 and won the Presidents' Trophy for the NHL's best overall record for the first time. The team record of 352 goals was set in 1980-81. That season, the Blues had ten players score 20 goals or more, just one short of the NHL record of 11 (set by the Bruins in 1977–78). The club's five 30-goal scorers was also one off the NHL record.

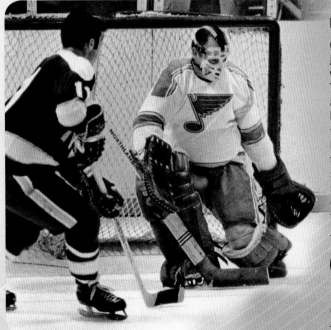

DOUBLE TROUBLE

Goaltenders Brian Elliott and Jaroslav Halak combined to win their first William Jennings Trophy in 2012. The duo yielded an NHL-low 165 goals while having a hand in a league-best 15 shutouts. Elliott (nine) and Halak (six) became the first tandem in NHL history to record six blankings apiece in the same season. The pair also set the club record for shutouts, besting the 13 set by Glenn Hall and Jacques Plante in 1968–69

After years of playing barefaced, Glenn Hall finally adopted a mask while sharing netminding duties with Jacques Plante in St. Louis in 1968–69.

TAMPA BAY LIGHTNING

Hall-of-Famer Phil Esposito was the man behind the move to put an NHL team in the Tampa-St. Petersburg area, laying the groundwork for acceptance throughout 1990. On December 6, 1990, it was announced that Tampa Bay and Ottawa had been awarded teams to begin play in 1992–93. (The NHL granted permanent membership status to both the Lightning and Ottawa Senators on December 16, 1991.) The team made the playoffs just once in its first 10 seasons before a breakout year in 2002–03. Led by Vincent Lecavalier, Brad Richards, and Martin St. Louis, the Lightning followed up with a Stanley Cup victory in 2004.

LADIES FIRST

During Tampa Bay's first training camp in 1992, Phil Esposito stunned the hockey world by signing Canadian women's national team goaltender Manon Rheaume to a tryout. On September 23, 1992, she played the first period of an exhibition game against the St. Louis Blues. Rheaume became the first women to play in any of the four major pro sports leagues in North America. In her only NHL appearance, she gave up two goals on nine shots.

▶ *Expectations were high when Vincent Lecavalier arrived in Tampa Bay as a number-one draft choice and developed into a top offensive threat.*

▶ *Brian Bradley had never scored more than 19 goals in a season before exploding for 42 during the Lightning's inaugural campaign.*

FIRST SEASON HIGHLIGHTS

The Lightning beat Chicago 7-3 in their first NHL regular-season game on October 7, 1992. Chris Kontos scored four goals, setting a club record that has never been matched. On November 7, 1992, defenseman Doug Crossman collected six points (three goals, three assists) in a 6-5 win over the Islanders to set another team record yet to be equaled. Brian Bradley scored 42 goals that season, the most ever by a player on an expansion team.

GOOD FOR GUDLEVSKIS

Goaltender Kristers Gudlevskis became the first player to compete in the East Coast Hockey League, American Hockey League, NHL and Olympic Games during one season when he made his debut with the Lightning on April 11, 2014. The 21-year-old played with Florida in the ECHL before recording a shutout in his debut with Syracuse of the AHL. Gudlevskis posted a pair of wins for upstart Latvia at the 2014 Sochi Games and then made 36 saves in Tampa Bay's 3-2 victory over Columbus.

EARLY HOMES

The Lightning played their first season of 1992–93 in the 10,425-seat Expo Hall on the Florida State Fairgounds in Tampa. The next year, they moved to the Florida Suncoast Dome in St. Petersburg, which was a baseball stadium reconfigured for hockey and would become known as "the Thunderdome." On October 9, 1993, the club set an NHL single-game attendance mark with 27,227 fans witnessing the Lightning home opener against the Florida Panthers.

CAPTAIN KID

Tampa Bay selected Vincent Lecavalier first overall in the 1998 NHL Entry Draft. On March 3, 2000, the Lightning named Lecavalier team captain. At age 19 and 10 months, he became the youngest captain in NHL history (Sidney Crosby was named captain in Pittsburgh at age 19 years and nine months in 2007). Lecavalier would have the "C" removed after 2000–01 to lessen the pressure on him, but would become captain again in 2008.

FREE AGENT

In 2000, Martin St. Louis signed as a free agent with Tampa Bay. He had a breakout year with 33 goals and 37 assists in 2002–03, when the Lightning won their first division title. In 2003–04, St. Louis led the NHL in scoring with 94 points (38 goals, 56 assists) to win the Art Ross Trophy and the Hart Trophy as MVP when Tampa Bay set club records with 46 wins and 106 points, and also won the Stanley Cup.

The undrafted Martin St. Louis continues to produce for the Lightning. The former Hart Trophy winner celebrated a pair of milestones during the 2011–12 season.

STAMKOS: OVERTIME THRILLER

Steven Stamkos netted his NHL-record fifth overtime winner when he scored 45 seconds into the extra session in a 3-2 victory over Winnipeg on March 31, 2012. Stamkos didn't just save his heroics for the extra five minutes of the game, however. The two-time Maurice Richard Trophy winner tallied 55 others times on his way to a remarkable 60-goal campaign.

FIRST TO 50 & 100

Brian Bradley's 42 goals in the team's first season of 1992–93 remained a club record until 2006–07. That year, Vincent Lecavalier became the first Lightning player to reach the 50-goal plateau, winning the Maurice "Rocket" Richard Trophy with an NHL-best 52 goals. Lecavalier also set a new club record with 108 points as both he and Martin St. Louis (43 goals, 59 assists, 102 points) became the first players in team history to top 100 points.

ROOKIE RECORDS

Brad Richards was Tampa Bay's second choice in the third round, 64th overall, after selecting Vincent Lecavalier in the 1998 NHL Entry Draft. Allowed to develop with less fanfare than Lecavalier, Richards set club rookie records with 21 goals, 41 assists, and 62 points in 2000–01. His 68 assists in 2005–06 also set a club record. Richards won the Conn Smythe Trophy when Tampa won the Stanley Cup in 2004 after setting an NHL playoff record with seven game-winning goals.

Brad Richards celebrates with the Stanley Cup after leading the playoffs with 26 points in 23 games in 2004.

LONG TIME COMING

Tampa Bay captain Dave Andreychuk was in his 22nd NHL season when the Lightning won the Stanley Cup in 2004. In his career, Andreychuk had played 1,759 games in the regular season and playoffs when he finally became a champion. Only Raymond Bourque had played more games before winning the Stanley Cup. Bourque was also in his 22nd season when he finally became a champion with the Colorado Avalanche in 2001, but he had played 1,826 games.

BISHOP'S IN CHARGE

After notching a franchise-best 40 wins in 2014–15, Ben Bishop became the first goaltender in league history to record a shutout in his first two Game 7 appearances. Bishop stopped 31 shots versus Detroit in the first round before upending the New York Rangers in the Eastern Conference final. He joined Colorado's Patrick Roy (2002) and Boston's Tim Thomas (2011) as the only netminders to accomplish the feat in the same playoff year.

TRIPLETS MAKE MARK

The line of Tyler Johnson, Nikita Kucherov and Ondrej Palat excelled during the 2014–15 playoffs, recording 31 of the team's 65 goals to propel the Lightning to their second Stanley Cup final appearance in franchise history. Johnson had a club-best 13 tallies – including six versus Detroit in the first round – while Kucherov netted six of his 10 against Montreal in the second, tying Ruslan Fedotenko's 2004 performance in the Eastern Conference final versus Philadelphia for the most in one playoff round. Palat added eight goals and as many assists to boot.

Brought along slowly as a rookie, Steven Stamkos exploded onto the scene during his second season of 2009–10 and has become one of the NHL's marquee stars.

TORONTO MAPLE LEAFS

Toronto was a charter member of the NHL when the League was formed on November 26, 1917 and went on to win the Stanley Cup in the spring of 1918. In 1920, the Toronto Arenas became the St. Patricks and won the Stanley Cup again in 1922. On February 14, 1927, the team was sold to Conn Smythe, who renamed them the Toronto Maple Leafs. Smythe built Maple Leaf Gardens at the height of the Depression in 1931 and launched the team into an era of greatness that would see them win the Stanley Cup 11 times in 36 seasons, from 1931–32 to 1966–67.

ACE & HAP

Ace Bailey and Hap Day were St. Patricks players who went on to star with the Maple Leafs. Hap Day was team captain from 1927–28 through 1936–37 and anchored the Toronto defense with King Clancy and Red Horner. Ace Bailey was the first Maple Leaf to win the scoring title when he led the League with 22 goals and 32 points in 1928–29, but became a key defensive forward when Toronto won the Stanley Cup in 1932.

THE KID LINE

Right-winger Charlie Conacher and left-winger Busher Jackson joined the Maple Leafs in 1929–30. Placed on a line with center Joe Primeau, the three youngsters quickly became one of the best lines in the NHL. Busher Jackson won the scoring title in 1931–32, while Conacher led the league in points in 1933–34 and 1934–35 and in goals five times between 1930–31 and 1935–36. Primeau led the NHL in assists three times between 1930–31 and 1933–34.

With his rugged playing style and powerful shot, Charlie Conacher was known as "The Big Bomber." He was a member of one of Canada's greatest sporting families.

GLORIOUS GOALIE

In 1941, Turk Broda was the first Toronto goalie to win the Vezina Trophy. In 1951, he became the first goalie with 300 career wins in the NHL. Broda was at his best when the pressure was highest, posting an impressive 1.98 goals-against average in 101 career playoff games and helping Toronto win the Stanley Cup five times between 1942 and 1951. Until surpassed by Jacques Plante in 1970, his 13 postseason shutouts were a modern NHL record.

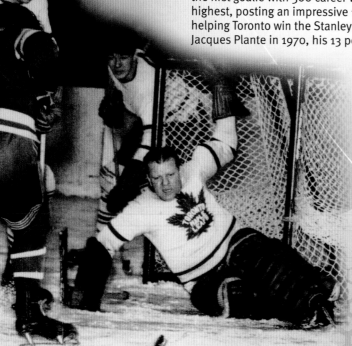

Turk Broda was the first goalie in NHL history to play in 100 playoff games. He posted 60 wins against 39 losses in the 101 postseason games he took part in.

COMEBACK OF COMEBACKS

Though the 1975 Islanders and 2010 Flyers (plus the 2004 Boston Red Sox in baseball) have all rallied to win a best-of-seven series after being down three games to nothing, only the 1942 Toronto Maple Leafs have done so to win a championship. The crowd of 16,218 at Maple Leaf Gardens for game seven on April 18, 1942 was the largest in Canada at that time and they witnessed the Leafs beat the Red Wings 3-1 to complete their comeback.

50-GOAL SCORERS

Frank Mahovlich scored 48 goals in 1960–61 and Darryl Sittler (45 in 1977–78) and Lanny McDonald (46 in 1976–77 and 47 in 1977–78) approached it as well, but the first Leaf to reach the 50-goal plateau was Rick Vaive. He scored 54 goals in 1981–82 and 51 and 52 goals in the next two seasons. Gary Leeman (51 goals in 1989–90) and Dave Andreychuk (53 goals in 1993–94) are the only other Leafs to score 50 goals.

100 POINTS

Darryl Sittler and Doug Gilmour are the only Leafs to score 100 points in a season and both did so twice. Sittler reached 100 points with 41 goals and 59 assists in 1975–76. Two years later, he established career highs with 45 goals, 72 assists, and 117 points. Doug Gilmour's 95 assists and 127 points set new Toronto scoring standards in 1992–93. A year later, Gilmour had 27 goals and 84 assists for 111 points.

▶ *Darryl Sittler cracked the top 10 in scoring five times for Toronto, reaching a high of third behind Guy Lafleur and Bryan Trottier in 1977–78.*

BIG GAMES

Darryl Sittler set an NHL record with 10 points in an 11-4 win over Boston on February 7, 1976, but his six goals only tied a Toronto record established by Corb Denneny with the St. Pats on January 26, 1921. Babe Pratt's team record of six assists in a game set on January 8, 1944 was equaled by Doug Gilmour, when he set up all six goals in a 6-1 win over Minnesota on February 13, 1993.

◀ *Doug Gilmour had a career-high 127 points and won the Selke Trophy as the NHL's best defensive forward in 1992–93.*

▶ *Mats Sundin led the Maple Leafs in scoring 12 times during the 13 seasons he spent in Toronto.*

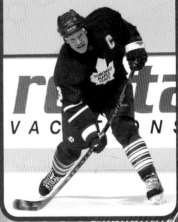

KESSEL'S REMARKABLE STRETCH

Phil Kessel recorded 13 multi-point performances during a 17-game point stretch in the 2013–14 season. He began with a goal and an assist against Washington on January 10 and scored a hat trick and an assist in the Maple Leafs' 6-3 win over Ottawa on February 1. The three-goal effort was his second of the season and he capped his 31-point stretch with a pair of consecutive two-point performances to bookend the Olympic break.

LOSING LEAFS

Toronto endured a tumultuous season in 2014–15 under the direction of new president Brendan Shanahan, setting franchise records with both an 11-game winless streak (0-10-1) and a 16-game road losing skid (0-14-2). The Maple Leafs limped to a 4-1 setback against New Jersey on February 6, 2015 to break the 10-game winless streak of the 1966–67 club, which rebounded to win the franchise's last Stanley Cup title later in the season. Peter Holland scored the go-ahead goal early in the third period of Toronto's 3-2 triumph over Florida on March 3, marking the team's first road victory since a 4-3 shootout win over Boston on New Year's Eve.

RETIRED NUMBERS

5	Bill Barilko	1946–1951
6*	Ace Bailey	1926–1934

HONORED NUMBERS

1	Turk Broda	1936–43, 45–52
	Johnny Bower	1958–1970
4	Hap Day	1926–1937
	Red Kelly	1959–1967
7	King Clancy	1930–1937
	Tim Horton	1949–50, 51–70
9	Charlie Conacher	1929–1938
	Ted Kennedy	1942–55, 56–57
10	Syl Apps	1936–43, 45–48
	George Armstrong	1949–50, 51–71
13	Mats Sundin	1994–2008
17	Wendel Clark	1985–94, 96–98, 2000
21	Borje Salming	1973–1989
27	Frank Mahovlich	1956–1968
	Darryl Sittler	1970–1982
93	Doug Gilmour	1992–97, 2003

*At Ace Bailey's request, Ron Ellis wore number 6 during his career.

VANCOUVER CANUCKS

When the NHL was getting ready to announce plans to expand into six additional hockey markets in 1965, Vancouver's representatives were front-and-center seeking a franchise to represent Western Canada. Vancouver was not included in the set of six teams that began play in 1967–68, but the Canucks and Buffalo Sabres were welcomed in the second phase of expansion on May 22, 1970. Players such as Stan Smyl, Thomas Gradin, and Richard Brodeur led the Canucks to the Stanley Cup Final in 1982, while Trevor Linden, Pavel Bure, and Kirk McLean led the team to the Final in 1994. The Canucks won the Presidents' Trophy in 2010–11 and 2011–12, but the Cup eluded them both times.

THE FIRST SEASON

Vancouver's first NHL regular-season game was broadcast live across Canada on October 9, 1970 when the Canucks hosted the Los Angeles Kings and lost 3-1. Barry Wilkins scored the first goal at 2:14 of the third period. Two nights later, the Canucks got their first win when Wayne Maki scored twice to lead them past Toronto 5-3. Andre Boudrais led the team in scoring with 66 points (25 goals, 41 assists). Rosaire Paiement was tops with 34 goals.

IN THE BEGINNING

The Canucks made Gary Doak from Boston their first selection in the NHL Expansion Draft on June 10, 1970. Other key players picked up in the Expansion Draft included Orland Kurtenbach, Ray Cullen, Pat Quinn, and Rosaire Paiement. A day later, the Canucks lost a spin of the wheel to Buffalo to determine the first pick in the NHL Amateur Draft. The Sabres took Gilbert Perreault first overall. Vancouver selected Dale Tallon with the second choice.

Orland Kurtenbach won the Cyclone Taylor Trophy as the fans' choice for MVP in each of the Canucks' first three seasons.

EARLY SCORING LEADERS

Bobby Schmautz set a new Canucks record with 38 goals in 1972–73, matched by Dennis Ververgaert who scored 38 goals, two years later. Ron Sedlbauer was first to score 40 in 1978–79 and Tony Tanti pushed the club record to 45 in 1983–84. That same season, Thomas Gradin set a club record with 57 assists and Patrik Sundstrom set a new team high for points, with 91 on 38 goals and 53 assists.

BURE BREAKS RECORDS

In 1991–92, Pavel Bure made his NHL debut with the Canucks and set a club rookie record with 34 goals. The next year, he became the first Vancouver player to reach both the 50-goal and 100-point plateaus with 60 goals and 110 points. Bure led the NHL in goals when he scored 60 again in 1993–94. He also scored 51 for the Canucks in 1997–98. Alexander Mogilny is the team's only other 50-goal scorer with 55 in 1995–96.

Zack Kassian got Vancouver off to a fast start at the Heritage Classic in 2014 before the bottom fell out.

PERFECT ATTENDANCE

Captain Henrik Sedin saw his ironman streak come to an end at 679 games after sitting out against Edmonton on January 21, 2014. The Swede injured his ribs in the previous contest and was also nursing a finger issue. Sedin was not accustomed to being out of the action, as his previous missed game came during the 2003–04 season – although he suited up and played 22 seconds in the regular-season finale to keep the streak alive. Doug Jarvis, who played with the Washington Capitals, Montreal Canadiens, and Hartford Whalers, holds the NHL record for longest streak of consecutive games (964).

THE SEDIN TWINS

Vancouver selected brothers Daniel and Henrik Sedin with the second and third picks overall in the 1999 NHL Entry Draft. In 2009–10, Henrik set club records with 83 assists and 112 points and became the first Vancouver player to win the Art Ross Trophy and the Hart Trophy as MVP. When Daniel won the Art Ross in 2010–11, the Sedins joined Charlie and Roy Conacher and Max and Doug Bentley as the only brothers who've won NHL scoring titles. They were the first to do so in back-to-back seasons.

CANUCKS' YOUNGEST CAPTAIN

Trevor Linden was the youngest player in the NHL in 1988–89, but became the first Canucks' rookie to score 30 goals. He was also the first rookie to be named the team's Most Valuable Player (MVP). Linden became the Canucks' youngest captain in 1991–92 at age 21. He would play 16 of his 19 NHL seasons with Vancouver during two stints with the team and holds the club record of 1,140 games played.

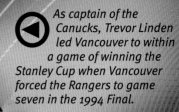

As captain of the Canucks, Trevor Linden led Vancouver to within a game of winning the Stanley Cup when Vancouver forced the Rangers to game seven in the 1994 Final.

ALL-TIME LEADER

Markus Naslund led the Canucks in scoring for seven straight seasons, from 1998–99 through 2005–06. In 2001–02, he finished second in scoring in the NHL and did so again in 2002–03, when he established career highs with 48 goals, 56 assists, and 104 points. Naslund is Vancouver's all-time leader with 346 goals and 756 points. On December 11, 2010, his number 19 was retired, joining Stan Smyl (#12) and Trevor Linden (#16) as the only Canucks to have received this honor.

VIG-TORIOUS

Alain Vigneault became the franchise's all-time winningest coach on November 23, 2011, when the Canucks breezed to a 3-0 victory over the Colorado Avalanche. The former Jack Adams Trophy winner recorded his 247th victory to move past Marc Crawford for the honor. Vigneault guided the Canucks to back-to-back Presidents' Trophies, but the Canucks bowed out in the Western Conference quarterfinals to eventual Stanley Cup-champion Los Angeles in 2012.

SIX & SEVEN FOR SUNDSTROM

Patrik Sundstrom collected a goal and six assists for a seven-point night, setting new team records for assists and points in one game in a 9-5 Canucks win over Pittsburgh on February 29, 1984. Sundstrom was just the third player in NHL history to earn six assists in a road game after Detroit's Billy Taylor (seven in 1947 versus Chicago) and Boston's Bobby Orr (six in 1973 against Vancouver).

VRBATA'S IMPRESSIVE INTRODUCTION

Radim Vrbata enjoyed his first season in Vancouver, scoring a team-high 31 goals and adding 32 assists for a career-best 63 points in 2014–15. The 33-year-old Vrbata made the most of playing with the superstar Sedin twins early in the campaign before being shuffled to the team's second line alongside Chris Higgins and Nick Bonino. Vrbata notched a pair of assists in a 6-5 victory over Edmonton in the season finale on April 11, 2015 to eclipse his previous high for a point total of 62 (career-high 35 goals, 27 assists with the then-Phoenix Coyotes in 2011–12).

Roberto Luongo and backup Cory Schneider allowed the fewest goals in the NHL in 2010–11 as the Canucks set club records with 54 wins and 117 points.

ROBERTO'S RECORDS

Roberto Luongo joined the Canucks in 2006–07 and promptly broke two long-time team goaltending records. His 76 games played surpassed Gary Smith's 72 (back in 1974–75) and his 47 wins shattered the record of 38 set by Kirk McLean in 1991–92. Luongo set a team record for shutouts with nine in 2008–09, including three in a row during a club-record scoreless streak of 242:36, from November 4–12, 2008. He also surpassed McLean's record for franchise victories on January 21, 2012.

KASSIAN COMES THROUGH

Having grown up in southern Ontario, Zack Kassian was prepared to play in the elements. Although rain forced league officials to order the retractable roof closed at B.C. Place Stadium, Kassian didn't disappoint by scoring a goal to give Vancouver a 2-0 lead in the Heritage Classic on March 2, 2014. The Canucks quickly yielded four goals in the loss to Ottawa for their ninth loss in 10 outings.

WASHINGTON CAPITALS

Many commentators were surprised when Washington landed an NHL franchise, but on June 8, 1972, the NHL announced it would place teams in the US Capital and in Kansas City for the 1974–75 season. Washington and Kansas City were officially welcomed on board on June 11, 1974. The Capitals were a woeful 8-67-5 in their first season, setting a modern record for fewest wins and points (21) in a season. Success was slow, as the team missed the playoffs for eight straight years before players such as Dennis Maruk, Mike Gartner, and Rod Langway began a breakthrough in the 1980s. The emergence of Alex Ovechkin in the 2000s gave the Capitals one of the most exciting players in hockey's history.

THE FIRST SEASON

The Capitals went through three coaches in their inaugural season. Among their 67 losses in 1974–75 and the record 446 goals the team surrendered, Washington allowed 10 goals in a game seven times and eight or nine goals on nine other occasions. Offensively, the Capitals' 181 goals ranked the team in last place in the NHL. On a team filled mostly with youngsters, veteran Tommy Williams led the scoring with 22 goals, 36 assists, and 58 points.

A BRIEF CAREER

The Capitals made defenseman Greg Joly the first pick in the 1974 Amateur Draft and selected high-scoring forward Mike Marson with their second-round pick. Marson was the second black player to reach the NHL, the first having been Willie O'Ree, who played briefly for Boston, beginning in 1957–58. Marson was Washington's third-leading scorer with 16 goals and 28 points as a rookie in 1974–75. Those would prove to be the best totals of his brief career.

 Washington's Mike Marson is watched by Boston's Brad Park (#22) and Bobby Schmautz.

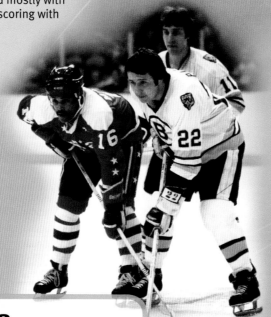

 *Dennis Maruk's 60 goals in 1981–82 ranked him third in the NHL behind Wayne Gretzky (92) and Mike Bossy (64). His 136 points were fourth behind Gretzky (212), Bossy (147), and Peter Stastny (139).*

NEW CLUB RECORDS

The Capitals acquired Dennis Maruk early on in their fifth season of 1978–79. Having twice topped 30 goals in his first three NHL seasons, Maruk scored 31 for the Capitals and set new club records, with 59 assists and 90 points. Two years later, he became the team's first 50-goal scorer and added 47 assists for 97 points. In 1981–82, Maruk shattered his own club records with 60 goals, 76 assists, and 136 points.

SINGLE-SEASON LEADERS

Most Goals	65	Alex Ovechkin (2007–08)
Most Assists	76	Dennis Maruk (1981–82)
Most Points	136	Dennis Maruk (1981–92; 60G, 76A)
Most Points, Right Wing	102	Mike Gartner (1984–85; 50G, 52A)
Most Points, Left Wing	112	Alex Ovechkin (2007–08; 65G, 47A)
Most Points, Defenseman	81	Larry Murphy (1986–87; 23G, 58A)
Most Points, Rookie	106	Alex Ovechkin (2005–06; 52G, 54A)
Most Wins	41	Olaf Kolzig (1999–2000)
		Braden Holtby (2014-15)
Most Shutouts	9	Jim Carey (1995–96)
		Braden Holtby (2014-15)
Most Penalty Minutes	339	Alan May (1989–90)

SECRETARY OF DEFENSE

The Capitals had never made the playoffs when they acquired Rod Langway from Montreal before the 1982–83 season, but they never failed to reach the postseason in the 10-plus years he played for the team. Langway was not much of an offensive threat, but his defensive play saw him become the first Washington player to earn a major award when he won the Norris Trophy in 1983. The Capitals' captain won it again in 1984.

EARLY LEADER

Mike Gartner spent the first 10 seasons of his 19-year NHL career with the Capitals after Washington selected him fourth overall in the 1979 Entry Draft. He led the team in goals five times and four times in points, scoring at least 35 goals in each of his nine full seasons in Washington. When he left the Capitals in 1989, he was the all-time leader in games played, goals, assists, points, powerplay, and game-winning goals at that time.

ALL-TIME CAREER LEADERS

Most Seasons	16	Olaf Kolzig
Most Games	983	Calle Johansson
Most Goals	475	Alex Ovechkin
Most Assists	427	Nicklas Backstrom
Most Points	895	Alex Ovechkin (475G, 420A)
Most Wins	301	Olaf Kolzig
Most Shutouts	35	Olaf Kolzig
Most Penalty Minutes	2,003	Dale Hunter

▶ *Olaf Kolzig bounced between Washington and the minors for eight seasons after the Capitals selected him in the first round (19th overall) in the 1989 NHL Entry Draft.*

OLLIE THE GOALIE

Olaf Kolzig emerged as a top goaltender during the 1997–98 season when he ranked among the NHL leaders in most statistical categories. He then emerged as a star during the 1998 playoffs, leading Washington to the Stanley Cup Final for the first time in franchise history. Kolzig, who is Washington's career leader in virtually every goaltending category, won the Vezina Trophy in 2000, joining Jim Carey (1996) as the only members of the Capitals to have been named the NHL's Best Goaltender.

BONDRA & BENGT

In 1994–95, Peter Bondra became the first Capitals' player to lead the NHL in goals when he scored 34 times in 47 games during the lockout-shortened, 48-game season. His 52 goals in 1997–98 tied Teemu Selanne for the NHL lead. On February 5, 1994, Bondra scored five goals in a 6-3 win over Tampa Bay, tying the club record set by Bengt Gustafsson in a 7-1 win over Philadelphia on January 8, 1984.

▼ *Peter Bondra spent 13-plus seasons with the Capitals and was Washington's leading goal scorer eight times in ten years from 1992–93 through 2001–02.*

ALEXANDER THE GREAT

In 2005–06, Alex Ovechkin joined Teemu Selanne and Wayne Gretzky as the only first-year players in NHL history to top 50 goals (52) and 100 points (106). He won the Calder Trophy as the NHL's top rookie ahead of Sidney Crosby (who also made his NHL debut that season).

Two years later, in 2007–08, Ovechkin won the Hart Trophy as MVP, the Art Ross Trophy as scoring leader (112 points), and the Maurice "Rocket" Richard Trophy with 65 goals. He won the Hart and Richard trophies (56 goals) again in 2008–09.

400 AND COUNTING

Alex Ovechkin became the sixth fastest player to reach the 400-goal plateau when he recorded the milestone tally on December 20, 2013. The captain's empty-net goal came in his 634th NHL game and sealed Washington's 4-2 triumph over Carolina. "(An) empty-netter is (an) empty-netter," Ovechkin said of his less-than-artistic tally. "Of course I (thought) about it, but it's over and it's time to move on." Ovechkin became the 12th player to reach 400 goals before the conclusion of his age-28 season.

▲ *Already the biggest star in Washington, Alex Ovechkin took on the added responsibilities of team captain on January 5, 2010.*

HOLTBY HOLDS THE DOOR

Braden Holtby enjoyed a career season in 2014–15, tying the franchise records of Olaf Kolzig for wins (41) and appearances (73) as well as Jim Carey's shutout total of nine. The Boston Bruins can attest to Holtby's dominance, as the goaltender denied all 88 shots en route to blanking them in all three meetings during the campaign. Holtby finished the season by making 25 consecutive starts, setting the club mark in that regard.

NIFTY NICKLAS

Nicklas Backstrom reached the 60-assist plateau for the second consecutive season and fourth time in his career after setting up captain Alex Ovechkin for a power-play goal in the last game of the 2014–15 campaign. The Swede has recorded four of the nine 60-assist seasons in franchise history, also doing so in 2008–09 and 2009–10. Backstrom's best asset continues to be his availability, as he played in all 82 games in the season for the fifth time in his career.

WINNIPEG JETS

On May 31, 2011, after 12 years in Atlanta, the Thrashers franchise was sold to True North Sports and Entertainment which would move the team to Winnipeg. On June 25, 1997, the NHL awarded expansion teams to Nashville, Columbus, Minnesota, and Atlanta to be phased in over the next few seasons. Atlanta would begin play in 1999–2000. The awarding of an Atlanta franchise saw NHL hockey return to Georgia, which first entered the League in 1972–73, but had seen the Atlanta Flames move to Calgary in 1980. Originally owned by Ted Turner, Turner Broadcasting Systems Inc. sold the team and the NBA's Atlanta Hawks to Atlanta Spirit LLC in 2004, but no local owner could be found to keep the Thrashers in Atlanta in 2011.

QUITE THE LADD

Captain Andrew Ladd has been a consistent contributor to the franchise since joining the then-Atlanta Thrashers following the Chicago Blackhawks' Stanley Cup-winning campaign in 2010. The fourth overall pick of the 2004 draft, Ladd was dealt to Atlanta for defenseman Ivan Vishnevskiy and a second-round pick in 2011 – and it was soon clear that the Thrashers got the better of the deal. Ladd posted 29 goals and 30 assists in his first season in Atlanta, and the following year finished second-best only to Evander Kane with 28 tallies. The lockout-shortened 2012–13 season did little to slow Ladd's production, as he notched team highs in both assists (28) and points (46).

FIRST THINGS FIRST

The MTS Centre was rockin', but the Montreal Canadiens proved to be rude visitors en route to a 5-1 win over the host Jets on October 9, 2011. Nik Antropov scored Winnipeg's only goal at 2:27 of the third period to cut the deficit to one before Yannick Weber, Travis Moen, and Max Pacioretty sent the home folks away unhappy. Winnipeg wouldn't taste victory until eight days later as Kyle Wellwood and Tanner Glass tallied in a 2-1 home triumph over the Pittsburgh Penguins.

SLUGFEST IN SOUTH PHILLY

After having trouble scoring goals during the first month of the season, the Jets decided to get nearly everyone involved in their game against the Philadelphia Flyers on October 27, 2011. Winnipeg saw nine different players score a goal – capped by captain Andrew Ladd's game-winner with 1:06 left in the third period – as the Jets posted a 9-8 triumph. Ironically, the former Winnipeg club also scored nine goals against the Flyers on October 23, 1993.

◀ Ondrej Pavelec was quite the workhorse during his first season in Winnipeg. The netminder played in 68 of the team's 82 games, posting a 29-28-9 mark with a 2.91 goals-against average.

THE MOVE TO WINNIPEG

The owners of the Atlanta Thrashers announced on May 31, 2011 that the club had been sold to True North Sports and Entertainment, operators of the minor-pro Manitoba Moose. For several years True North had worked behind the scenes to bring an NHL team back to Winnipeg, home of the Jets in the WHA from 1972–73 to 1978–79 and in the NHL from 1979–80 to 1995–96. The MTS Centre, a modern 15,000-seat arena located in downtown Winnipeg, is home to the club that took Atlanta's spot in the Southeast Division in 2011–12 and shifted to the NHL's Western Conference in 2012–13.

ONDREJ THE GIANT

Ondrej Pavelec turned aside all 34 shots he faced as Winnipeg recorded its first shutout with a 3-0 victory over the New York Islanders on November 3, 2011. Evander Kane provided all the offense Pavelec would need by poking in a rebound nearly 4 1/2 minutes into the first period. The blanking was the first of four for Pavelec this season.

FINISHING STRONG

Winnipeg (43-26-13) enjoyed its best season to date in 2014–15, recording a franchise-high 99 points and matching the club mark in wins en route to the securing the second postseason berth in the team's history. The Jets' point total was two more than the 2006–07 club, which posted a 43-28-11 mark to win the Southeast Division title as the Atlanta Thrashers. Coach Paul Maurice was in his first full season at the helm after being hired in January 2014, replacing Claude Noel behind the bench.

KANE & WHEELER PACK A PUNCH

Named after a former heavyweight champion, Evander Kane joined Blake Wheeler in taking their potent punch from Atlanta to Manitoba. The fourth overall pick of the 2009 draft, Kane has seen his goal totals increase with every season in the league – with Wheeler more often than not lending a hand. Kane collected a team-leading and career-best 30 goals in 2011–12, while Wheeler was more than happy to hold the club honors with 47 assists.

Evander Kane didn't just score goals for the Jets in 2011–12, he also contributed with career bests in plus/minus (+11) and hits (173).

Blake Wheeler nearly doubled his previous career high with 47 assists during the 2011–12 season. His 64 points were 19 better than his previous career best of 45, which was set during his rookie campaign with Boston.

19 YEARS IN THE MAKING

With snow falling outside of MTS Centre, Winnipeg enjoyed its famed "whiteout" inside the building while hosting its first playoff game in almost 19 years. Unfortunately for the Jets, there was no happy ending as they squandered a third-period lead for the third straight contest in the Western Conference first-round series to lose 5-4 in overtime to Anaheim in Game 3 on April 20, 2015. Lee Stempniak scored midway into the first period to send the crowd into a frenzy, as the playoff contest marked the first in Winnipeg since April 28, 1996.

LONG-OVERDUE HOMECOMING

Teemu Selanne was a stud right out of the blocks. The 10th overall pick of the 1988 draft, Selanne set rookie records with 76 goals and 132 points during his 1992–93 season with the Jets. The Finnish Flash would eventually head to Anaheim, but he was welcomed back with open arms in his first trip to Manitoba in 16 years. "It was something that I could never imagine," Selanne said of his return. He notched a pair of assists – to which the "home" crowd roared its approval – in the Jets' 5-3 victory over the Ducks on December 17, 2011.

WELCOME HOME DOAN

Shane Doan certainly knows the city of Winnipeg. After all, the 16-year veteran was selected by the original Jets with the seventh overall pick in 1995 draft. Upon returning to Manitoba on December 1, 2011, the captain of the Phoenix Coyotes received a standing ovation from the MTS Centre faithful – although Doan later joked it was because he turned the puck over to result in the lone goal of the game. Winnipeg won 1-0.

Despite playing for the opposing team, Teemu Selanne was embraced in his return to Winnipeg. Selanne was drafted by the original Jets in 1988.

DEFUNCT CLUBS

On January 2, 1918 (and less than a month into the NHL's first season), a fire destroyed the Montreal Arena. The Montreal Canadiens moved to a smaller rink on the other side of town, but one of the game's first elite clubs (the Montreal Wanderers) disbanded after playing just four games in the NHL. During the 1920s, the NHL grew to 10 teams before relocation and other franchise foldings saw the League reduced to just six teams. In more modern times, several franchises have been relocated but no team has truly disappeared since the Cleveland Barons were merged with the Minnesota North Stars in 1978.

MONTREAL WANDERERS

Gone for nearly 100 years, the Montreal Wanderers remain one of hockey's legendary clubs. Sixteen future Hockey Hall of Famers played for the Wanderers during their 15-year existence and the team took the Stanley Cup in 1906, 1907, 1908, and 1910. The Wanderers were formed in December of 1903 and helped create the NHA and the NHL, but player losses, poor economics during World War One, and an arena fire forced the franchise to suspend operations.

QUEBEC BULLDOGS

The history of hockey in Quebec City dates back to at least the first Montreal Winter Carnival of 1883 and the roots of the Quebec Bulldogs can be traced to 1886 and the formation of the Amateur Hockey Association of Canada. Quebec played in the NHA but did not join the NHL until the third season of 1919–20. Joe Malone led the NHL with 39 goals, but Quebec went just 4-20-0 that season and the franchise subsequently folded.

HAMILTON TIGERS

In 1920, Hamilton businessmen paid $5,000 for a franchise to replace Quebec. After four last-place seasons, Hamilton finished first in 1924–25, but when the Tigers went on strike before the playoffs to protest they had not received pay raises when the season was lengthened, they were suspended by the NHL. New York interests purchased the team from the NHL in September 1925, though new ownership was sought to keep a team in Hamilton until November.

Art Ross played only three games in the NHL, but starred for the Montreal Wanderers for seven seasons in leagues that predated the NHL. He later had a long career as coach and general manager of the Boston Bruins.

Joe Malone starred for eight seasons with the Quebec Bulldogs in leagues that predated the NHL. He later returned to the team for its lone NHL campaign.

The 1924–25 Hamilton Tigers were the last team to represent the southern Ontario steel town in the NHL.

NEW YORK AMERICANS

On February 6, 1925, *The New York Times* reported on a deal to bring an NHL team to the city. The New York Americans were officially welcomed to the NHL at League meetings in September. Though they were the first NHL team in Manhattan and had a few good years, the Americans played second fiddle to the New York Rangers during most of their existence. The team folded in 1942 after playing one season as the Brooklyn Americans.

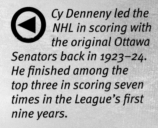

Roy Worters spent three seasons with the Pittsburgh Pirates and nine seasons with the New York Americans during his Hall of Fame career in the 1920s and '30s.

Cy Denneny led the NHL in scoring with the original Ottawa Senators back in 1923–24. He finished among the top three in scoring seven times in the League's first nine years.

PITTSBURGH PIRATES

The NHL's third franchise in the United States was granted on November 7, 1925, when Pittsburgh formally joined the Boston Bruins and New York Americans in the seven-team circuit. Featuring future Hall of Famers in Lionel Conacher, Roy Worters, and Frank Fredrickson, the Pirates twice made the playoffs in three years but struggled for two more seasons before the combination of a last-place finish and the 1929 stock market crash meant the Pittsburgh team was doomed.

PHILADELPHIA QUAKERS

Twelve players who had worn the yellow and black of the Pittsburgh Pirates in 1929–30 suited up in orange and black with the Philadelphia Quakers when the team moved across Pennsylvania in 1930–31. During its last season in Pittsburgh, the team was 5-36-3 in 44 games but fared even worse in Philadelphia, going 4-36-4. The Quakers withdrew from the NHL prior to the 1931–32 season although the Pittsburgh/Philadelphia franchise was not formally disbanded until May 7, 1936.

OTTAWA SENATORS

In 1883, the original Ottawa Senators began as the Ottawa Hockey Club and already boasted numerous Stanley Cup titles when they became charter members of the NHL in 1917. Featuring stars such as Clint Benedict, Eddie Gerard, Frank Nighbor, and Cy Denneny, Ottawa won the Stanley Cup again in 1920, 1921, 1923, and 1927, but soon fell on hard economic times. After suspending operations in 1931–32, the Senators played two final seasons before relocating to St. Louis in 1934.

MONTREAL MAROONS

During 14 seasons in the NHL, the Montreal Maroons boasted some of the top stars of the era, including Nels Stewart, the NHL's first 300-goal scorer. In 1926 and 1935, they won the Stanley Cup. The Maroons entered the NHL with the Boston Bruins in 1924–25 and played out of the newly constructed Montreal Forum. In 1938, they suspended operations due to economic losses during the Great Depression and officially folded on May 13, 1939.

RELOCATION DATES OF CURRENT NHL TEAMS

Current Team	Date	Previous Name
Calgary Flames	June 24, 1980	Atlanta Flames
Carolina Hurricanes	June 25, 1997	Hartford Whalers
Colorado Avalanche	June 21, 1995	Quebec Nordiques
Dallas Stars	June 9, 1993	Minnesota North Stars
New Jersey Devils	June 30, 1982	Colorado Rockies
	August 25, 1976	Kansas City Scouts
Phoenix Coyotes	July 1, 1996	Winnipeg Jets
Winnipeg Jets	May 31, 2011	Atlanta Thrashers

SEALS & BARONS

The Oakland Seals were the only new NHL expansion team never to be in playoff contention during the 1967–68 season. They reached the playoffs for the next two years, but the franchise continued to struggle. Sold and renamed the California Golden Seals in 1970, the team missed the playoffs for six straight seasons before moving to Cleveland in 1976. After two more non-playoff years, the Cleveland Barons merged with the Minnesota North Stars in 1978.

ST. LOUIS EAGLES

On September 22, 1934, the NHL granted permission to move the Ottawa Senators to St. Louis. Unfortunately, St. Louis already had a top team in the American Hockey Association and the last-place Eagles struggled to draw fans. At the end of the 1934–35 season, the owners asked to suspend operations for one year. The NHL governors instead decided to terminate the team, buying out the franchise and staging a draft to distribute its players throughout the League.

PART IX INTERNATIONAL ICE HOCKEY

From just four members in 1908 to nearly 70 today, the International Ice Hockey Federation oversees the men's and women's game around the world.

Promising phenomenon Connor McDavid's spirited play helped Canada claim gold at the 2015 World Junior Championship.

THE WORLD CHAMPIONSHIPS

Founded in Paris in 1908 under the name *Ligue International de Hockey sur Glace*, the International Ice Hockey Federation today boasts more than 50 national federations as full members, and nearly 70 when associate or affiliate members are included. While most of these member nations are in Europe, the growth of the game worldwide has seen membership spread to Asia, Africa, South America, and, in North America, Mexico as well. The objectives of the IIHF are: to govern, develop, and promote hockey (and inline hockey) throughout the world and to promote friendly relations among the member national associations.

ALL-TIME EUROPEAN CHAMPIONS

27	USSR
14	Bohemia/Czechoslovakia
10	Sweden
4	Great Britain
	Switzerland
2	Germany
	Austria
1	France
	Belgium

Note: 1912's results were later removed from the record book because of the participation of Austria, then not an IIHF member. Bohemia won the 1912 championship.

FOUNDING OF THE IIHF

The International Ice Hockey Federation was founded in Paris, France, on May 15, 1908 as the *Ligue International de Hockey sur Glace*. Representatives from Belgium, France, Great Britain, and Switzerland signed the founding document. Later the same year, Bohemia (which became Czechoslovakia) joined as the fifth member. Louis Magnus, a Frenchman, was the organization's first president. The first congress was held in Paris in the same year and the second took place in Chamonix, France, in 1909.

THE EUROPEAN CHAMPIONSHIPS

The first official European Championship was played in January, 1910, on the frozen ice of Lake Geneva in the Swiss Alps. Great Britain, Germany, Belgium, and Switzerland all took part, with Great Britain winning. With the exception of the years of World War One, the European Championships were held annually until 1932. From 1933 to 1991, the event was held as part of the World Championships. In all, there were 66 European Championships between 1910 and 1991.

▲ Hungary had a competitive national hockey team during the 1930s that tied Canada's gold medal-winning team 1-1 at the 1938 World Championship.

◄ Bohemia (which became the core of Czechoslovakia after World War One) was an early European hockey power.

BIRTH OF THE WORLD CHAMPIONSHIPS

Canada and the United States joined the IIHF in 1920, when they took part in the hockey tournament held that spring in conjunction with the Antwerp Olympics. In 1983, the IIHF ruled that the 1920 Olympics would be considered the first World Championship. The IIHF had already decided in 1930 that the 1924 and 1928 Olympics would also count as World Championships. The first World Championship to be held independently from the Olympics took place in 1930.

THE 1930 WORLD CHAMPIONSHIP

In 1930, the IIHF decided that it would hold an annual World Championship. In order to gain World Championship status, at least one non-European team would need to take part. A Toronto team sponsored by the CCM sporting goods company was touring Europe in the winter of 1930 and represented Canada. Given a bye directly into the finals, the Canadians beat European champions Germany 6-1 to claim the World title.

A NEW CHAMPION

Including the Olympics and World Championships, between 1920 and 1932, Canada had won six straight international tournaments and had never lost a game. Their winning streak ended at the 1933 World Championship in Prague. Both the Toronto National "Sea Fleas" and the Boston-based American team were undefeated heading into the final. The score was 1-1 through regulation time before John Garrison scored the only goal in a full 10-minute overtime session to give the USA a 2-1 victory.

CZECH CHAMPIONSHIPS

Canada did not send a team overseas in 1947, when the World Championships resumed for the first time since 1939 following World War Two. A weak American team left the field wide open for the Europeans and Czechoslovakia emerged as champions. Czechoslovakia would tie Canada at the 1948 Winter Olympics and have to settle for a silver medal, but they beat Canada for the first time at the 1949 World Championship to once again claim the world title.

A NEW WORLD ORDER

The Soviet Union made its international hockey debut at the 1954 World Championship in Stockholm. Canada had not sent a team in 1953, and sent only a Senior B club in 1954. Still, the East York Lyndhursts remained undefeated until they were shocked 7-2 by the Soviets in the final game. The only blemish on the Soviet record was a 1-1 tie with the host Swedes and their victory over Canada gave them their first world title.

THE NATS

After the Soviet victory in 1954, Canadian club teams would win the World Championships again in 1955, 1958, 1959, and 1961. However it had become obvious by 1963 that a stronger squad was needed to compete with the Soviets. Father David Bauer (a hockey coach, teacher, and priest) inaugurated a Canadian national team program for the 1963–64 season. Though poorly funded and often ignored at home, the Canadian Nats won bronze medals in 1966 and 1967, and at the 1968 Grenoble Winter Olympics.

PROS VS. AMATEURS

The IIHF had long been more lenient than the International Olympic Committee on the use of professional players. As such, retired Canadian pros could have their amateur status reinstated and play for Canada at the World Championships. However, when agreements allowing more professionals to compete at the 1970 World Championships were eventually reversed, Canada protested by withdrawing from all international competitions. Active NHL pros were finally allowed to compete at the World Championships in 1977. Today, many national teams competing at the World Championships draw on NHL players whose clubs missed the playoffs or were eliminated in the early rounds.

RUSSIA REIGNS SUPREME

Washington Capitals superstar Alex Ovechkin overcame a knee injury earlier in the tournament to help Russia win the 2014 IIHF World Championships in Minsk, Belarus. Ovechkin scored the tying goal in the second period before Pittsburgh Penguins stud Evgeni Malkin netted the go-ahead tally eight minutes later as the Russians skated to a 5-2 triumph over Finland on May 25. Russia won its fourth tournament in seven years (2008, 2009, 2012, 2014), outscoring the opposition by a 42-10 margin en route to winning all 10 of its contests. Russian President Vladimir Putin was in attendance as the club exacted a bit of revenge for being ousted by the Finns in the quarterfinals of the 2014 Sochi Winter Olympics just three months earlier.

CROSBY JOINS TRIPLE GOLD CLUB

Sidney Crosby collected a gold and an assist as Canada completed an unbeaten 10-game run with a 6-1 victory over Russia in the gold-medal game of the 2015 World Championship in Prague, Czech Republic, to win gold for the first time since 2007. The Canadians' triumph allowed the Pittsburgh Penguins phenom to gain entry into the legendary Triple Gold Club, which requires players to have won a Stanley Cup (2009), an Olympic gold medal (2010 and 2014) and a World Championship (2015).

WOMEN'S WORLD CHAMPIONSHIPS

Since at least the late-1880s, women have been playing hockey in Canada. Like women's baseball in the United States during World War Two, women's hockey became popular in Canada during World War One and was played quite competitively in Canada and parts of the US into the 1920s and 30s. The game took a downturn in the 1950s when more conservative attitudes toward women returned after World War Two, but by the late 1960s, women's hockey was once again gaining in popularity, though it received little support at any official level. It was not until the 1980s that women's hockey truly began to break through.

EARLIEST DAYS

One of the earliest photographs of women's hockey dates back to about 1890 and depicts Isobel Stanley, the daughter of Lord Stanley, playing hockey on an outdoor rink at Rideau Hall, residence of the Governor-General in Ottawa. Only a month after Lord Stanley and his family witnessed their first hockey game at the Montreal Winter Carnival in 1889, Isobel Stanley played for a Government House team in a victory over the Rideau ladies' hockey club.

THE FIRST MODERN STAR

Shirley Cameron was the first women's hockey superstar of the modern era. A founding member of the Edmonton Chimos in 1973, she played at the highest level of competition for 20 years, including the first IIHF-sanctioned Women's World Championships in 1990. The Chimos lost in the finals when the Canadian Women's National Championship was reintroduced in 1982, but Cameron led them to the title in 1984, 1985, and 1992 before retiring to coach the team.

THE UNOFFICIAL CHAMPIONSHIP

The first Women's World Championship was held in Toronto in April of 1987, but the event was not recognized by the IIHF. Teams from Canada, the United States, Sweden, Switzerland, and Japan were on hand, as well as a team from the province of Ontario. The Ontario team eliminated the USA in the semifinals before losing to Canada, but Ontario was not given a final ranking, so the USA was considered the second-place finisher.

THIS TIME IT COUNTS

In March 1990, the first official IIHF Women's World Championship was held in Ottawa. Team Canada wore bright pink uniforms and although some of the women found these outfits embarrassing, they did help to bring attention to the tournament. After romping through their group play, Canada edged Finland in the semifinals before beating the USA to take the title. Leading the Canadians were Angela James and Heather Ginzel. Cammi Granato was the top American star.

THE GAME GROWS

During the 1890s, women's hockey teams were formed all across Canada. In 1900, the first-known league for women was organized in Quebec, with teams in Montreal, Trois-Rivières, and Quebec City. The first international women's ice-hockey tournament was held in Cleveland, Ohio, in 1916 and featured teams from the US and Canada. In 1921, the University of Toronto defeated McGill University in the first intercollegiate women's hockey tournament.

EARLY STARS

The Preston Rivulettes were the women's hockey champions of Ontario for 10 straight years in the 1930s. During the decade, they are said to have played 350 games and lost only two. Hilda Ranscombe was the team's top star and led Preston to six Canadian championships. Another star of the era was Bobbie Rosenfeld, who also won two Olympic medals in track and field in 1928, and was named Canada's Female Athlete of the Half-Century in 1950.

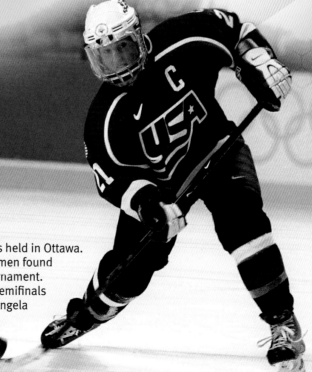

▼ *Cammi Granato was the youngest of five children in a hockey-playing family that included her brother Tony who grew up to play in the NHL.*

NO MIRACLE THIS TIME

Though they had lost at the 1998 Nagano Olympics, Canada was still a perfect six for six at the Women's World Championships through 2000. With a team led by Cammi Granato, Krissy Wendell, and Jenny Schmidgall, the USA looked to end that streak at Lake Placid in 2001. The Americans were dominant throughout the tournament and outshot Canada 35-18 in the gold medal game, but goalie Kim St-Pierre was brilliant in a 3-2 Canadian victory.

THE BIG FOUR

Originally held just once every three or four years, a Women's World Championship has been scheduled every year (except in Olympic years) since 1997. Outside of the Women's World Championships, the biggest annual international event in women's hockey is the Four Nations Cup. First introduced as the Three Nations Cup in 1996, the tournament features Canada, the United States, Finland, and Sweden, who have been the four top nations in women's hockey.

THE TIDE FINALLY TURNS

Canada suffered its first loss at the 2004 Women's World Championship, losing to the United States in a qualifying round game, but bounced back to win gold for the eighth straight time. Canada and the US faced off again in the final of the 2005 Women's World Hockey Championship, with the Americans coming out on top. Canada did not allow a goal in the tournament until surrendering three in a shootout to lose the championship game 1-0.

TWO TOP STARS

Hayley Wickenheiser was just 15 years old when she made the Canadian women's national team in 1994. By the next World Championship in 1997, Wickenheiser was a star. Canada won gold in 1997, as it had in every tournament up to that point, and Wickenheiser finished second in scoring behind Finland's Riikka Nieminen. Nieminen, who also led the 1994 tournament in scoring, is consider by many to be the best female player Europe has ever produced.

KESSEL TO THE RESCUE

After falling to Canada in the 2012 gold-medal game, the United States was not going to be denied in the following year. Amanda Kessel scored on a 2-on-1 rush to snap a tie early in the third period as the Americans skated to a 3-2 triumph over the Canadians in Ottawa. The North American rivals have grown accustomed to meeting each other in the final, having done so since the tournament's inception in 1990. Canada, which enjoys a 10-6 advantage in gold medals, garnered its revenge by rallying from a late two-goal deficit to best the United States at the 2014 Sochi Olympic Games.

GOOD KNIGHT INDEED

Hilary Knight collected a goal and an assist as the United States continued its recent domination of Canada to win the 2015 Women's World Championships in Malmo, Sweden. Knight scored seven goals and set up five others in five games en route to being named the tournament's MVP. Linemates Brianna Decker and Kendall Coyne each tallied in the third period for the Americans, who claimed gold at the expense of their neighbors to the north for the fifth time in six tournaments. Finland felled Russia by a 4-1 score in the third-place game.

▲ *Amanda Kessel proved to be too much to handle as she guided the United States past rival Canada in the 2013 women's world hockey championship.*

HALL OF FAMERS

In 2007, Cassie Campbell became the first female hockey player inducted into Canada's Sports Hall of Fame. She had starred for the Canadian national women's team from 1994 to 2006. In 2008, American Cammi Granato and Canadians Geraldine Heaney and Angela James were the first women to be inducted into the IIHF Hall of Fame. James was known as "the Wayne Gretzky of women's hockey." In 2010, James and Granato were inducted into the Hockey Hall of Fame.

U-20 WORLD JUNIOR CHAMPIONSHIPS

Officially known as the World Under-20 Championship, the event that has become an annual Christmas holiday tradition is more commonly known as the World Junior Championship. The Soviet and Czech hockey federations first proposed a World Junior tournament for players under 20 in 1973. Unofficial events were held from 1974 to 1976 before the first IIHF-sanctioned tournament took place in 1977. Over the years, the USSR/Russia and Canada have dominated the event, with the United States, Finland, Sweden, and the Czech Republic also winning on occasion. Many top players from the World Junior Championships have gone on to star in the NHL.

SOVIET DOMINATION

After winning all three unofficial tournaments, the Soviet Union won the first four official World Under-20 Championships for a streak of seven straight titles from 1974 to 1980. The first official tournament in 1977 marked the true international coming out for Viacheslav Fetisov, who was named Best Defenseman and would star against Wayne Gretzky and the Canadian team in 1978. Vladimir Krutov was the top scorer and best forward at the tournament in 1979 and 1980.

STAR-STUDDED SQUADS CAN'T STOP SOVIETS

A Canadian team boasting Mario Lemieux, Steve Yzerman, and Dave Andreychuk could finish no better than third at the 1983 World Junior Championship. Czechoslovakia was led by best goaltender Dominik Hasek and top scorer Vladimir Ruzicka but finished second. Sweden boasted best forward Tomas Sandstrom, but wound up fourth. The Soviets beat them all, posting a perfect record of 7-0-0 on home ice in Leningrad to win the gold medal once again.

PUNCH-UP IN PIESTANY

The Canadian team led by Theo Fleury and Brendan Shanahan could have clinched the gold medal with a win over the Soviets in the final game of the 1987 World Junior Championship. However, the game was halted midway through the second period after a huge brawl in which the two teams were left to slug it out in the dark after the lights were doused in the arena. Both teams were suspended by the IIHF and, as a result, Finland won its first gold medal.

HOW SWEDE IT IS

Ottawa Senators draft selection Mika Zibanejad scored 10:09 into overtime to lead Sweden to its first World Junior Hockey Championship title in 31 years with a 1-0 triumph over Russia on January 5, 2012, in Calgary, Alberta. The sixth overall pick of the 2011 NHL draft, Zibanejad stole the puck from Russian defender Nikita Gusev and backhanded a shot past netminder Andrei Makarov for the lone tally. Host Canada settled for the bronze medal after cruising to a 4-0 victory over Finland.

WORKING OVERTIME

After five straight championships, Canada fell to a shocking eighth-place finish in 1998. Finland dominated on home ice and beat Russia 2-1 in overtime in the gold medal game. A year later, in Winnipeg, Russia beat Canada 3-2 in overtime to take the title, and in 2000, the gold medal game remained scoreless through overtime and went to a shootout. Milan Kraft scored the winner and Zdenek Smid starred in goal to lead the Czech Republic over Russia.

CANADA COMES THROUGH

In the early years, Canada did not send a true national team to the World Junior Championships and would often send champion junior club teams instead. Finally, in 1982, coach Dave King and assistant Mike Keenan led a true national junior team and the result was Canada's first World Junior title. The team included future NHL players such as goalie Mike Moffat, defensemen Gord Kluzak, and James Patrick, and forwards Mike Moller, Marc Habscheid, and Scott Arniel.

NEW FORMAT, SAME RESULTS

Ten teams took part at the 1996 World Junior Championships in Boston, up from eight teams in past years. The tournament also featured the first elimination-style playoff round, with quarterfinals and semifinals leading to a definitive gold medal game. Canada received brilliant performances from Jose Theodore (who was named Best Goalie) and from scoring leader and Best Forward Jarome Iginla to win the fourth of five straight championships. Sweden's Mattias Ohlund was named Best Defenseman.

NUGENT-HOPKINS EXCELS, BUT CANADA FINISHES FOURTH

The top overall pick of Edmonton in 2011, Nugent-Hopkins participated in the 2013 tournament due to the NHL's work stoppage. Despite a tournament-best 15 points in six games – including a goal and three assists in the bronze-medal game – Canada saw its 14-year medal streak come to an end with a 6-5 overtime loss to Russia. Led by tournament MVP John Gibson, the United States ultimately skated to its third title, besting Sweden.

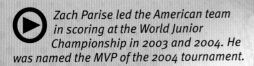

Zach Parise led the American team in scoring at the World Junior Championship in 2003 and 2004. He was named the MVP of the 2004 tournament.

Jordan Eberle helped Canada win its fifth straight gold medal in 2009 but had to settle for silver in 2010 despite being named tournament MVP.

SHOOTING FOR SIX STRAIGHT

In 2009, Canada tied its own record with a fifth straight championship in Ottawa. Facing elimination in the semifinals against Russia, Jordan Eberle tied the game 5-5 with just five seconds remaining and later scored the winning goal in a shootout. Canada then beat Sweden 5-1 to win gold. Eberle starred again in the finals of 2010, but John Carlson's overtime goal gave the USA a 6-5 victory to deny Canada a sixth straight gold medal.

FIRST FOR THE AMERICANS

After losing to Russia in the gold medal game in 2002 and 2003, Canada reached the finals again in 2004 only to find a new rival. Considered by many to be the pre-tournament favorite, the American lineup led by Zach Parise boasted many of the same players who had won the 2002 World Under-18 Championship. Still, Canada led 3-1 going into the third period before Patrick O'Sullivan capped a three-goal rally that gave the USA a stunning victory.

CANADA'S BACK ON TOP

Connor McDavid and Sam Reinhart each scored a goal to lift Canada to its record 16th title with a 5-4 victory over Russia in the 2015 World Junior Championship final in Toronto. The Canadians claimed their first gold since the 2009 tournament, and their first medal since 2012. McDavid's tally put Canada up 3-1 and Reinhart's fifth goal of the tournament extended the lead to four before the Russians scored three times in 3:16 to trim the deficit. Denis Godla was named the tourney's MVP after leading Slovakia to the bronze medal.

THE GREATEST TEAM EVER?

With the NHL in the midst of a season-long lockout, Canada sent a powerful team to the 2005 World Junior Championship in North Dakota. The Canadians boasted 12 returnees from the 2004 squad, including captain Mike Richards, and romped to the championship with six straight wins, beating a Russian team led by Alex Ovechkin and Evgeni Malkin 6-1 in the final game. Patrice Bergeron played on a line with 17-year-old sensation Sidney Crosby and was named tournament MVP.

THREE TIMES TOEWS

Goalie Carey Price led Team Canada to a third straight World Junior title in 2007 as the Canadians went undefeated for the third straight year. The key victory came in the semifinals, where the Americans outplayed Canada but were tied 1-1 through overtime before being defeated in a thrill-packed shootout that featured three goals by Jonathan Toews. In the gold medal game against Russia, Canada jumped out to a 4-0 lead and held on for a 4–2 victory.

WORLD UNDER-18 CHAMPIONSHIPS

The World Under-18 Championship began as a European Junior Championship for players under the age of 19. Like the World Junior Championship, the Soviet and Czech hockey federations first proposed the idea. An unofficial tournament was held in 1967, with the event gaining official IIHF status the following year. When the World Junior Championship for players under 20 became official in 1977, the age limit for the European Junior Championship was lowered to 18, which led to the tournament being heavily scouted for the NHL Draft. The tournament became the World Under-18 Championship in 1999, when the United States entered. Canada made its first appearance in 2002.

ALL-TIME EUROPEAN JUNIOR CHAMPIONSHIP TITLES

12	USSR/Russia (1969–70–71–73–75–76–80–81–83–84–89–96)
10	Sweden (1972–74–77–82–85–87–90–93–94–98)
5	Czechoslovakia (1968–79–88–91–92)
4	Finland (1978–86–95–97)

SEDINS' SPARK SWEDEN

The final European Junior Championship was played in April of 1998. Sweden needed to win its final game over Russia by at least four goals or the gold medal would go to archrival Finland. With twin brothers Daniel and Henrik Sedin leading the way, Sweden won by a score of 5-1. Daniel finished tied for the tournament's leading scorer with three goals and eight assists for 11 points, while Henrik had five goals in six games.

WHITE FUELS RED, WHITE AND BLUE

Colin White scored 12:44 into overtime as the United States secured its ninth gold medal - and sixth in seven years - with a 2-1 victory over Finland on April 26, 2015. White converted Jeremy Bracco's backdoor feed for the winner and Jack Roslovic also tallied for the Americans, who outscored their opponents 46-13 in the tournament and put a whopping 62 shots on goal in the finale. Evan Sarthou finished with 19 saves and Auston Matthews (15 points) was named the tournament's Most Valuable Player.

US INVOLVEMENT

In 1996, USA Hockey introduced its National Team Development Program. The plan was to bring the best 16- and 17-year-old hockey players in the country to Ann Arbor, Michigan, to train together year-round and prepare these student athletes for participation on US national teams. The USNTDP paved the way for American involvement at the 1999 World Under-18 Championship and has led to Team USA's improved results in recent years at the World Junior Championships.

FINLAND'S FIRST

Prior to the 1978 European Junior Championship, Finland had never won a gold medal in any team sport at the World or European level. But after wins against Switzerland, Norway, Sweden, and Czechoslovakia, the Finns found themselves playing the Soviets for a chance to win the tournament. Tied 3-3 after regulation time and 5-5 after a full 20-minute overtime period, Jari Kurri scored just 1:42 into a second sudden death, overtime session to give Finland its first championship.

Ilya Kovalchuk's performance at the 2001 World Under-18 Championship helped to solidify his position as the top pick in that year's NHL Entry Draft.

KOVALCHUK COMES THROUGH

After Finland won the World Under-18 Championship in 1999 and 2000, a future NHL star took Russia to the top in 2001. Ilya Kovalchuk, who had won gold with Russia at the 2000 Under-17 Challenge, led the 2001 Under-18 event in goals (11) and points (15) as Russia won the gold medal with a 6-2 win over Switzerland in the final game. Six weeks later, the Atlanta Thrashers picked Kovalchuk first overall in the NHL Entry Draft.

ALEXANDER THE GREAT

Alex Ovechkin was only 16 years old when he set scoring records at the 2002 World Under-18 Championship with 14 goals and 18 points in just eight games. Fellow Russian and future Washington Capitals teammate Alexander Semin was second in scoring at the tournament that year with 15 points on eight goals and seven assists. Ovechkin played at the Under-18 event again in 2003 and finished tied for the tournament lead with nine goals in six games.

USA A-OK

Team USA needed to beat Russia by at least two goals in the final game to claim the gold medal at the 2002 World Under-18 Championship and did so with a 3-1 victory. It was a dramatic improvement for a team who had finished no better than sixth at three previous tournaments. Patrick O'Sullivan led the offense with eight goals and seven assists, while Zach Parise scored seven times. Ryan Suter was named Best Defenseman.

CANADA'S FIRST TITLE

After finishing sixth in its first appearance in 2002, Canada won gold at the 2003 World Under-18 Championship. Despite a slow start, the Canadians got on a roll and caught a break when Slovakia upset Russia in the semifinals. Canada then defeated the Slovaks and goalie Jaroslav Halak 3-0 in the gold medal game. Future Olympic gold medalists Ryan Getzlaf and Brent Seabrook, along with Jeff Carter and Mike Green, were among Team Canada's future stars.

ONE-SIDED WIN

Canada won its second gold medal at the World Under-18 Championship in 2008, beating the Russians 8-0 in the most lopsided gold medal game in tournament history. The Canadian roster was full of future first-round draft choices, including future World Junior star Jordan Eberle (who scored two goals in the finale), Cody Hodgson (who led the tournament in scoring with two goals and 10 assists), and 2010 first-overall NHL Draft pick, Taylor Hall.

STARS EARN THEIR STRIPES

Phil Kessel, the highest-scoring American player in the history of the World Under-18 Championship, led the tournament with nine goals and 16 points when the United States won gold in 2005. Patrick Kane was the leading scorer the following year as the Americans repeated as champions. The US started a string of four straight gold medals in 2009 – capped by Nicolas Kerdiles collecting two goals and three assists in a 7-0 rout of Sweden on April 22, 2012.

▲ *Cody Hodgson won gold medals and led the tournament in scoring at the 2008 World Under-18 Championship and the 2009 World Junior Championship.*

▲ *With 104 goals and 180 points in his two years with the program, Phil Kessel is the highest-scoring player in the history of the US National Team Development Program.*

▶ *With 102 points (52 goals, 50 assists) in 68 games in 2005–06, Patrick Kane enjoyed the highest scoring single season in the history of the USNTDP.*

WORLD CUP OF HOCKEY

In 1976, the NHL, the NHL Players Association, and Hockey Canada created the Canada Cup. It heralded Canada's official return to international hockey after a boycott that began in 1970. Staged before the start of the NHL season, the tournament offered hockey fans their first chance to see top NHL players (and WHA stars) representing their respective countries. The Canada Cup was held five times in total: 1976, 1981, 1984, 1987, and 1991. In 1996, the tournament was rebranded as the World Cup of Hockey. It was expanded to include eight national teams and saw some games played in Europe. A second World Cup was held in 2004.

▼ Goalie Mike Richter backstopped the United States to victory with a brilliant performance in the final game of the 1996 World Cup of Hockey.

ALL-TIME CANADA CUP/WORLD CUP RESULTS

Year	Winner	Runner-up	MVP
1976	Canada	Czechoslovakia	Bobby Orr
1981	Soviet Union	Canada	Vladislav Tretiak
1984	Canada	Sweden	John Tonelli
1987	Canada	Soviet Union	Wayne Gretzky
1991	Canada	United States	Bill Ranford
1996	United States	Canada	Mike Richter
2004	Canada	Finland	Vincent Lecavalier

CANADA CUP, 1976

The inaugural Canada Cup featured Canada, the Soviet Union, Czechoslovakia, Sweden, Finland, and the United States. After losing to Czechoslovakia at the World Championship that year, the Soviets were a team in transition and they failed to make the finals. The Czechs beat the Canadians 1-0 in round-robin play, but Team Canada got its revenge in the finals by sweeping the best-of-three series with 6-0 and 5-4 victories. Bobby Orr was brilliant for Canada throughout the series.

THE 1976 FINAL

Czech stars such as Milan Novy, Ivan Hlinka, Jiri Bubla, and Peter Stastny had all won the World Championship in 1976, but the team could not get past Bobby Orr, Bobby Hull, Bobby Clarke, and one of the greatest Canadian hockey teams ever assembled. Still, after a 6-0 win in the opener of the finals, it took an overtime goal from Darryl Sittler for Team Canada to wrap up the first Canada Cup championship.

◄ Bobby Orr's stellar play at the 1976 Canada Cup marked the last great moment of his spectacular career.

CANADA CUP, 1981

Five years later, the same six countries were back for the second Canada Cup. Once again, the Soviets were in rebuilding mode, though they did reach the finals this time despite a 7-3 loss to Team Canada in the last game of round-robin play. The tournament featured a one-game final that year and the Soviets stunned the Canadians with a lopsided 8-1 victory. Sergei Shepelev led the way with three goals, while Igor Larionov scored twice.

CANADA CUP, 1984

After a fifth-place finish at the World Championships earlier in the year, West Germany replaced Finland at the third Canada Cup. Team Canada limped through the round robin with only two wins and a tie in five games, but upset the undefeated Soviets in the semifinals, while Sweden crushed the United States 9-2 in their semifinal. Canada finally found its form in the finals and swept the best-of-three series with 5-2 and 6-5 victories.

CANADA-USSR, 1984

The Soviets capped the first perfect 5-0-0 run through the Canada Cup round robin with a 6-3 win over Team Canada in their last game. Three nights later, the two teams met again in the semifinals. Canada dominated through two periods, but led only 1-0. They would then need a goal from Doug Wilson with little time remaining to tie the game 2-2 before winning on a goal by Mike Bossy at 12:29 of overtime.

CANADA CUP, 1987

The 1987 Canada Cup featured the emergence of Mario Lemieux as a true superstar. Teamed with Wayne Gretzky, Lemieux's talents were on display in a tournament that featured some of the most exciting hockey in history. Lemieux set a Canada Cup record with 11 goals in nine games, while Gretzky set records with 18 assists and 21 points. The two stars combined on the tournament-winning goal in Canada's thrilling 6-5 final-game victory against the Soviets.

Wayne Gretzky (front) and Mario Lemieux helped produce some of the greatest hockey ever seen at the 1987 Canada Cup.

CANADA-USSR, 1987

For the first time in Canada Cup history, the best-of-three finals went the distance ... and each game was more exciting than the one before! The Soviets won the opener 6-5 on an overtime goal by Alexander Semak before Team Canada tied the series with a 6-5 victory on a Mario Lemieux goal in double overtime. In game three, Wayne Gretzky set up Lemieux again with 1:26 remaining for another 6-5 victory that clinched the series.

CANADA CUP, 1991

Led by Mike Modano, Brett Hull, Brian Leetch, and Pat Lafontaine, Team USA lost only to Canada during the round-robin portion of the tournament, and after downing Finland 7-3 in the semifinals, was looking for revenge against Canada in the finals. Team Canada won game one 4-1 but lost Wayne Gretzky when a cross-check by Team USA defenseman Gary Suter put him out of action. Even without The Great One, Canada won the second game 4-2 to sweep the series.

Vladimir Krutov, Igor Larionov, Sergei Makarov, and Sergei Babinov celebrate a goal during the Soviets' 8-1 rout of Canada in the final game of the 1981 Canada Cup.

WORLD CUP OF HOCKEY, 1996

An American team starring Tony Amonte, John LeClair, and Keith Tkachuk won the inaugural World Cup of Hockey. After defeating Canada, Russia, and Slovakia in the North American pool, Team USA beat Russia again in the semifinals. Canada knocked off Germany and Sweden in playoff games, then opened the finals with a 4-3 overtime win in Philadelphia. However, the Americans bounced back with a pair of 5-2 victories in Montreal to win the tournament.

Tony Amonte scored in the third period as the US rallied from a 2-1 deficit into a 3-2 lead en route to a 5-2 victory in the final game of the 1996 World Cup.

WORLD CUP OF HOCKEY, 2004

Led by executive director Wayne Gretzky and coach Pat Quinn, who had run Team Canada at the 2002 Salt Lake City Olympics, the 2004 World Cup team featured many of the same stars as the recent gold medal squad. The Canadians went undefeated through the tournament, but needed an overtime goal by Vincent Lecavalier to beat the Czech Republic 4-3 in the semifinals and a third-period goal from Shane Doan to defeat Finland 3-2 in the one-game final.

Vincent Lecavalier was Canada's top scorer with seven points (two goals, five assists) in six games and was named MVP of the 2004 World Cup of Hockey.

INDEX

CREDITS

The publishers would like to thank the following sources for their kind permission to reproduce the pictures in this book.

Getty Images: 187BR; /AFP: 26, 27T, 29T; /Dave Abel: 70BL; /Graig Abel: 7BC, 32-33, 77BR, 167R; /Justin K Aller: 121BR; /Claus Andersen: 108, 161TL, 167L, 176-177; /Scott Audette: 57L, 164TR, 165T; /Joel Auerbach: 153R; /Brian Babineau/NHLI: 112-113; /Steve Babineau: 7BL, 19TL, 34L, 55T, 56B, 59TL, 65TR, 72B, 79C, 88TR, 89TR, 101R, 109BL, 119C, 119BL, 120C, 120BR, 121L, 122TR, 134B, 140L, 145L, 157T, 158, 162L, 170C; /Brian Bahr: 100BR, 129B, 180; /Al Bello: 28L, 28BC, 77BL; /Bruce Bennett: 6BL, 6BR, 7BR, 12, 13, 14TR, 16R, 17TL, 18L, 18BR, 21R, 21BR, 28TR, 29BL, 31L, 34BL, 35TL, 35R, 36BL, 38, 39L, 39BR, 40R, 41, 42, 43C, 44TL, 48L, 48BR, 49T, 50, 51B, 52, 53BL, 54TR, 54BL, 57TR, 57B, 58B, 60B, 61BL, 64BR, 65L, 65BR, 67, 68, 69C, 69BR, 71TL, 71TR, 73C, 78TR, 78BL, 80L, 80R, 80B, 81T, 83TL, 84TR, 84BL, 85, 86R, 89L, 90-91, 95TL, 95BL, 95R, 96L, 97, 98, 100L, 101TL, 102B, 103L, 103TR, 103B, 106BL, 106BR, 110, 111B, 115TR, 122L, 127C, 134TR, 136BL, 116BR, 140BR, 141B, 144TR, 145TL, 149TL, 150L, 150R, 151C, 151BL, 152, 153BL, 157BL, 159TR, 162R, 163B, 166TR, 166BL, 167T, 170TR, 171BL, 183C, 186BL, 186BR, 187TR; /Paul Bereswill: 73TL; /Denis Brodeur: 16BL, 40B, 53R, 55BR, 60TR, 61TR, 62R, 66TR, 70C, 87BR, 109TR, 117L, 122BR, 135R, 157R, 169T; /Ralph Cane/Time & Life Pictures: 25C; /Chicago Tribune: 127BR; /Julio Cortez: 22-23; /Glenn Cratty: 114TR, 139TL, 159BL, 186R, 187C; /DK Photo: 59BL; /Andy Devlin/NHLI: 72L, 137BR; /Melchior DiGiacomo: 19BR, 20L, 20BR, 37TR, 83TR; /Bob Donnan/Sports Illustrated: 124; /Tony Duffy: 111T; /Elsa: 51T, 62L, 77R, 148, 149C, 163T, 165L; /G. Fiume: 115L; /Focus on Sport: 17BL, 27R, 30BR, 31TL, 36BR, 96BR; /Gregg Forwerck/NHLI: 146C; /Fox Photos: 24L; /Richard T Gagnon: 104-105; /Gamma-Keystone: 11, 178BL; /General Photographic Agency: 30L; /John Giamundo/Bruce Bennett: 37C, 127R, 151BR; /Noah Graham: 64L; /Otto Greule Jr: 45BR; /Jeff Gross: 115BL, 130BL; /Norm Hall/NHLI: 117T, 127BL; /Grant Halverson: 125R; /Andy Hayt: 159L; /Marianne Helm: 173BL; /Harry How: 114L, 160BR; /Hulton Archive: 14BL, 45L, 49BR; /Imagno/Austrian Archives: 178R; /Jed Jacobsohn: 146BR; /Glenn James/NHLI: 133BR; /Tasos Katopodis: 126; /David E Klutho/Sports Illustrated: 136C; /Robert Laberge: 39BL, 44B, 89BR; /Francois Lacasse/NHLI: 74-75, 165B; /Rich Lam: 168BL; /Kellie Landis: 141C; /Mitchell Layton: 82BL; /Scott Levy/Bruce Bennett: 21C; /Andy Marlin: 79BR; /Andy Martin/NHLI: 149BR; /Michael Martin: 128B, 142, 161BR; /Ronald Martinez: 132BL; /Jim McIsaac: 87L, 141TL, 164L, 171C, 185BR; /Al Messerschmidt: 6BCL, 58R, 82BR; /Francis Miller/Time & Life Pictures: 17R; /Ronald C Modra/Sports Imagery: 59R; /Montreal Gazette/AFP: 93; /NHL Images: 130R; /New York Daily News Archive: 8-9; /Juan Ocampo/NHLI: 140BC; /Christopher Pasatieri: 172; /Silvia Pecota/NHLI: 102TL; /Doug Pensinger: 73B, 77TL, 123L, 147R, 184; /Hy Peskin/Sports Illustrated: 70BR; /Christian Petersen: 43BL; /Pictorial Parade: 56TL; /Mike Powell: 25B; /Len Redkoles: 99, 118, 156; /Dave Reginek/NHLI: 35BL; /Robert Riger: 83L, 179; /Andre Ringuette/NHLI: 46-47, 155TL, 155C; /Rogers Photo Archive: 88BL, 168L; /Martin Rose: 181; /John Russell: 143BR, 147TL, 147BL; /John Russell/NHLI: 116L; /Jamie Sabau/NHLI: 129C, 131L, 131R; /Dave Sandford: 137L, 154, 155TR, 185L; /Eliot J Schechter: 66BR, 138, 139R; /Harry Scull Jr: 81R, 121TR; /Gregory Shamus: 6BCR, 61BR, 86B, 125BL, 131T, 159TL, 159BR; /George Silk/Time & Life Pictures: 145B; /Bill Smith/NHLI: 128TR; /Don Smith/NHLI: 161TR; /Sports Illustrated: 119TL; /Jamie Squire: 31BR, 87TR; /Rick Stewart: 63BR, 139BL, 160L, 162BL; /Mike Stobe/NHLI: 144B; /Bob Thomas: 27B; /Gerry Thomas: 123R, 143TL; /Lance Thomson/NHLI: 173TL; /Joe Traver: 133T; /Yoshikazu Tsuno/AFP: 63TL; /Aert van der Neer/The Bridgeman Art Library: 10; /Jeff Vinnick: 135BL, 169L, 171TR; /Bill Wippert/NHLI: 143C, 173R; /Richard Wolowicz: 183B, 185TR

Hockey Hall of Fame: 107; /Imperial Oil-Turofsky: 175T; /Le Studio du Hockey: 92, 174TR, 174BR, 175L; /James Rice: 174L

Press Association Images: /Tony Gutierrez/AP: 132C

Private Collection: 24BR, 76

Every effort has been made to acknowledge correctly and contact the source and/or copyright holder of each picture and Carlton Books Limited apologises for any unintentional errors or omissions that will be corrected in future editions of this book.